# ADVANCE PRAISE FOR *DIVINE DUALITY*

At the heart of humanity's present evolutionary challenge is the need to heal and transform the relationship between women and men. Not only does this relationship affect all the other social, political, and economic realities of our world, it influences the larger relationship of humanity with the Earth, with the larger whole of life. It is a crucible for the entire drama. For just this reason *Divine Duality* is a crucial book for our time. This is a courageous work, describing the profound journey of transformation that Will Keepin and his colleagues have been skillfully facilitating and undergoing with hundreds of pioneering men and women. Its message is both unflinching and full of hope. May this book send its ripples into the world far and wide.

> — **Richard Tarnas, Ph.D.**, author of *The Passion of the Western Mind* and *Cosmos and Psyche*

The poet Rainer Marie Rilke envisioned a distant future when men and women would no longer be drawn to each other as opposites, but rather, "freed of all misconceptions and antipathies" able at last "to share the heavy sexual burden that has been laid upon them, simply, seriously, and with patience." Rilke would be enormously heartened, I believe, by the pioneering work of the Satyana Institute and by the simplicity, seriousness, and tremendous patience of those who are leading it.

> — **Carol Lee Flinders, Ph.D**, author of *Enduring Lives: Portraits of Women and Faith in Action* and *At the Root of this Longing: Reconciling a Spiritual Hunger and Feminist Thirst*

Few things challenge the inherent structures of patriarchy more than gender reconciliation—the deep meeting of masculine and feminine experiences and values on every level and in every realm. Will Keepin's pioneering, passionate, deeply thoughtful work has been on the cutting edge for years. Now his book gives us all access to his profound insights and effective methods. This is crucial work.

> — **Andrew Harvey**, author of twenty books including *Way of Passion*, *Return of the Mother*, and *The Direct Path*

Will Keepin makes an extraordinary contribution to fostering gender reconciliation and increases tolerance surrounding issues of sexism. This is a practical and empowering book which delivers people out of their polarization and into their character and humanity.

> — **Angeles Arrien, Ph.D.**, cultural anthropologist and author of *The Four-Fold Way* and *The Second Half of Life*

# Divine Duality

## The Power of Reconciliation
## Between Women and Men

**William Keepin, Ph.D.**

with Cynthia Brix, M.Div.,
and Molly Dwyer, Ph.D.

**HOHM PRESS**
Prescott, Arizona

Cover and interior design: Zachary Parker, Kadak Graphics
Cover art: Lowell Brook, www.Becomingfree.com
Layout: Becky Fulker, Kubera Services

Library of Congress Cataloging in Publication Data:

Keepin, William.
 Divine duality : the power of reconciliation between women and men / William Keepin with Cynthia Brix, and Molly Dwyer.
    p. cm.
 Includes bibliographical references and index.
 ISBN-13: 978-1-890772-74-1 (trade pbk. : alk. paper)
 1. Sex role--Religious aspects. 2. Reconciliation--Religious aspects. 3. Sex dif-ferences--Religious aspects. I. Brix, Cynthia. II. Dwyer, Molly. III. Title.
 BL65.S4K44 2007
 305.3--dc22

                              2007031631

HOHM PRESS
P.O. Box 2501
Prescott, AZ 86302
800-381-2700
http://www.hohmpress.com

This book was printed in the U.S.A. on recycled, acid-free paper using soy ink.

11 10 09 08 07          1 2 3 4 5

To my parents
Madge and Bob Keepin,
Who gave me the gift of life
and kept on giving and giving . . .


And to the Nameless One,
Who gave me the gift of Life,
and to Whom
i give my life.

# CONTENTS

# INTRODUCTION

## *Call of the Beloved*

*The future of humanity will be decided not by relations
between nations, but by relations between men and women.*

—D. H. Lawrence

Whether or not D. H. Lawrence was overstating the case in making this prophetic pronouncement, he was pointing to something very real. The crisis in relations between women and men is of massive proportions and is creating profound misery for literally billions of people across the planet. Many deeply committed individuals and organizations are actively engaged in all manner of inspiring projects to ameliorate this situation, and the work reported in this book presents perhaps another step toward that goal.

People often ask me how, as a physicist by profession, I came to organize a project on healing and reconciliation between women and men. The journey from there to here began when I was awakened to women's issues as a young man in college, and later to men's issues. As I read some of the early classics in feminist and "masculinist" literature, I was astounded by the sheer magnitude of gender oppression and amazed that these insights were only just emerging in the late twentieth century. Subsequently, I awoke to the magnitude and impact of my own gender conditioning, and I was forced to begin personal healing work in the face of two marriages that did not last. I never regarded these as "failed marriages," however, because I learned so much, and the lessons of the heart sometimes cannot be learned any other way. I owe a tremendous debt of gratitude especially to my first wife, and also to other women in my personal life through whom I learned many vital lessons early in life. For this I am forever grateful.

After completing my doctorate in mathematical physics and conducting research on quantum theory and chaos theory, I joined an international scientific think tank, where my professional focus shifted to sustainable alternatives to nuclear power and fossil fuels. Before long I found myself embroiled in a scientific controversy, and became a reluctant whistle blower when I uncovered unscrupulous data manipulation to advance the political objectives of the nuclear industry. I returned to graduate school in the late 1980s to study Eastern philosophy and transpersonal psychology, and trained for three years in Holotropic Breathwork with Stanislav Grof, who was an important teacher for me. Other key teachers and influences along the way have included Ravi Ravindra, Joanna Macy, Richard Tarnas, Barbara Findeisen, and, more recently, Llewellyn Vaughan-Lee and Father Thomas Keating, as well as many students and colleagues I have been privileged to work with over the years.

For six years I had the privilege of working closely with two clinical psychologists in Atlanta: Sharyn Faro and Bonnie Morrison, whose clientele included many lesbian and gay clients, as well as victims of sexual trauma and abuse. We utilized Holotropic Breathwork extensively in clinical settings for deep experiential healing, and I experienced firsthand the unbelievable suffering perpetrated through sexual violation and gender oppression. Profound healings occurred frequently in this work, and this clinical background became part of the foundation for building Satyana's gender reconciliation work.

I began Zen meditation in the early 1980s, followed by several Vipassana meditation retreats and, later, Tibetan Buddhist retreats. Then I was introduced to the mystical wisdom of India, and was profoundly blessed to receive firsthand guidance from a little-known Indian spiritual master. This changed my life completely and flowered into a passionate commitment to the spiritual journey and to serving the Divine. This ripened into a deep commitment to the mystical path, which was further enriched by encounters with the Sufi and Christian mystical traditions. In the process, my involvement in gender reconciliation work has been thoroughly transformed, and the present book is a direct outgrowth of this experience. For all this, my gratitude knows no bounds.

The masculine/feminine consorts in the deities of the Hindu and Buddhist mystical traditions have inspired me greatly, along with the ravishing beauty of mystical poetry by Rumi, Jnaneswar, Ramprasad, Rab'ia, Kabir, Mirabai, and others. I have been astounded by how poorly women are treated in many of these societies that have produced such profound devotional poetry to the Divine Feminine.

I have been fortunate to be closely involved with several intentional communities since 1984, especially Findhorn (Scotland) and more recently Maher (India) and Damanhur (Italy). I was blessed to participate with several colleagues in the founding of the Global Ecovillage Network in the early 1990s. In visiting numerous spiritual and intentional communities across the globe I have witnessed the tribulations and triumphs of various communities grappling deeply with the complex nexus of gender, sexuality, intimacy, and spirituality, which has informed the development of Satyana's gender reconciliation work.

Taken together, all of these experiences and factors have instilled in me a passion for deep healing and transformation of relations between women and men. Once awakened to the magnitude of the need, coupled with the paucity of substantive responses in most societies across the globe, I felt compelled to offer whatever contribution might be possible, and the work documented in this book is the result. Let the readers be the judge of its value, and build further upon this work if they find it worthy.

The gender reconciliation work of Satyana Institute evolved over a period of fifteen years, beginning with early prototypes and collaborations with various colleagues. In the early 1990s I collaborated with social activist Heart Phoenix and Australian deep-ecologist John Seed, who organized a series of prototype workshops that brought male and female environmental activists together to explore the nexus of gender and ecology. Over the years, other collaborators became involved, including (in alphabetical order) Liz Bragg, Davis Chapman, Raphael Tillman Fox, Kay Grindland, Harriet Rose Meiss, Bill Pfeiffer, Ben Robin, and Jeffrey Weisberg.

In the mid-1990s I began developing gender reconciliation work-shops for wider venues in collaboration with Johanna Johnson, Allen Kanner, Amy Fox, Anne Yeomans, and others, and I published an article on gender reconciliation in *ReVision* magazine (Winter 1995). Meanwhile, some of the early colleagues also continued to develop the work, including Heart Phoenix and Jeffrey Weissberg, who cre-ated a series of gender workshops entitled "Beyond the Veil," which they have offered regularly at Kripalu Center in Massachusetts and elsewhere.

In the late 1990s my longtime friend and colleague Diane Haug began collaborating with me on this work, and then Molly Dwyer joined Satyana Institute while completing her Ph.D. dissertation on the cosmology of gender. Molly made important contributions to the work before moving on in 2003 to pursue her passion for writ-ing fiction, and Diane continues to collaborate with us periodically. Cynthia Brix joined Satyana Institute in 2001 as Administrative Coordinator, and upon completing divinity school, Cynthia became Program Director for Satyana Institute.

Many guest faculty have added their insights to this rich mix over the years, including Peter Rutter, Carol Flinders, Andrew Harvey, Christopher Kilmartin, Lucia Ticzon, Rina Swenson, Mahnaz Afkhami, Larry Robinson, and Stuart Sovatsky. All of these col-leagues brought their unique gifts to the gender reconciliation work, which has grown and benefited through many stages of its evolution, and now the work seems poised to reach out to yet wider and more diverse audiences through this book.

Given the magnitude of the healing required between women and men across the globe, I am acutely aware of the limitations of our gender reconciliation work and of its limited scope when com-pared to the vast need for global gender healing. Nevertheless, it has been a deep privilege to witness the remarkable courage, integrity, and sheer audacity of nearly seven hundred women and men from many different cultures as they forged new ground to engage in this work. It has been incredibly inspiring to watch these wonderful men and women as they grappled—sometimes humblingly, sometimes triumphantly (usually both!)—with some of the most daunting challenges facing human society today.

To all these wonderful pioneers who had the courage and vulnerability to embark upon this work together, let me say *Thank You* for making this work what it has become, and for providing the inspiration to write this book. May the fruits of your "heart"-earned labor inspire and benefit men and women across the world!

*Note to the Reader*

Throughout the book, the names of workshop attendees, and some minor details, have been changed to protect the identity of all participants.

# CHAPTER 1

# Oasis of Truth:
# The Call for Reconciliation
# Between Women and Men

*The Beloved is with those whose hearts
are broken for the sake of the Beloved.*

—Sufi saying

"Can a woman become enlightened?" asked the bright, aspiring student with keen enthusiasm. Her shining eyes revealed her heart's exuberant passion for spiritual realization. This burning desire had led her to northern India, where she had joined the exiled Buddhist community that had fled Tibet to escape Chinese persecution.

"No," came the solemn reply from the wizened senior lama. He was one of the most venerated masters in the Tibetan Buddhist tradition, and his sonorous voice imparted a commanding authority and measured calm. "A woman can advance to a very high spiritual stage, just prior to enlightenment," he continued in deep resonant tones. "Then she must die and be reborn as a man, in order to attain enlightenment."

*Why??* wondered the young woman inwardly, her crestfallen heart sinking rapidly with profound disappointment. She reluctantly accepted the answer from the wise old lama with quiet resignation. She had no choice: the lama's spiritual integrity, depth, and authority were beyond question. He was a highly revered teacher whose very presence exuded profound qualities of deep wisdom and compassion, qualities to which her yearning heart ardently aspired. She could even feel his compassion for her tragic plight, as a woman aspiring for the impossible. The very word for "woman" in the Tibetan language means literally "lesser birth."

*But why must a human being be a man in order to become spiritually enlightened?* She continued to puzzle over the question, deeply in fact, for many years. The more she pondered the question, the less sense it made. She tried to rationalize it, comforting herself with the thought that the enlightened state is beyond all reason and sense of mind, so perhaps this deep truth could only be realized after a woman dies and is reborn a man and becomes enlightened herself . . . er . . . *himself*! Or perhaps it's like a Zen koan, she mused, something that transcends all logic and mental comprehension altogether. Meanwhile, like the other Tibetan nuns, she was relegated to cooking, cleaning, and supporting the monks. But the question would not let her rest, and she continued to wrestle with it for years, from many different angles.

She found another lama who initiated her into the esoteric practices of Tibetan Buddhist meditation. Her sincerity and depth of commitment led her to move into a cave, high in the Himalayas at thirteen thousand feet, where she lived alone for twelve years. There she meditated for twelve hours every day, spending a total of more than fifty-two thousand hours in meditation. Profound depths of spiritual and mystical consciousness were awakened within her. Over those twelve years, she almost died twice, first when her cave was sealed shut in a huge snowstorm, but she was able to dig herself out. The second time was from a large falling rock. She was sitting quietly when suddenly she heard an inner voice say, "Move." When she did not respond immediately, the voice repeated itself urgently. "Move, *now!*" She moved, and a gigantic boulder suddenly fell exactly where she had been sitting.

But the voice was silent on other matters, such as her dilemma of being a woman striving in vain for spiritual enlightenment. Her commitment to spiritual realization was absolute. Yet she could not attain the ultimate goal. Why? Because she was a woman. Not because she was perhaps insufficiently pure of heart. Not because she was maybe not committed deeply enough, or insufficiently disciplined in her meditation practice. Not because she was imperfect in her austerity or aspiration or prayers—all of which were plausible reasons she could readily accept and understand. But because she was a woman. She carried her dilemma into deep meditation. Yet, unlike other quandaries or issues that she took inward into deep contemplation, this one did not resolve itself. The situation did not become ever clearer and self-evident. Instead it became all the more bewildering and confusing. The more she pondered it, the more befuddled it became—even ludicrous. The bottom line boiled down to a simple, ridiculous question that posed itself in her mind starkly: *What is so spiritually special about a penis that it is impossible to become enlightened without one?*

Finally, one day she had the opportunity to ask her question of other senior lamas. She had come down from the mountain after twelve years in meditation, having achieved something that few senior lamas had ever done. Indeed, her intensive solo retreat high in a mountain cave for twelve years was something all the lamas had been convinced was impossible for any woman to accomplish. She was now afforded tremendous respect among the leaders of the Tibetan Buddhist tradition. At one point, she was invited to a high-level meeting of many of the highest lamas in the tradition. She was the only woman present.

There she again asked the same question: "Can a woman become enlightened?" And again, three of the senior lamas told her, "No." So she asked them to please go into meditation, and in all seriousness to ponder this question in earnest: *Why is it that a woman cannot attain enlightenment? In particular, what exactly is it that is so spiritually special about the male reproductive organs that it is impossible to become enlightened without them?*

The three lamas went away and duly meditated upon the question for several days. Then they came back and told her, "We do not know." The woman gazed intently at each lama in turn, searching for any further clues or insights. None were forthcoming.

"We could not discover the answer," they concluded.

"Ah, yes," she responded, "and this is because it isn't true." She then announced to these senior lamas that she was making a firm commitment to continue to incarnate in female form until she became a fully enlightened buddha in a woman's body.

This is the true story of Tenzin Palmo, a Tibetan Buddhist nun born in Britain who still lives in northern India today, where she runs a nunnery she founded to train Tibetan nuns in the esoteric Buddhist practices that have been denied women for more than a thousand years. Tenzin Palmo's Dongyu Gatsal Ling Nunnery, together with a few other pioneering projects, is reversing centuries of patriarchal precedent in Tibetan Buddhism. And the nunnery has now received the blessing of the Dalai Lama, who, by the way, has told Tenzin Palmo that a woman can indeed become enlightened.

**Essence of Gender Reconciliation**

The foregoing anecdote reveals, in its bare essentials, the nature of gender healing and reconciliation between women and men. In essence, the process is simple: women and men gather together—on equal terms, in integrity, dropping the usual conditioned denials, taboos, and excuses—and jointly explore the truth of their experiences, vulnerabilities, insights, and aspirations. Through this process, they make discoveries together and allow new awareness to dawn. They allow these new revelations to change them, embracing whatever healing is required and taking full responsibility for the consequences of whatever is jointly discovered and experienced. When this work is conducted with integrity and sensitivity by even a small number of women and men, the resulting benefits are not for them alone but filter back into the community to benefit the larger society.

While Tenzin Palmo's story may seem charming, almost whimsical, and certainly comical in hindsight, living through those challenging years was very real and deeply painful for her. She was denied the transformative esoteric practices of Tibetan Buddhism—one of the most profound and beautiful schools of spiritual wisdom in human history—simply because she was a woman. Those were the loneliest years of her life, far lonelier than her extended solitude in the cave. Meanwhile, the Tibetan people—men and women alike—had never questioned the gender inequity in their tradition because for them it was based on the "reality" of who women and men are. Yet, it was sheer illusion, sitting right there at the core of a tradition committed to dispelling illusions—and for many centuries this illusion had unjustly denied Tibetan women, and especially Tibetan nuns, their spiritual birthright.

Neither Tenzin Palmo nor the lamas could have achieved this breakthrough on their own. They needed each other. She needed sincere, well-intentioned male lamas to whom to pose the question. The lamas needed her to ask the question in earnest in order for them to even embark upon the inquiry. She further needed the men to respond with integrity, and they did so—thereby honoring her and upholding the spiritual principles of their tradition. Together, Tenzin Palmo and these few lamas achieved a profound breakthrough—not only (or even primarily) for themselves, but for the Tibetan people and the entire Vajrayana Buddhist tradition, as women are admitted into the ranks of spiritual mastery. This breakthrough has helped change the Tibetan Buddhist tradition forever.

Of course, in other cases of gender reconciliation the process can and usually does look very different, depending on the circumstances. It may entail cathartic emotional releases, or powerful dynamic energies coming into play, or the profound spiritual grace that pours forth at times. But the essence of the process at its best is basically the same: women and men join together as equals, they get deeply honest with each other about their experiences, and through this process they heal past wounds, awaken to new realizations together, reach a place of reconciliation and forgiveness, and are thereby mutually transformed.

**Oasis of Truth: The Need for a New Forum for Women and Men**
The forum that Tenzin Palmo was finally afforded—a context in which she was taken seriously and where she could ask the unaskable questions—is something that every human being longs for: an oasis of truth where the deep questions can be asked in earnest and where one can drink directly from the wellsprings of truth, free of the conditioned responses and cultural thought-forms that shape and distort so much of our experience of being human. In the case of gender, such an oasis would be a forum in which women and men

can gather in integrity, raise challenging questions about gender and sexuality, discuss the undiscussable, and allow healing and reconciliation to unfold naturally. Societies everywhere need just such a forum—yet virtually nowhere does it exist. Even in spiritual communities or groups or similar contexts where we might expect such an open forum to be present, frequently there are taboos on speaking openly about gender issues and dynamics, particularly in cases where the leadership may be engaged in gender power dynamics or sexual activities that are kept hidden from view.

Gender reconciliation work seeks to provide this needed forum—an oasis of truth and healing where issues concerning masculine and feminine; lesbian, gay, bisexual and transgender (LGBT); cultural conditioning and power dynamics around sexuality and gender can finally be addressed openly and honestly. A forum where real stories can be told, in uncensored detail, and be truly heard. A forum that is not limited to dialogue alone but welcomes the consequences of asking the deep questions—where tears, outrage, embarrassment, anguish, shame, absurdity, forgiveness, compassion, healing, and spiritual grace can all come forth in their innate and flowing wisdom. A place where the heart can melt or soar as needed and the human spirit can triumph through the trials and tribulation of thousands of years of gender oppression and injustice.

Such a forum is needed in every culture across the globe. It must go beyond mere verbal exchange and conceptual understanding into a place of mutuality, compassion, forgiveness, and communion. This book documents a modest first step in this direction.

## Satyana Institute's Power of Reconciliation Project

To begin creating a forum for gender healing and reconciliation, the author and various colleagues founded a project initially called Gender Reconciliation, and more recently Power of Reconciliation, hosted by the Satyana Institute, a nonprofit service organization founded by Will Keepin and Jed Swift that is currently based near Seattle, Washington. Over time, Satyana Institute has developed a gender-collaboration process for healing and reconciliation of gender-based conflict and injustice. The process is founded on universal principles of love and forgiveness, and the methodology weaves a broad mix of modalities, including psychological and therapeutic techniques, contemplative disciplines, experiential exercises, and transpersonal and spiritual approaches. This diverse methodology has proven vital to the success of the work. To limit gender healing to cognitive or dialogical modalities would tend to derail the process and preclude a deeper, transformative process. The latter occurs when men and women transcend the tensions and divisions of gender duality through a shared emotional, psychological, and spiritual breakthrough into a higher unity.

Over the past fifteen years, Satyana Institute and its earlier incarnations have convened more than forty gatherings for women and men to jointly explore "gender reconciliation." Most of these events were five-day intensive residential workshops; the rest were of shorter duration, including weekend workshops, daylong events, and conference presentations. These gatherings provide a unique forum for women and men to jointly confront the realities of gender disharmony and engage in constructive dialogue and healing work on some of the most divisive and seemingly intractable gender issues. The process has been found to work equally well both in affluent Western countries and in societies of severe gender injustice such as India and South Africa. This book describes what we have experienced and learned in these gatherings. We offer it in hopes that it will inspire further work that builds on the promising results we have witnessed thus far.

The fundamental premise underlying Satyana's gender reconciliation work is that both women and men suffer the effects of gender injustice and that women and men need each other for a true and complete healing and reconciliation. Although major strides forward have been taken by both the women's and men's movements in the past several decades, neither group working alone can create gender balance in society. The sexes must work together for this balance to be realized, collaborating in courageous new forms of experimental and transformative modalities. A whole new approach is needed that goes beyond the more traditional methods of social and political reform.

In this book, we use the term "gender reconciliation" or "gender healing" to refer to the particular form of healing and reconciliation work that is documented herein for women and men (regardless of

participants' sexual orientations). The terminology "gender reconciliation" is quite new, as an Internet search quickly shows. The term
could potentially be interpreted in a variety of ways and may have
different meanings in other contexts. Sometimes when people hear
this term they assume it has to do with reconciling conflicts about
one's own gender identity, which is not what we mean here. For our
purposes, we adopt the term "gender reconciliation" as a shorthand
way to refer to the particular form of healing work between women
and men described in this book.

The purpose of gender reconciliation is to transform the roots of
gender imbalance at multiple levels: within the individual, in interpersonal relationships, and in the larger society. Gender reconciliation seeks to provide a safe and skillfully facilitated forum where
women and men can jointly examine the subtle knots of cultural
conditioning around gender and sexuality, support each other in
healing the roots of negative gender dynamics, and address the associated inequities and injustices in the world. In carefully designed
and facilitated group process exercises, issues rarely discussed aloud
are openly shared and collectively addressed. The process entails the
power of mindful, heartfelt truth-telling in community coupled with
the mysterious grace of loving witness, forgiveness, and compassionate presence to facilitate deep healing and reconciliation. A detailed
outline of the design and stages of Satyana Institute's gender reconciliation model is presented in Appendix A.

The gender issues and dynamics that arise in our gender reconciliation events are nothing new in themselves. Gender injustice
is age-old and universal, and the key issues have been frequently
addressed in women's and men's groups—working in isolation from
each other—as they strive to bring consciousness to the hidden gender injustices of our society. This separation of women's groups and
men's groups was historically necessary because authentic gender
healing work could not have begun in any other way, and indeed
such work must continue.

Now the time has come to take a next step: forging creative
ways for men and women to collaborate on mutual gender healing.
Powerful new dimensions of transformative work between women

and men become possible when difficult gender issues are confronted with integrity and sensitivity in mixed groups.

To our knowledge, the work reported in this book represents one of the very few organized, sustained efforts in collaborative gender healing with women and men working together. Other gender healing work that bears some relation to Satyana's work has utilized various methods, primarily different forms of dialogue. Examples include a series of successful weekend workshops for women and men entitled Essential Peacemaking, developed during the 1990s by Danaan Parry and Jerilyn Brusseau prior to Parry's untimely death in 1996.[1] Another series of gender dialogue workshops was developed by the Stone Center in Wellesley, Massachusetts, culminating in the book *We Have to Talk*, by Samuel Shem and Janet Surrey.[2] Marion Woodman and Robert Bly conducted a series of experiential, mytho-poetic workshops for men and women, and co-authored the book *The Maiden King: The Reunion of Masculine and Feminine*.[3] An interesting weeklong gender dialogue experiment in the form of a camping trip is chronicled in the book, *What Women and Men Really Want*, by Aaron Kipnis and Elizabeth Herron.[4] Riane Eisler and David Loye have pioneered what they call the "partnership" model for gender relations in their book *The Partnership Way*.[5] Beyond these, there are of course innumerable popular books on gender and intimate relationships, most of which are less directly relevant to our work, such as the *Men Are from Mars/Women Are from Venus* series by John Gray and the books on gender communication styles by Deborah Tannen. Several books on conscious sexuality by authors such as Miranda Shaw, Georg Feuerstein, Barry Long, David Deida, and Amarananda Bhairavan are quite useful. Other books relevant to various aspects of our work will be cited as we proceed.

The work reported in this book is practical and experiential in nature rather than analytical or theoretical, and the results are applicable in a wide range of theoretical or philosophical contexts. Theories abound about the nature of gender differences, and of course these theories often contradict each other. The essentialist theory, for example, proposes that in their basic nature women and men are fundamentally different—biologically, psychologically, and spiritually. In contrast, the constructivist theory proposes that women and men are fundamentally the same, with the apparent differences resulting from social constructions. For the present work, it matters little which theoretical, philosophical, or spiritual perspective the reader holds about the nature of gender, or related questions. As the reader will discover, what transpires in the events reported in this book does not depend for its validity on any particular philosophical perspective or spiritual orientation.

## Casualties in the "Gender War"

While this book presents an optimistic and positive message, it is nevertheless important to begin by acknowledging the extremely painful manifestations of gender injustice in our society today. Although many of us are familiar with the realities of gender violence, it is instructive to review a few of the sobering statistics, focusing in particular on the distinct ways in which different subgroups of the population are afflicted.

## Women's Gender-Trauma Statistics

- In the United States, a woman is raped or sexually assaulted every minute—usually by a friend or acquaintance. One out of every five women is a victim of rape in her lifetime. Worldwide, 40 to 60 percent of sexual assaults are committed against girls fifteen years of age or younger, regardless of region or culture.
- Domestic violence is the leading cause of injury and death to women between the ages of fifteen and forty-four worldwide. At least one out of every three women and girls worldwide has been beaten or sexually abused in her lifetime. These rates are higher in Africa, Latin America, and Asia, where UN statistics indicate up to 58 percent of women have experienced physical violence.
- Between 40 and 70 percent of all female murder victims are killed by their intimate partners. In the United States, FBI data indicate that at least half of the 5,328 women murdered in 1990 were killed by their husbands or boyfriends.
- "Honor killings" by male family members claim the lives of thousands of girls and women in Hindu, Middle Eastern and Asian cultures every year.

- An estimated twenty-five thousand women are doused in kerosene and set ablaze each year in India by their husbands or inlaws. These excruciating murders are generally dismissed as kitchen accidents by a patriarchal justice system.
- In the United States, nearly twice as many women (12.4 million) as men suffer from depression each year.

## Men's Gender-Trauma Statistics
- The victims of men's violence are mostly other men, accounting for 80 percent of male violence.
- Men commit suicide four times more often than women.
- In the United States, 6.4 million men suffer from depression each year.
- Male depression more often goes unrecognized and untreated.
- In 2007 the Boy Scouts of America was legally forced to reveal, for the first time, its secret archives on sexually abusive scout leaders—exposing a vast history of pedophilia perpetrated against young scouts that required the dismissal of at least 5,100 scout leaders since 1946.
- Among teenagers, males account for fully 90 percent of completed suicides, a statistic that speaks volumes about the pressures on young men coming of age.
- Men have higher death rates than women for all fifteen leading causes of death.
- Men account for 60 percent of traffic fatalities, 79 percent of murder victims, 95 percent of workplace fatalities, and 99.993 percent of deaths in armed combat.
- The average life span for men is 11 percent shorter than for women. Male stress is the decisive factor.

## Lesbian-Gay-Bisexual-Transgender Trauma Statistics
- In sixteen U.S. cities, reported incidents of violence against lesbian/gay/bisexual/transgender (LGBT) individuals recently increased by an average 242 percent over a single year. Incidents of further harassment and abuse of LGBT victims by police increased by 155 percent over the same period (NCAVP study).

• At the 2007 World Social Forum in Nairobi, violence against the LGBT community in Africa was highlighted as a major concern. Human Rights Watch recently documented sharp increases in anti-lesbian violence in South Africa.

These statistics reflect grim social realities of gender injustice and associated human rights violations. They also reflect cultural pressures on both women and men to submit to unhealthy and dis-empowering models of femininity and masculinity. In societies across the globe, people of both sexes and every gender identity are boxed into narrowly defined roles, and in most countries there are strong reprisals for those who dare to step beyond these rigid restrictions. These pressures inevitably produce widespread self- and gender conflict, which takes an incalculable toll on all societies. Even in the West, despite the supposed emancipation of women, there are strong cultural forces and pressures that favor men and uphold masculine values disproportionately. Western societies are thus far from gender balanced, and the pretense that they are is one of the obstacles to making further headway.

**Domestic Misery: The Iceberg Underlying Domestic Violence**
Terrorism is a widely publicized threat in many countries of the world today. Yet, this danger is minuscule compared to the daily terrorism of domestic violence, which plagues at least one in three households across the globe. In the United States today, for example, the public is obsessed with the potential threat from foreign terrorists. Yet in purely statistical terms, most citizens have a far greater chance of being murdered or attacked by their own intimate partners or family members than by a terrorist. Where is the public outrage about this? How are Americans mobilizing to ameliorate this far more urgent threat that claims far more lives than terrorism?

In any war, the wounded always far outnumber the dead. Whatever number of people are killed, there are always many more who are wounded, usually by a factor of ten or more. And the wounded are yet again far outnumbered by those who are psychologically damaged or stricken.

Consider what this means for the "gender war" of domestic violence. As reflected in the statistics above, domestic violence is the leading cause of murder for women in the United States. Similar patterns hold in most other countries across the globe. Tragic as they are, these deaths are only the most severe casualties in the gender conflict. Beyond these "war dead," there are many thousands or millions more who are wounded and injured every year through physical and sexual abuse perpetrated by those who supposedly love them most. And again, quite beyond these "wounded" are many more millions, or rather billions, who are psychologically damaged, depressed, stricken—living under oppressive or threatening conditions in their own homes and communities. Thus massive numbers of people are suffering deeply in their closest intimate and family relationships.

What we call domestic violence is but the tip of an iceberg of vast suffering that afflicts billions—a phenomenon that could be called "domestic misery." Precisely in those relationships where one is supposed to feel the most loved and accepted, many people are the most miserable and vulnerable—all across the globe. Much of this domestic misery is created and sustained by dysfunctional relations between women and men—often held in place by oppressive gender, social, and religious conditioning within the society—from which its hapless victims know not how to escape.

This vast collective misery is then projected outward, which fuels corresponding forms of misery and oppression in social institutions and in relations among nations. It is a cliché but true that "peace begins at home." Yet "home" is precisely where billions experience no true peace whatsoever. As Mahatma Gandhi emphasized, if we practice love and nonviolence in the outer world but we don't manifest these principles in our daily home life, then any success in the outer world is a chimera.

What all this points to is a global crisis in "right relations" of such gigantic proportions it is almost inconceivable. This crisis cries out for a massive societal response, but compared to the magnitude of the suffering involved it seems to receive comparatively little attention. Domestic violence is tearing up our communities, yet we live almost as if it weren't there—rather like living next to a gigantic mountain that is so huge everyone takes it for granted and barely even notices it.

## The Unfathomable Power of Love

A major factor that helps keep all this domestic misery firmly in place is not talking about it. Individuals, families, and society collude to keep this stupendous suffering well hidden. For example, a key lesson borne out for the authors from years of facilitating gender reconciliation work is that there exist large and crucial gaps in women's awareness of men and in men's awareness of women. These gaps in mutual awareness are kept in place by all manner of taboos and forbidden topics of conversation or inquiry in society—especially in mixed company, but also within each gender grouping. As a result, men do not realize the depth and nature of the suffering endured by women, nor do women realize the nature and depth of men's suffering, nor do heterosexuals realize the nature and extent of suffering in LGBT populations. Women do not grasp the devastating pain and incapacitation that boys and men suffer as they are conditioned to become "real men": how their emotions are denied them, how their inner sensitivities are bludgeoned in masculine competition, how their sexuality is brutalized and desacralized through masculine conditioning—be it in the schoolyard, the family, the church, the military, or the workplace. Nor do men realize the magnitude of women's and girls' suffering in relation to the incessant threat (or experience) of rape, physical abuse, and psychological violence; the denial of girls' and women's authentic voices and intuitive powers; the oppressive conditioning around female beauty; fears around body image; the painful realities of sexual harassment and the glass ceiling in the workplace—to name a few. In all societies, both women and men are powerfully conditioned to repress the daily realities of these experiences and to collude with the rest of society in keeping these dimensions of shared experience hidden. Similar patterns apply in relation to the suffering of LGBT populations, to which the heterosexual population is often completely oblivious.

Yet it is precisely in bringing courageous and compassionate light to these taboo arenas that deep healing and transformation of social gender conditioning can take place. As Martin Luther King, Jr., emphasized, social change does not happen by keeping corruption and injustice hidden, but rather by confronting darkness with the power of love. No matter how challenging the ensuing process may become at times, the inner light and love in the human heart always has the power to dispel darkness and ignorance. The process calls forth—indeed *demands*—the highest from the human heart, which for lack of a better term we can call "divine consciousness," something that dwells deeply within every human being regardless of race or of cultural or religious heritage. This divine consciousness manifests as the awakening of a universal love, the *agape* that transcends all human weakness, darkness, and obscurity. Gender healing and reconciliation consciously invokes this universal love of the heart, which in the end has the capacity to overcome the very real and formidable challenges of gender oppression and injustice that have tormented human societies for literally thousands of years. In King's words, if "pessimism concerning human nature is not balanced by an optimism concerning divine nature," then we "overlook the cure of grace." The power of love invokes this grace, which in turn facilitates deep healing and fosters authentic social change. Without conscious cultivation of love, the grace does not come, and the social healing does not last.

Although Martin Luther King spoke of this process in Christian terms, precisely the same process is described in Hindu terms by the twin principles of *ahimsa* and *satyagraha*, articulated by Mahatma Gandhi. Gandhi emphasized that *ahimsa* and *satyagraha* confer a "matchless and universal power" upon those who practice them. Satyana's gender reconciliation work draws upon these universal spiritual principles. As such, our work draws from all spiritual traditions, and is not beholden to any one tradition. This spiritual orientation is discussed more fully below and in the next chapter.

**The Alchemical Nature of Gender Reconciliation**
How is the power of this universal love activated and invoked in practice? We adopt the term "collective alchemy" to describe how it unfolds in the gender healing process. The ancient tradition of alchemy has been widely discredited and mischaracterized in modern

society as an arcane physical science that sought to turn lead into gold. Yet the deeper significance of alchemy has little to do with physical transformation and is instead a spiritual process in which the "lead" of the human psyche—the inner darkness and repressed "poisons" lodged in the mind and heart (called "prima material")—are confronted directly and transmuted into the golden light of love. As sages across the traditions have affirmed, when the dross of the false self burns, it becomes part of the light. Alchemy refers to this process, which operates by the unfathomable power of love. The process has long been known by spiritual masters in various traditions, yet only relatively recently, through the work of pioneers such as Carl Jung, has alchemy been recognized in the West as having any legitimacy.

Traditionally, alchemy refers to a process of spiritual transformation that takes place within an individual. As Sufi master and Jungian scholar Llewellyn Vaughan-Lee describes the process, the divine light or spark of the soul is directed to areas of blocked awareness or unconsciousness within the individual. As the light of the soul is directed inward, it illuminates and eventually dispels the darkness within. At first this process brings to conscious awareness what has been repressed and pushed away. This is often quite a painful and humbling process, because it typically unmasks a large amount of repugnant "shadow" material in the consciousness of the individual. Yet deep within this very darkness dwells an innate light, which Jung termed the "lumen natura." As the alchemical process continues, this latent inner light is awakened, and over time it completely transforms the individual into a being of light. Although greatly oversimplified in this description, in essence the darkness within is transmuted into light and love.[6]

In gender healing work, an analogous process takes place on a collective or community level. We gather in a diverse group—as women and men, for example—and after setting the context and creating a safe space for the work, we begin by skillfully exploring arenas that are usually avoided or unacknowledged in relation to participants' experiences of gender in their lives. We confront the collective darkness in our society in relation to gender conditioning, sexuality, and the oppression of the feminine that has predominated since antiquity. The process is initially painful, which is why it is usually avoided in our society or, if entered, rarely carried beyond this stage. In gender healing work we keep going and continue to examine key issues directly and openly, without flinching, yet with compassion, as men and women together. In so doing we bring the light of our personal and social consciousness to dark corridors of human pain that have long been neglected and suppressed. As the process continues, something remarkable eventually begins to happen. There is an awakening of a new light, an unexpected healing energy and grace that arises in some form. This is surprising to many participants because often, just when it appears that the group is beginning to tread the most intractable or hopeless territory—territory that seems utterly beyond our limited capacity to embrace—there is an infusion of healing presence and grace that suffuses each person with love and opens the door to new pathways together as a group. This ushers in powerful group experiences of healing, reconciliation, and forgiveness that constitute the "gold" of this collective alchemy.

The process of collective alchemy takes some time to understand and must be witnessed repeatedly to be understood deeply. Although it takes place within a group and includes a strong element of healing, it is fundamentally different from a collective psychological process such as group therapy. In group therapy, the therapist is a trained professional who holds clinical authority in the group and works with each individual as the group process unfolds. The role of the therapist is, in part, to point out what needs healing in each individual and to be the "expert" on each person's process.

In gender reconciliation work, if there is a "therapist" present at all, it is the group wisdom itself. When someone bares his or her soul before the rest of the group or community, it is not the role of the facilitators or other participants to analyze that person's story or experience. Rather, the story is witnessed and received by everyone in the group, which often precipitates some further opening or sharing from others in the group. The process then evolves organically within the group, building a synergistic momentum that may unfold in any number of creative directions. Over time, as trust builds in the community, the personal disclosures and stories begin to unmask ever more vulnerable truths or hidden secrets, and as the community attends to these, the alchemical nature of the process begins to unveil itself. From within the inevitable darkness and distress, light begins to shine forth.

This bears similarity to a process the Sufis call "light upon light," in which the inner light of the soul is met and amplified by a corresponding light from the Divine. The Indian sage Sri Aurobindo describes this same process in his Integral Yoga, where the grace of spiritual aspiration stretching "upward" from the human heart is met and greatly amplified by a spiritual grace that "descends" from the Divine plane. In gender reconciliation work, this process takes place within a group or community rather than in one person's interior spiritual journey.

As people turn the light of collective attention toward their interior vulnerabilities and hidden secrets, the initial shock and outrage they may feel soon dissolves into a deep, abiding comfort that comes with facing truth directly. Then a sense of the real begins to take hold, and people are comforted and even nurtured by this unmasked truth far more than they are scandalized by whatever disclosed secrets or dashed illusions are entailed, most of which they already knew deep down in their hearts anyway. The power of the work comes through this alchemical process in which the darkness is transmuted into light, and the energy that was trapped in maintaining rigid social strictures and unhealthy cultural conditioning becomes freed up and released.

This alchemical process characterizes group reconciliation work of any kind, but it is especially intensified when working with gender issues. This is because in gender and sexuality the intimacy of the heart is involved as well as the body and mind. Wrapped up in gender is the longing of the human heart for love and intimacy, embracing all levels from the desire for a beloved partner or spouse to universal forms of love for God or the Divine.

Gender reconciliation work is not for everyone. It requires a high degree of willingness to be personally challenged, to have one's secrets revealed, and to stretch and become vulnerable. Not everyone is open to this or ready for it. As one friend and colleague remarked to us wryly with a sheepish grin, "I'd sooner lie down naked in a pit of scorpions than do gender reconciliation work." Yet for those who are ready for it, the process can be deeply rewarding and is generally experienced as powerfully transformative and liberating.

## Masculine, Feminine, and Gender

In the course of our gender reconciliation work we strive to maintain an open mind to the intrinsic value inherent in all spiritual and philosophical perspectives, particularly because our work is practical and does not seek to advance any particular theoretical position. Nevertheless, as authors it is important for us to make our philosophical, psychological, sexual, and spiritual orientations and biases explicit in regard to this work. We draw heavily from the teachings and wisdom of spiritual and mystical traditions from both East and West, coupled with elements from Jungian and transpersonal psychology. As for the nature of sex difference, we lean toward what might be called a neo-Taoist perspective, affirming the complementarity of masculine and feminine principles, and we regard physical sexuality as a specific manifestation of a more universal complementarity, which could be thought of as a generalized yin/yang approach. This perspective suggests that complementary masculine and feminine principles or qualities dwell together in every human being, regardless of their conditioning and whether they have a male or female body. We hold this and all perspectives lightly.

A corollary of this perspective is that a dynamic balance between masculine and feminine principles and qualities is necessary for a healthy functioning person, relationship, or society. When there is a systematic imbalance between masculine and feminine, as has been the case in Western culture for more than three millennia, profound social malaise is the inevitable result, and this is the condition we find our society in today.

A healthy balance between masculine and feminine dimensions of life is fluid and dynamic, rather than fixed and static. At times the masculine principle prevails, at other times the feminine principle prevails, and the two energies are mutually interpenetrating (masculine) and mutually inter-receptive (feminine) in their eternal dance. Esoterically, masculine and feminine energies are linked together in the abandon of a profound love, rather than a struggle for power.

Exoterically, the dynamic balance of feminine and masculine manifests at multiple levels simultaneously: from the innermost solitude of the individual, to the family and community, and on up through the broadest domains of culture and civilization. Just as a bird can fly only by using both wings in a coordinated, dynamic balance, humanity can rise to its full potential and live in lasting peace only when a harmonious balance between feminine and masculine is realized.

Regarding gender and sexual orientation, we view these categories as encompassing a broad spectrum of legitimate possibilities and expressions that transcend a narrow masculine/feminine polarity. In general, we view "sex difference" as referring to biologically determined differences in bodily characteristics and physiology, whereas "gender" refers to a wide variety of related and socially constructed categories. While the author's personal life experiences have been heterosexual, the gender work itself has attracted people of diverse sexual orientations, including lesbian, gay, bisexual, and transgendered persons (LGBT). We value all of these diverse sexual orientations, as discussed more fully below. Interestingly, we have observed that the practical results of gender reconciliation work generally seem to unfold in broadly similar patterns for people from diverse philosophical, sexual, and spiritual backgrounds. The core of this work is the inner work of the heart, which transcends sexual orientation, body identification, and lifestyle and philosophical differences.

The purpose of Satyana's gender reconciliation work has not been to analyze or theorize about the nature of gender differences, but rather to convene forums in which women and men can enter into a deep exploration of and openhearted communication about their experiences as women and men and to move from this foundation through creative dynamic interaction to a place of mutual healing, forgiveness, and reconciliation.

**The Need for Change**
It almost goes without saying that the work reported in this book is just a beginning step. The need for healing and rebalancing of the feminine and masculine is vast and multidimensional, extending to

virtually every human society across the globe. The key issues of gender imbalance in women and men are deep, ancient, and complex; they are archetypal constructions that span all cultures and eras throughout human history. Clearly, the scope and depth of transformation required to achieve a harmonious gender balance in society is profound—far beyond what could be encompassed in any one project.

Nevertheless, while acknowledging the magnitude of the daunting challenge, this book outlines an initial, admittedly humble, step that can be taken toward this larger goal of social and cultural healing between women and men. While it is impossible to know exactly how such a comprehensive healing might eventually unfold, we do believe we have found an appropriate place to begin.

Sincere communication and honest exchange about challenging or delicate matters can be a transformative experience in itself. As the philosopher Martin Buber observed, genuine dialogue requires that all parties involved bring a willingness to be changed by the dialogue process itself. These changes take place because the participants create new meaning together—a meaning that is discovered afresh through their mutual interaction. Thus, participants coming out of such an exchange are different people from who they were going in, and the resulting meaning is shared, rather than belonging to any one participant. The requisite condition for this to happen is a willingness to be changed by the process. Without this willingness, true dialogue cannot take place.

The purpose of our gender reconciliation work has been to convene events wherein just such dialogues and related forms of healing and reconciliation can take place. This is not to suggest that profound experiences of this nature always happen in our gatherings. Such moments in shared or collective consciousness cannot be forced or preordained. The most we can do is to create the invitation and the requisite conditions for a genuine healing and reconciliation to take place. What then emerges is dependent on a wide range of factors—most especially, the intentions and readiness of the participants involved.

## Collective Healing of Gender Injustice

No human being escapes the affliction of cultural gender conditioning and associated injustice. It is so pervasive that it is taken for granted and assumed to be a normal and inevitable part of life. Most people are at least vaguely aware that our society tends to value the masculine over the feminine, yet few of us are aware of how powerfully this imbalance shapes our personal, family, and social realities on a daily basis. After thousands of years of structural injustice related to gender and sexuality, the level of systemic healing and transformation required to properly address this cultural imbalance can only be done in the collective—in the society from which it has emerged.

However, because no forum or vehicle exists for this level of healing in our culture, the burden falls upon every marriage and intimate partnership, as well as every professional or interpersonal relationship. These avenues are of course woefully inadequate to the task, through no fault of their own. In the privacy of every couple's bedroom, for example, the entire archetypal history and drama of the "battle of the sexes" is present. Every couple is saddled with a burden they can barely discern or comprehend, much less transform on their own. Having little or no direct awareness of this collective human pain, the couple nevertheless experiences its power and negative impact. Typically they do not recognize when the conflicts and tensions arising between them are not unique to their particular circumstances but rather are a manifestation of this collective human pain being channeled through them.

To escape from the pressure of this isolation we need to place the burden of gender healing back where it belongs—in the collective, with women and men working together in conscious community to foster the necessary healing. The possibility of such collective healing holds tremendous transformative power that remains as yet untapped. It is difficult for people to imagine the freedom and energy that would be released if our society were to seriously embrace this task of collective gender healing in community. The foundational fabric of society would be unraveled and rewoven anew; women and men could walk the streets alone in safety, children would be raised with an intrinsic respect for the sacred mystery of gender diversity in their schools and homes. Sexuality would be liberated as an expression of shared intimacy in a larger cultural context of harmony and balance—an environment that would support couples and intimate partnerships to reach to the heights of sublime communion and divinity in their experience of love. Yet, in the absence of this societal gender healing, none of these remarkable transformations can take place, except perhaps in rare isolated exceptions for a fortunate few.

Our society is thus called to embark upon a new venture in gender healing and transformation. After decades of separate women's and men's movements—valuable though they have been—another step is urgently needed: the time has come for women and men to band together to jointly create gender harmony. We must gather in mixed groups to plumb new depths of relational awareness, courageous truth-telling, compassionate listening, empathic sensitivity, and mutual healing. This form of gender work is almost entirely absent in our society, even in progressive social change movements and otherwise highly conscious spiritual communities. Yet there is a powerful yearning on the part of women and men of all sexual orientations—many of whom have done years of work in separate women's or men's groups—to now take this next step.

### Reconciliation: Moving Beyond Conflict Resolution

There is a growing body of literature today in the rapidly emerging field of reconciliation, which is becoming recognized as a crucial step beyond conflict resolution. Detailed review of this literature is beyond the scope of this book. Our purpose here is to present a practical body of work that cultivates reconciliation in the realms of gender healing. Nevertheless, a few summary remarks about reconciliation are appropriate.

Reconciliation is a step beyond the domain of conflict resolution, which, as traditionally defined and practiced, is coming to be viewed as inadequate for creating true healing, harmony, and effective community in arenas where there has been long-standing conflict. The work of reconciliation recognizes that a deeper level of community healing and bonding work is required that goes beyond agreements and resolutions between adversarial leaders. An altogether different kind of leadership is required to create pathways for relationships to flourish, and to heal wounds so as to support mutual growth between parties that have traditionally been in conflict.

A phenomenon reported in the reconciliation literature is that the leaders in this new field are rarely the same leaders who prevailed during processes of negotiation and conflict resolution. We have observed a parallel phenomenon in the nascent field of gender reconciliation. Leadership in gender reconciliation is not coming primarily from leaders in the women's movement or men's movement, as might be expected at first blush. Rather, the leadership is coming from small groups of women and men who are moving beyond the frameworks and agendas of the women's and men's movements and embarking upon an unprecedented level of healing and reconciliation across the gender divide. These women and men are not interested in mere conflict resolution, nor in winning concessions from the "other side," but rather in building an altogether new level of integrity and harmony between women and men that will one day enable humanity to reclaim the magic of a balanced communion between masculine and feminine. In their hearts, emerging leaders of gender reconciliation naturally draw back from partisan interests and are instead fueled by a passion for unity and communion among all peoples. Many of these emerging leaders have never had a strong involvement with either the women's movement or men's movement, and many who did have such an involvement report having grown weary of the one-sided struggles, coupled with a general absence of deep listening on both sides. Meanwhile, established leaders of women's and men's movements are often held back from this emerging reconciliation work, even if they are inclined in this direction, because they are beholden to constituencies with vested interests who expect their leaders to represent those interests.

Emerging leaders in reconciliation frequently have a strong commitment to spiritual transformation in their personal and professional lives and to manifesting an inclusive vision of social harmony for all. They are striving for practical unity and oneness within the entire human family—across all divisions of gender, race, religion, nation, creed, and class. Many are motivated by an inner conviction of an emerging universal spirituality that uplifts the noblest teachings common to all religions, while decrying rigid dogmas or exclusivist beliefs promulgated by any one religion or spiritual tradition. They tend to establish their primary collegial relationships and professional commitments not so much based on recognized standards of professional credentials and accomplishments but rather on the highest standards of ethical values, motivation, humility, and personal integrity—and they collaborate with those who can join them there. They do not rely upon their own intelligence and often considerable skills as their primary means of practical guidance and decision making, but rather they cultivate a powerful discernment and deep inner silence that enables them to pick up subtle cues that come from a larger universal wisdom. Finally, they recognize that all human beings are ultimately far more alike than they are different— regardless of gender difference, sexual orientation, race, class, and so forth—and that overcoming selfishness in every form and uniting people across their differences is the only path that will lead to a peaceful humanity. They regard all human beings as their brothers and sisters, and they tend to shun any social, religious, or economic practices that privilege any group or sect of human beings over the rest of humanity.

A key example of the reconciliation process in practice is the Truth and Reconciliation Commission (TRC) in post-apartheid South Africa. Led by Archbishop Desmond Tutu, the TRC represents one of the most unique experiments in human history on a national scale working explicitly with reconciliation and forgiveness. While the process was not without its flaws, the TRC fostered remarkable healing in a country that had been severely ravaged by systematic racial violence. The mandate of the TRC was not only to discover the truth, but also to go beyond truth finding to "promote national unity and reconciliation in a spirit of understanding which transcends the conflict and divisions of the past." Several important books analyzing the TRC experience have emerged recently, so there is no need to review the TRC in depth here. Nevertheless, it is important to note that the TRC's approach to reconciliation was shaped by and imbued with religious content, and it has facilitated a deep experience of healing that has enabled a fresh beginning in South African society in regard to racial integration.

The process of reconciliation is an inherently inclusive and spiritual process. It does not neglect traditional methodologies of conflict resolution such as negotiation and compromise, but it strives to move beyond these more expedient means to invoke spiritual principles and practices of compassion, wisdom, forgiveness, and expanded consciousness. These spiritual qualities are viewed not as unattainable ideals that are the province of saints alone, but rather as realistic and practical avenues for achieving unprecedented results in transforming human conflicts.

Just as the TRC in South Africa was underpinned by potent religious principles, so Satyana's gender reconciliation work is grounded in spiritual content of a universal nonsectarian nature, with a similar goal of fostering deep healing, reconciliation, and a fresh beginning. Perhaps this is one reason that Satyana's gender reconciliation work has been enthusiastically embraced in South Africa among leaders in the government, faith communities, and activist communities. It seems that in light of their pioneering leadership in reconciliation, the people of South Africa are ready to embrace another needed level of reconciliation in relation to gender. These issues are discussed more fully in Chapter 10, which describes Satyana Institute's work in South Africa.

## Working with Shifting Sexual Orientations and Gender Identities

Traditional gender identities and sexual orientations are being profoundly questioned and widely deconstructed today, particularly among younger generations in Western societies. Lesbian, gay, bisexual, and transgender (LGBT) concerns have come much more into public view over the past few decades as the cultural dominance of heterosexuality and the binary male/female dichotomy have come under increasing scrutiny and criticism. Within a few short decades, societies across the globe have been awakened to a much greater level of acceptance of diverse sexual orientations, quite beyond traditional heterosexual values and biases.

These sweeping changes have made a major contribution to dismantling some of the most destructive forms of gender conditioning. Alternatives to the traditional rigid masculine and feminine gender roles are emerging, giving people greater freedom to express their uniqueness and explore new forms of gender identity and sexuality beyond heterosexual norms. Taboos on homosexuality are being lifted, and several countries are implementing pioneering legislation to sanction same-sex marriages, or at least civil unions.

The orthodox separation of all human beings into two distinct biological categories of male and female is coming into scientific question. About one in every fifteen hundred newborn infants is "intersexed," meaning that their genitalia do not conform to the usual male or female anatomy. Since the nineteenth century intersexed infants have been surgically altered to make them either male or female (usually the latter). However, this practice is coming under intense criticism, as the intersexed individuals have often grown to feel as adults that their sexual identity was mistakenly forced upon them by the medical community. This contentious arena is raising challenging new scientific and medical questions about male and female biology and anatomy.

Despite growing acceptance, LGBT populations have been severely persecuted in most if not all societies across the globe, including the supposedly advanced Western countries. LGBT individuals have also been the target of increasing "hate crimes," homophobia, and long-standing discriminatory policies that constitute systematic violations of their fundamental human rights. These abuses of human rights have been increasingly reported in the media and press in recent decades, and new legislation is slowly being implemented in many countries to protect these vulnerable populations. In May 2007 the U.S. House of Representatives passed a bill to prevent hate-crimes that included "gender diversity." Nine U.S. states and the District of Columbia now have anti-discrimination laws that protect transgender people, and three more states have legislation pending. In some countries such as South Africa, gender justice is guaranteed as a basic human right for all citizens in the Bill of Rights, including choice of sexual orientation, yet the

society has a long way to go in practice to catch up with the ideals
of its Constitution.

Over the years in Satyana's gender reconciliation work, we
have worked with participants of all sexual orientations, although
the majority of our clientele have been heterosexual women and
men. We have also collaborated with several bisexual, lesbian, and
gay co-facilitators and guest faculty. Six years of intensive healing
work with lesbian and gay clients (mentioned in the introduction)
greatly sensitized the author (Will) to LGBT concerns. In Satyana
Institute's yearlong professional training program in gender reconciliation, eleven out of thirty-three trainees identified as either
bisexual (seven), lesbian (two), gay (one), or transgender (one). This
invaluable experience has provided deep learnings and vital contributions to our gender reconciliation work. Satyana Institute has
always welcomed LGBT individuals to our programs, and we uphold
the importance and legitimacy of LGBT issues. Nevertheless, of the
approximately seven hundred participants in our gender reconciliation programs over the years, more than 80 percent have identified as
heterosexual. Although Satyana's gender reconciliation model works
well for bisexual, lesbian, and gay participants, some of these clients
have understandably preferred to explore other modalities of gender
work that are focused more exclusively on LGBT issues. Satyana's
gender reconciliation model is less ideally suited for transgender
participants who do not identify as either women or men except in
cases where there is a substantial number of transgender participants,
in which case we have completely reconfigured the model in some
events, with promising results. Variations in the model to accommo-
date these situations are discussed in more detail in Appendix A.

In summary, the dynamics within a gender-diverse group have the
potential to become a source of creative tension within the group,
and if properly handled, this can serve to move all participants into
a powerful experience of awakening, healing, and transformative
learning. In most of Satyana Institute's gatherings that have combined heterosexual and LGBT participants, a profound level of gender healing work has resulted that would not have occurred in the
same way if the group had not been so diverse.

**Spiritual Basis of Gender Reconciliation**

Our work regards the spiritual dimensions of human consciousness and society as fundamental to gender healing and reconciliation. This commitment is not rooted in any particular religious ideology or spiritual philosophy. Rather, we seek to invoke universal spiritual values that are not tied to any particular tradition but which underpin all authentic spiritual traditions. Such an inclusive perspective is becoming increasingly recognized as vital to the understanding of spiritual consciousness in human society. It represents what is sometimes called "the perennial philosophy," "interfaith spirituality," "integral spirituality," or "ageless wisdom"—terms that refer to a broad synthesis of universal truths in cross-cultural spiritual wisdom. Such a synthesis of the world's wisdom traditions is certainly not new but is today gaining a much wider recognition as vital to awakening a deep and urgently needed level of global consciousness and human unity.

The present book is not a theoretical volume, and our purpose is not to argue for any philosophical or spiritual framework over another. We simply draw upon the primacy of Spirit in human consciousness as reflected throughout the world's wisdom traditions, and affirm that for authentic gender reconciliation to take place—whether on the individual, family, societal, or cultural level—it is essential to include the spiritual dimension of human consciousness. Without consciously taking account of Spirit and invoking this transformative dimension of human existence, the dilemma of gender disharmony and injustice—which has afflicted human societies across the globe for thousands of years—will never be resolved. Psychological and social reforms alone—whether in legal, political, or theological garb—will not suffice.

In our work, we draw upon many different spiritual traditions and practices, applying them as seems appropriate to our task of cultivating the domain of gender reconciliation. All cultures and societies—from the most ancient to the most industrial or the most esoteric—have grappled with the polarity and complementarity of masculine and feminine, and each has contributed important insights and practices. Thus we draw on specific contributions from different traditions and perspectives as appropriate, including, for example: silent meditation practices (such as Vipassana meditation), the yin-yang duality of Taoism, the lover/Beloved of Sufism, the timeless wisdom of Hindu and Buddhist traditions, Christian mystical symbolism, the Goddess traditions, and the indigenous Native American traditions, including the tradition of *berdache* (third or fourth genders, beyond male and female).

Certain archetypal representations of masculine and feminine polarity and dynamic unity are of special value at times in gender reconciliation work, such as the half-male/half-female deity of Ardhranarishvara in Hindu mysticism, the *conjunctio oppositorum* of alchemy, the Christian tradition of bridal mysticism, the rich symbolism of the *Mahabharata* in Hindu mythology, Mother Earth and Father Sky in indigenous wisdom, the tree of life in the Jewish Kaballah, the Gnostic gospels' representations of male and female, the *heiros gamos* (sacred marriage), and the tantric union of male and female deities in Hinduism and Vajrayana Buddhism. Recognizing that spiritual wisdom itself evolves, we do not limit ourselves to these codified traditions alone, because new insights are emerging all the time.

In this process, we are deliberate in applying specific insights or invoking particular archetypes with care at points where they emerge through the work naturally, or when they illuminate our purpose. However, we never impose any particular perspective. Our goal is decidedly not to develop or propose a universal, all-encompassing framework for understanding the spiritual dimensions of masculine and feminine as they manifest in different cultural traditions and contexts. On the contrary, we sense that, ultimately, feminine and masculine aspects of existence are portals to a much larger mystery whose deepest roots are utterly sacred and far beyond any capacity for expression in conceptual models or frameworks. Thus, "gender" is but a doorway to a vast inner universe of ultimate relationships between oneness and duality, manifest and divine, being and nonbeing, temporal and eternal.

We have found that this eclectic spiritual approach works well in practice, but we invoke this inclusive pluralism without making a dogma of such a model or framework. "All models are wrong, but some are useful," as the saying goes. We draw upon universal models as potentially insightful frameworks, but we do not impose them as a set of universal truths that must be accepted before the work of gender reconciliation can begin.

Our work in gender reconciliation has been hands-on and experiential, not theoretical or conceptual. Participants require no common spiritual framework to embark upon gender healing work together. We have worked equally comfortably with staunch Catholics, devout Muslims, Zen meditators, secular humanists, Western scientists, clergy of various denominations, New Age visionaries, as well as with groups that mix all of these up together. The gender conditioning we have all experienced cuts across these categories and unites us in a common work to be done together as human beings. From this foundation, gender healing work proceeds naturally.

For participants who do not have a strong spiritual background or orientation, gender reconciliation work can sometimes serve as a natural pathway to awakening spiritual insight. To give an example, when a community of women and men explore gender dynamics together, contradictory truths and perceptions often emerge—both across the sexes and within each sex grouping. Such moments of apparent impasse provide significant opportunities for breakthrough. As the community stays with the uncomfortable tension of contradiction, individuals begin to perceive the truth of "the other" as their own experience, and the polarities of conflicting positions often dissolve into an unexpected emergence of a deeper underlying unity: a profound recognition that, ultimately, there is no "other." We are all one. This remarkable realization occurs not infrequently in the course of gender healing work—as a direct perception, rather than as a mere concept or philosophical principle. Thus "gender" can serve as a powerful vehicle for awakening transformative insights and realizations.

In practice, working from a foundation of universal spiritual values that underpin gender reconciliation helps male and female participants embrace the goal of transforming—rather than "winning"—gender conflicts and facilitates a deeper trust in the more confounding or mysterious elements of the process. It helps people to embrace the interpenetrating spiritual, cultural, and psychological dynamics of gender work and the complex subtleties that inevitably arise. Pascal's famous adage, "The heart has reasons of which reason has no knowledge," aptly characterizes the spiritual dimension of gender reconciliation work.

Let us now launch this work by invoking a prayer from the great mystical poet Jnaneswar:

I honor the God and the Goddess,
The eternal parents of the Universe . . .
What beauty! Both are made of the same nectar,
And share the same food.

Out of Supreme Love,
They swallow each other up,
But separate again,
For the joy of being two.

The are not completely the same,
But neither are they different.
None can tell exactly what they are.

How sweet is their love!
The entire universe is too small to contain them,
Yet they live happily together
In the tiniest particle,
and in the heart of every being.
They dwell together,
Both wearing a garment of light.
From the beginning of time they have been together
Reveling in their own Supreme Love . . .[7]

# CHAPTER 2

# Cultivating Compassion: Principles of Gender Reconciliation

*When you make the two into one, and when you make the male and female into a single one, so that the male will not be male nor the female be female, then shall you enter the Kingdom of Heaven.*

—Gospel of Thomas (Logion 22)

In the Jain spiritual tradition there is a parable about a man who becomes very ill. His wife cares for him diligently, giving him nurturing meals and body rubs and tending to his every physical need. The doctor comes and gives him medicine. Other family members visit, giving him loving attention. In spite of all this, he gets worse and worse. Then one day he experiences a powerful opening in his heart to the presence of God, and when this happens, he is healed. As he quickly recovers, all those who cared for him feel vindicated that their loving ministrations finally succeeded. The doctor smiles confidently in his conviction that his medicine has been effective, and the wife rests assured that the healthy food and loving massage she has given her husband are responsible for his recovery. Yet all of them are mistaken in attributing the healing to themselves. The man's inward opening to the presence of Spirit actually created the healing.

This parable underscores the essence of healing, which is intrinsically mysterious to our cognitive minds. We do not know how healing "works." It is quite beyond our rational capacity to understand. We cannot direct it, yet we can participate in its unfolding. We may develop certain theories about it and recognize certain aspects of the process, but, in practice, the most we can do is to align ourselves with the deeper wisdom of the healing process. We invite and invoke and support the healing process, and then it inevitably takes its own course.

*Just as a physical wound knows how to heal itself, so too the human psyche instinctively knows how to heal itself.* This principle is foundational to gender healing work, and perhaps to all healing work, as it reflects the existence of a larger force or mystery that is responsible for healing. Our task in gender reconciliation work is to allow this mysterious healing process to unfold in its own organic, natural manner—and to be directed by it rather than attempting to direct it.

The metaphor of a physical wound is apt. When we get a cut or laceration, we keep it clean and covered to keep the dirt out. The cut then heals of its own accord; we don't do the healing ourselves. We could not even begin to tell the blood vessels how to reconnect, or the skin how to regenerate itself. The most we can do is create an environment conducive for the healing to take place. Our bodies, not our minds, know internally what to do to heal.

The process of healing the human psyche, including the kinds of wounds that trouble the masculine and the feminine—both within individuals and between women and men in society—is much the same. We do not have to consciously understand all the subtle intricacies of the healing process in order to participate in it. Nor can we consciously direct the healing in the ways we are accustomed to orchestrating or managing other endeavors. The invisible fuel for this healing process is our heartfelt compassion and loving presence and the sincerity of the collective intention that we bring to it.

## Principles of Gender Reconciliation

Five foundational themes have arisen over the years in our work with gender reconciliation—key understandings that have emerged through observation and experience. These ideas ground the philosophical underpinnings of the work and motivate its practical application. All five reflect patterns we've seen repeatedly or pitfalls that have emerged time and again. Taken together, these five principles contribute to our emerging perspective about working with women and men together and to the manner in which the overall process of gender reconciliation unfolds. We offer these principles here, not as definitive truths or axioms but rather as guidelines gleaned from our explorations into the rich domain of gender reconciliation.

1. *A spiritual foundation is essential for gender reconciliation.*

Gender imbalance is, at its root, a collective spiritual crisis. Hence, spiritual principles and practices, universal and nonsectarian, are essential to transforming gender relations. By "spiritual foundation" or "divine consciousness," we simply mean recognition of the existence of some form of larger presence or higher wisdom that is fundamental to all life and existence. It is something beyond what the mind can comprehend directly, but this makes it no less real. No matter how it is named—whether we call it God or Goddess, the Divine, Tao, Spirit, or simply the Universe—there is an essential mystery of consciousness, creative genius, and universal love that permeates all of existence. In gender reconciliation work, this ineffable mystery is consciously invoked and embraced, and we rely upon and align ourselves with it.

Every religious tradition affirms some version of this mystery. There is something "out there" or "in here" that is omnipresent and all powerful, and which must be our guide if we are to be instruments for the transformation of the unhealthy dynamics at play in our species. If we ignore this hidden mystery and depend solely on our own devices, our vision is myopic and our work is rendered ineffective or incomplete.

A striking contemporary formulation of this universal consciousness or wisdom is given in the work of the Snowmass Conference, a pioneering group of spiritual leaders from nine major world religions. Founded by Benedictine monk Thomas Keating, the group has been meeting over a period of twenty years and is comprised of leaders from diverse religions, including Protestant, Catholic, Eastern

Orthodox, Islamic, Jewish, Native American, Hindu, Theravadan Buddhist, and Tibetan Buddhist. This group created a list of points of universal agreement shared by all. The first of these points is the existence of an Ultimate Reality to which different names are given in different traditions but which cannot be limited by any name or concept and which is the source of the infinite potentiality and actualization of all human beings. Suffering, ignorance, weakness, and illusion are the result of our experiencing the human condition as separate from this Ultimate Reality.

Thomas Berry reiterates this principle, stating that in order to grapple effectively with the destructive conditions that are engulfing the planet we must "lean on the Universe." This is another way of saying, "Not my will but Thy will"—which requires surrender to the larger wisdom of the forces that gave rise to all existence. There is something beyond the human being that we must embrace if we are going to find our way to genuine healing or positive change that will endure.

This is not to say that agnostics, atheists, and others who consider themselves "nonspiritual" cannot participate in or benefit from gender reconciliation work. Indeed, the work itself generally entails an opening of the heart, which speaks in its own language to a deeper universal experience. Keating's Snowmass conference affirms that "Ultimate Reality may be experienced not only through religious practices, but also through nature, art, human relationships, and service to others." In many traditions a practice of "formative community" can facilitate initiatory experiences of deep insight or awakening, and this is frequently experienced in the work of gender reconciliation.

Perhaps the most fundamental duality in human existence is that of male and female. Working with women and men together allows for the possibility of a profound communion across the duality of masculine and feminine and an awakening into a deeply shared understanding and experience. Gender reconciliation is thus a form of training that begins by moving individuals out of their own self identifications and into a kind of empathic connection with "otherness," and from there eventually into an experience of Oneness.

Lasting harmony between the sexes cannot be achieved through social, psychological, or political reform alone. These modes are certainly valuable and necessary for realizing gender equality in society, but they are not sufficient in themselves because gender reconciliation entails an inherent spiritual dimension. Gender disharmony is vast and pervasive; its symptoms are manifest in myriad ways in virtually every culture across the globe. For authentic gender reconciliation, we aspire to a comprehensive approach that includes but also transcends traditional modes of social change, invoking a larger universal intelligence or grace. For this, we must consciously place ourselves in relationship to that larger wisdom.

In the New Testament there is a parable about a sick woman who reaches out as Christ walks by, and she touches the hem of his robe. He spins around and says, "Who touched me? Power has gone out of me." Trembling, the woman acknowledges her action—and, in fact, she is healed. She had no idea how this healing would come about; she simply knew that Jesus was passing nearby and that her only hope was to stretch out to touch that which could heal. Her action, her faith, and her conviction—not the robe of Jesus—brought about her healing.

When we convene a group for gender healing and reconciliation, we are collectively taking similar action. We stretch ourselves to a larger consciousness and grace that is *beyond our capacity, but within our reach.* This action and experience is related to what mystics speak of in referring to union with the Divine: an annihilation of self in which the "I" is dissolved altogether and merged into a higher experiential unity. All true healers know that when healing unfolds at its best, there is no egoistic self that does the work; rather it is simply being done, as the spirit or Divine moving on earth. In gender reconciliation groups, we collectively reach for an unknown power or grace that has a healing potential far beyond our own capabilities or understanding. We invite this power and presence, knowing from experience that something transcendent and universal can and does work through us and it dwarfs our own mechanisms for healing, thinking, fixing, and/or reconstructing what needs to be healed. As with all spiritual healing, the gender wound of humanity will one day heal not because we know how to fix it, but through its own mysterious capacity, coupled with our collective consent and openness to the process.

*2.  Gender healing and reconciliation require that equal value be placed on feminine and masculine perspectives, and that intrinsic differences between the sexes be honored and appreciated.*

In gender reconciliation work it is crucial to maintain a dynamic balance between the masculine and feminine perspectives and to avoid any systematic bias toward either. Both men and women are damaged, and each needs the other for true and complete healing. Maintaining gender balance does not mean that the different perspectives should provide the same kind of information or awareness. An essential aspect of gender reconciliation work is to "hold the tension of opposites," as Jung put it. This means giving equal support to fundamentally different or opposing perspectives in a collective container so that the alchemy of opposites can work its creative magic. Indeed, the male and female perspectives are often fundamentally different in ways that make for synergistic depth and clarity, creating something that neither perspective could accomplish on its own. As physicist Niels Bohr has expressed this principle, "The opposite of a profound truth is often another profound truth."

Still, a bias toward either a masculine or feminine perspective can creep into this work. Much has been done in the last several decades to articulate an essential feminist critique of our culture, yet this critique can inadvertently leave us failing to recognize the damage that has also been done to men. We have often seen reflected in our gender workshops the impasse that currently exists between the women's and men's movements. Each side demands to be heard by the other; then, not feeling heard, each side articulates the same points again and again. To break through this impasse, each group must clear its collective mind of its own gender-focused bias or agenda and listen deeply to receive the other.

Too often when men and women engage in dialogue, the result is merely cognitive exchanges of information, heard by the other side through the filters of its own gender bias and conditioning and often dismissed without being truly received. When women and men listen with the heart, however, a liberating or cleansing process comes about in the collective, and something transformative moves through both parties and into the dialogue.

In personal development and spiritual work, awareness of one's own "shadow" is essential to the process, serving as grist for the mill of transformation. In the same way, a collective awareness of the gender shadow is grist for the mill of gender reconciliation. It is essential that we look at this shadow directly, without denial or defensive posturing. It is vital that women and men—heterosexuals, lesbians, and gays—learn to listen to each other in a deep and authentic way. To do so we must look together at what each of us carries in our collective shadow and examine the parts of ourselves that we don't necessarily want to share. If we can create forums where such sharing is possible—where such things can come forward in an atmosphere free of judgment and blame—we can then begin to create the conditions for a collective transformation around gender consciousness that our culture urgently needs.

Every human being embodies both masculine and feminine qualities. To be whole, each person must ultimately create a balanced integration of these qualities that is unique to her- or himself. Sadly, our society still perpetuates the false ideal that a real man should be all masculine, and a real woman all feminine. Neither is possible, nor desirable. As Jung and many others have emphasized, every individual integrates a combination of personal qualities drawn from a broad spectrum ranging from the "essential" masculine to the "essential" feminine. And because each individual integrates masculine and feminine characteristics differently, a rich diversity and collective power emerges in a group or community of women and men that brings these multiple combinations into dynamic synergy.

To be a real man or a real woman simply means to become fully human. And this entails integrating a dynamic balance between what have traditionally been identified as feminine and masculine qualities. In very general terms, men need to integrate qualities that have been traditionally associated with the feminine, such as compassion, sensitivity, and nurturing; and women need to integrate qualities that have traditionally been associated with the masculine, such as leadership, assertiveness, and risk-taking. When these qualities are balanced in any human being, the result is a dramatic rise in empowerment, creativity, and well-being.

Just as a man and a woman must be united to create a child, so too masculine and feminine qualities must be united to create the fullness of a human being. Gerda Lerner has pointed out that "when we see with one eye, our vision is limited in range and devoid of depth." Just as visual acuity is achieved by combining the information coming through both of our eyes, so depth of human experience arises from synthesizing the gifts of both masculine and feminine qualities.

*3. Transforming the cultural foundations of gender imbalance is best done in groups or communities.*

In today's world, when we encounter challenging gender dynamics in personal relationships, we generally seek to resolve these struggles on a personal or interpersonal level. We reflect on our personal issues and failures, or we focus on the failures of our partners and friends, and/or we may go into couple's therapy. In so doing, we collapse the situation into the private and the personal sphere, giving insufficient attention to the fact that we are all profoundly impacted by social and cultural conditioning in relation to gender. This conditioning is so ubiquitous that we take it for granted, and so fully integrated into our surroundings that we are hardly aware that it exists.

Because gender disharmony is a cultural affliction that affects the collective social consciousness, gender reconciliation is necessarily collective work. It asks participants not only to consider their individual experience but also to harmonize with collective energies and work with the diversity and range of perspectives that each individual brings to the group. Working in groups, participants find that their boundaries begin to expand outward from the personal dimension and benefit from a collective synergy and energetic spaciousness. When gender issues are introduced into this context, individuals begin to realize that many of the gender challenges they struggle with are systemic: hidden forces operating in the collective that are quite beyond their own personal failings or understandings. For many, this is a major revelation—a shocking realization of the extent to which they were socialized and conditioned at every stage of life, from earliest childhood onward.

No one escapes gender conditioning. Most of us unwittingly carry the cultural gender shadow into our important relationships, and we end up in struggles with our partners, family members, friends, and colleagues that aren't really about us as individuals. When women and men do gender reconciliation work in community, they begin to see the power of this cultural baggage in a new light. They realize the prevalence of overarching social patterns and conditioning in much of their experience—and comprehend that, in this larger context, they are not alone in what happened to them. This is a profound realization that has to be embraced holistically. It is not enough to understand it cognitively; it must be experienced emotionally and psychically. It must become wisdom of the heart. Gender reconciliation potentially allows each individual to see—in a deeper way—just how great a disservice their cultural conditioning has been.

Another key reason that gender reconciliation work is best done in groups or communities is that communities are the fertile ground for the coming era of humanity's awakening. Vietnamese Zen master Thich Nhat Hanh has said that the next Buddha will come not as an individual but in the form of a community—a group of people living together in loving kindness and mindful awareness. Many contemporary mystics are echoing this view, including Sufi teacher Llewellyn Vaughan-Lee, who says there is a new divine energy coming into humanity that will operate only in communities and groups, and the "rules" for spiritual awakening have changed. Communities are now fundamental vehicles for that awakening.

Indeed, humans have reached a point where different forms of synergistic cooperation may be the only way to survive. This awareness points to the need for women and men to join in community and discover together the ways in which the gender shadow has made itself manifest. Gender reconciliation work, and the power of our collective intention, create a crucible for catalyzing the necessary healing in the larger society.

4. *The process of gender reconciliation requires the fullness of our humanity—integrating physical, emotional, intellectual, and spiritual dimensions—to create the conditions for genuine transformation.*

If any essential aspect of our humanity is omitted in gender reconciliation work, the resulting transformation will be neither authentic nor lasting. Our society often ignores or sidesteps challenging truths, dilemmas, or difficult emotional expressions when they arise. Entire institutions are created to formalize and reify these omissions. Our religious institutions frequently deny the physical dimension in an attempt to "transcend" this "lower" part of ourselves. Our academic and political systems tend to downplay our intuitive or spiritual parts in a quest to be "rational" or scientific. Most social institutions tend to inhibit our emotional and artistic expression and often systematically suppress the uniqueness of each human being.

This socialized repression helps to keep structural gender injustice and imbalances in place. As a corrective, we must develop constructive ways to give full voice and expression to the spectrum of responses associated with our gendered experience—including the challenging emotions of anger, grief, fear, sorrow, shame, despair, and vulnerability. Indeed, a critical aspect of gender work is skillful facilitation of intense emotional process. This means embracing our humanity in its own experiential currency—and not rationalizing, repressing, sublimating, or denying the emotional or less "tidy" parts of ourselves.

Over the years we have encountered numerous attempts at gender healing work that limit their methodology to dialogical or cognitive modalities alone. We have found that restricting the work in this way often derails the process entirely. For example, two psychotherapist colleagues, a man and a woman, had each been running separate men's and women's groups for several years. The two colleagues decided to initiate a gender reconciliation process for their clients by combining their two groups. After only two meetings, and a classic gender confrontation, the project came to an abrupt end. What happened? At the first meeting, one of the men told one of the women that she had beautiful hands. The woman felt objectified, rather than seen for who she really was. The man felt he was innocently reaching out in sincerity to give an innocuous compliment to the woman.

A verbal exchange between the two spread into the larger group and rapidly escalated into a heated conflict that divided the group along gender lines and was left unresolved. The same discord arose again in the second meeting, and the ensuing dialogue deteriorated into a gridlock from which the group simply could not recover, despite the genuine goodwill that had brought the two groups together. The organizers felt they had no choice but to abandon the project altogether. From our perspective, this outcome was the result of the process being limited to dialogue and verbal exchange. The tensions that were triggered in the mixed group required a deeper level of processing that could not be reached through words alone.

To take another example: one of the authors (Will) once attended a workshop on Bohmian dialogue led by Lee Nichol, a skilled facilitator who presented dialogue workshops all over the United States and abroad. Developed by physicist David Bohm, Bohmian dialogue is a powerful method designed to support collective inquiry and creative communication in groups. One of its foundational principles is that there is never a prescribed agenda for the dialogue—the focus of the conversation must be free to go wherever the group takes it. After the workshop, Will asked Nichol if he ever intervened on the content of the conversation, rather than merely on process. Nichol replied that there is only one area in which he does intervene: the "man/woman issue." As Nichol explained, this is the one issue with the capacity—if not the tendency—to draw the group into a nonconstructive quagmire in which the dialogue process itself breaks down.

This anecdote hints at two telling realizations: first, that to explore the "man-woman issue" is precisely what many groups need to do in order to discover a whole new level of group consciousness and depth of experience; and second, that dialogue alone is not an adequate methodology to take the group there.

In gender reconciliation work there are times when powerful emotional expression and releases of various kinds are necessary. To inhibit them is to obstruct or block the reconciliation process. There are other times when contemplative silence, group meditation or prayer, breathwork, psychodrama, spontaneous ritual, or other forms of nonverbal group work are absolutely essential to the skillful resolution of what arises in the process. Throughout this book we describe some of the practices we have employed that go beyond the cognitive and verbal levels to help free up the psychic and energetic blockages that inevitably surface in gender healing work.

The need for nonverbal forms of group process and facilitation applies not only to creating a safe space for the release of challenging emotions but also to allowing the presence of ecstatic dimensions of consciousness. These aspects of the work can be tremendously healing, and arise in ways that are often quite startling to those who have little experience in deep group process work. Indeed, a primary motivation for insisting on appropriate experiential avenues for processing challenging emotional energies is not for their own sake alone but also because, in so doing, we simultaneously create the possibility for the expression of highly benevolent emotional and spiritual energies, which often follow naturally on the heels of deep emotional release work. Such positive energies can manifest in a variety of ways, including richly moving or inspiring forms of creative, artistic, or ecstatic expression. It is not enough simply to tell inspiring stories or read beautiful poems celebrating the qualities of the masculine and feminine and their eternal dance. It is vital to create experiential contexts in which people can actually touch these dimensions directly, witness them living in one another, and celebrate the birthright of our full humanity as men and women on the earth.

5. *Transforming gender relations is uncharted territory. No experts, road maps, or guidebooks exist.*

Gender disharmony is vast and ancient, and the implications touch every aspect of human society. As conveners and organizers of gender reconciliation work we make no claim to have found definitive answers for transforming gender relations. After fifteen years of facilitating gender work, our methods and approaches continue to evolve, and there is certainly no definitive formula that applies to all situations. Yet, one thing we have learned is this: bringing compassionate, unflinching awareness to gender dynamics in groups and communities is a remarkably powerful place to begin. As in all spiritual practice, deepening awareness is itself transformative.

This point may seem self-evident. Yet we have consistently observed that there are large gaps in women's fundamental awareness of men's experience, and corresponding gaps in men's awareness of women. The two sexes are quite ignorant of various dimensions of each other's social reality and individual experience. And there are equally large gaps in mutual awareness of heterosexual and homosexual/lesbian experience. Furthermore, there are social taboos and tacitly forbidden subjects for discussion in our culture that prevent women and men from exploring many realms of gendered experience—not only in mixed company, but also within each gender group. These taboos range from issues like rape and pornography to issues of fundamental identity and essence and experience of sexuality and intimacy.

There are myriad ways in which gender injustice is unconsciously supported and perpetuated in society. We mentioned in Chapter 1 a few ways in which men and women are unaware of one another's social reality. Beyond this, both men and women are socialized to unconsciously perpetuate harmful myths within their own gender. For example, men need to examine among themselves the insidious ways in which men are conditioned to ridicule or dominate women and reject the feminine through habitual socialized behavior and humor and to foist reprisals upon those men who don't buy into the dominant model of "macho" patriarchal conditioning. And women need to examine their complicity in exploiting and enforcing injurious cultural norms around physical beauty and sexual attractiveness, sometimes using these energies to manipulate men and each other, thereby exacerbating the very objectification from which women seek to escape. These and other learned socialized behaviors are so routine and pervasive they often escape our conscious notice. Hence, many of us unwittingly perpetuate gender disharmony in innumerable subtle ways while holding the sincere conviction that we are not personally complicit in the spread of gender injustice.

Today's widespread social disharmony in relation to gender is not inevitable for human society, although it is the inevitable product of thousands of years of systemic gender injustice across the globe. Because we have never known anything else, it is difficult or impossible for us to imagine what life would be like if we had grown up in a society that was truly integrated and healthy in relation to gender and sexuality. The entire fabric of human society would be vastly different from what we know today. The forums for social interaction, the depth and intimacy of interpersonal relationships, the structure and roles of family and community, the exalted expression and celebration of the erotic, the nature and forms of religious worship and spiritual ceremony—all these aspects of life would likely be profoundly different from today's cultural norms and socialized patterns. Taken together, these elements would comprise a rich and fulfilling community life that we can only guess at, yet is often glimpsed in gender reconciliation work.

Perhaps there do exist a rare few individuals who were fortunate enough to grow up in a truly gender-healed community, tucked away somewhere in an isolated society far removed from the cultural mainstream. But the vast majority of us—whether from the West or the East, North or South—have no experience of life in such a harmonious social context, and we carry the multiple wounds and confusions of an unhealed humanity deep in our hearts. We carry this challenging burden not only in the form of our own personal histories and socialization, but also in the larger archetypal legacy of generations of humanity's collective pain around gender and sexuality. This leads to an incredible challenge when it comes to unraveling and healing these issues in society.

For young people, the challenge is especially daunting as they come of age and struggle to understand what is going on all around them, and how they should live. Their dilemma in relation to gender and sexuality is aptly described by the Tibetan Djwhal Khul:[1]

Our young people, especially the idealistic types and the clear-thinking boys and girls, find themselves faced with a situation that defies their best efforts. They do not know what to think or what to believe. They look into, or form part of, homes which are sanctified by legal marriage, and find (on a large scale) nothing but unhappiness, legalized prostitution, ill-health, the seeking of illicit relations outside the home, neglected and unwanted children, the friction produced by wrong mating, divorce, and no answer to their many intelligent questions. They then look elsewhere, into the lives of those who have avoided the responsibility of marriage, and find discontent, frequently a secret and hidden sex life, ill-health as a result of the frustration of the natural instincts, psychological conditions of the worst kind, sometimes illegitimate children, sexual perversions . . . They ask the worldly minded for a solution and for help, and get no clear reply, no sound philosophy and no fundamental instruction. The moralities of the past may be pointed out to them, or they may have the virtues of "straight living" eulogized to them. But no true solution is offered, and no light is thrown upon their problem. They may turn to the religious minded people, and be told to be good; the example of saints may be cited to them, or they may find themselves deluged in a flood of puritanical injunctions and righteous platitudes with unsatisfying explanations, based often on personal prejudice and predilection. But seldom is a clear note sounded, and seldom is it possible to do more than enunciate the great Mosaic law, "Thou shalt not . . ." Who can speak to them with real wisdom and understanding about this universal problem? Who truly comprehends the true significance of the sex life, its place in the great scheme of things, and the relation between the sexes? Who can say with true vision what the next evolutionary step will be, whither humanity is going?

Yet, despite this daunting morass and unenviable cultural heritage in relation to gender, it is also true that we are all experts on what needs to be healed, because we all have direct personal experience of the inequities and injustice. As Joanna Macy has observed, "Our wounds are our credentials." Indeed, we are collectively quite astute about the specific challenges and subtleties of what needs to be transformed in society. Yet, precisely because we have not lived in a gender-healed society, none of us are experts on how such a society would actually look, or what new forms social organization and interpersonal relations might take. Nor do we know how to accomplish the necessary healing and transformation to get us there. In short, we know what needs to be done, but we don't know how to do it.

For all these reasons, we must begin with the recognition that there are no experts in gender reconciliation, because (to borrow the vernacular) no one has "been there, done that" yet. This is equally true of the authors of this book. We make no claim to have found definitive "answers" for gender reconciliation, and thus we see ourselves as beginners rather than "experts" in this nascent field. From our perspective, no such experts currently exist. Nor are there maps or handbooks that can lead us out of the dense forest of gender injustice into the promised land of a healthy society of gender harmony.

However, that said, we do believe we have found a way to begin the process. And we don't believe it is necessary or even desirable to know in advance the details of where the process will ultimately lead. What is essential is to stay present for the task and maintain impeccable integrity in the gender healing process as it unfolds.

In the face of so many unknowns, how can we ensure even this integrity? How do we proceed in practice? The answers are simple enough, if challenging to implement at times: speaking our truth, witnessing with compassion, staying present throughout the process, bearing with its agonies as well as its ecstasies; not flinching from the difficult realities; trusting the emerging wisdom of the community; leaving nothing out, including anyone who participates in earnest; and, perhaps most of all, maintaining an unshakable faith in the human spirit. As facilitators and organizers, we have lived through many challenges in this work over the years. Yet, the healing moments have always outweighed the difficulties and provided the inspiration and confidence that helps us persevere on a path that will lead to the reconciliation and harmony that we all yearn for and which is our birthright as human beings.

### Ethical Guidelines and Agreements

To help support the implementation of the above principles of gender reconciliation in practice, we have developed a set of ethical guidelines and agreements which we ask participants to uphold throughout our events. These protocols or community rules support the integrity of the gender reconciliation process and help to ensure a safe, effective "container" in which to engage the group work. When registering for a workshop or training, participants are asked to commit themselves to these community agreements for the duration of the event.

For the most part, our guidelines and agreements reflect the kind of protocol often found in experiential healing or group process work in community. They include agreements to maintain confidentiality about what transpires during the event, to take responsibility for one's own experience and to respect the experience of others, to be mindful about one's own communication style and allow room for others to share, and to stay present for the duration of the process.

In addition to these more typical agreements, there are also some agreements or practices specific to this work that we ask participants to commit to during our time together. These include honoring the power of silence and recognizing that moments of silence often reveal deeper levels of meaning and subtlety in what transpires. We also ask participants to recognize that gender reconciliation work is uncharted territory for all of us and so it is essential to allow for ambiguity and uncertainty as we proceed and to learn to "hold the tension of opposites"—sitting with discomfort without necessarily rushing in to try to resolve or "fix" things.

Finally, we make an unusual request: we ask participants to refrain from romantic or sexual interactions during our gender reconciliation workshops, except in cases of established couples with a long-standing prior commitment. There is much to be learned about intimacy that cannot be experienced in the face of powerful forces of cultural conditioning around sexuality and intimate relations. By temporarily suspending society's unwritten rules of engagement pertaining to romantic and sexual pursuits, participants are supported to step beyond habitual behavior and familiar territory and enter into something altogether different.

The purpose of this temporary sexual moratorium is not to deny or denigrate sexuality in any way. Quite the contrary, it serves to create an exceptionally safe and intimate environment for comfortable discourse and collective inquiry on highly delicate or vulnerable matters relating to gender and sexuality. It also cultivates a deeper mindfulness of this powerful arena of life. When a group of people choose to consciously step back from habitual cultural conditioning around sexual energy and relations, a remarkable opportunity emerges to witness the profound impact of the daily onslaught of sexual innuendo and romantic ideals that are promulgated in mainstream society.

If the sun never set, we would have no perception of the vast depths of space, which become visible only at night when we are able to see what is obscured by the bright daylight. In similar fashion, we refrain from sexual interaction in gender reconciliation work in order to discover hidden depths of intimacy and subtlety that are otherwise obscured in our daily lives. Over the years, we have found that working in community with this agreement tends to cultivate new modes of shared intimacy, mutual inquiry, and collective healing on levels that are rarely experienced otherwise in normal social environments.

These guidelines and agreements have served to strengthen the gender reconciliation process, and of course they become particularly important when a crisis or conflict emerges within the group. At such moments, we often lean heavily upon these shared agreements as a foundation to maintain the integrity of the community as we carefully explore difficult and potentially divisive issues.

In closing this part of our consideration of gender healing, we quote the mystic poet Rainer Maria Rilke, who expressed the general philosophy underpinning our gender reconciliation work with great eloquence: "Have patience with everything unresolved in your heart, and try to love the questions themselves. Don't search for the answers, which could not be given to you now, because you would not be able to live them." Rilke's words capture the real purpose of our gender reconciliation work: not to search for the answers, or try to fix all that needs healing, or presume to know how to address the many ills afflicting us in relation to gender and sexuality, but rather to gather together in community to confront the difficult questions directly, and to love the questions themselves. "Perhaps then," as Rilke intimates, "someday far in the future, you will gradually, without even noticing it, live your way into the answer."

# CHAPTER 3

# *Bearing Witness to Gender Wounds*

*The world situation today, where sex is concerned, is so critical and so serious that there are no thinkers to be found who can yet see the solution, or who can find—no matter how clear their brains or erudite their minds—the way out of the present impasse.*

—Djwhal Khul (Alice Bailey)

Looking out at some two hundred upturned faces, now divided into separate women's and men's groups, we asked everyone in the auditorium to turn their chairs so they were no longer facing the podium, but rather were facing the other group across the aisle. There had been a general commotion only moments before as the conference participants had risen to their feet and walked to the side of the aisle where their gender group was gathering. This partition alone ushered in a tangible presence of archetypal energies as the men gathered on one side and the women on the other.

The setting was an international conference entitled "The Alchemy of Peacebuilding," held in Dubrovnik, Croatia, in June of 2002. The conference brought together activists, politicians, academics, and concerned citizens from several countries to explore new pathways to peace. Included among the participants was an impressive contingent of youth from around the Balkan region and an equally impressive group of young American leaders from the Watts neighborhood in Los Angeles. Many of these young people had experienced firsthand the violence of war or civil conflict. It was humbling to hear their stories, and inspiring to see their commitment to building a just peace in the world.

The energy level in the room intensified, and people were stimulated with both the curiosity and the slight trepidation that always accompanies the beginning of gender work. Instead of our usual opening presentation, we had given this group only a brief introduction to the wider cultural and historical framework of gender injustice. Time was limited—we had two and a half hours—and our goal was to give this earnest group an experiential glimpse into the process of gender reconciliation as a component of building peace in the world.

As the men and women turned to face one another, a paradoxical combination of heightened tension and deeper intimacy could be felt simultaneously as the group began a subtle shift toward becoming more of a community and less of an audience. We asked each person to pay attention to how it felt to consciously sit among her or his "own sex," and to notice whatever feelings arose simply from being placed in these groupings, opposite one another. We asked them to reflect on whether they felt at home within their ascribed gender group and to become aware of the tremendous gender diversity inherent within each group, acknowledging the broad range of life experience, sexual orientation, and body biology that each group embodied.

Next, we asked the participants to close their eyes and reflect inwardly on their experience of the world through their particular body and mind, including their unique biology, sexuality, gender identity, and spiritual orientation. During this silence we gently guided participants to be mindful of the inner terrain of their own most private and personal feeling states, taking note of whatever awareness or inner dialogue was present within them. We then invited a deepening of the silence, asking participants to enter into any practice of silence, meditation, or contemplation they found comfortable.

After sitting together in silence for several minutes, we read a poem from the Indian poet Jnaneswar celebrating the union of the sacred masculine and the sacred feminine (quoted at the end of Chapter 1). As we opened our eyes some minutes later and looked about the room, there was a sense of clear recognition that we were a group of earnest women and men who had gathered to explore and discover how to build bridges across diversity and difference in order to create more peace in our war-weary world. And present among us was this fundamental difference, common to all human beings in every culture, both ancient and modern: the duality of being incarnated in either male or female bodies.

**Silent Witnessing**
The conference community was now prepared to move into a process we call "silent witnessing." This practice tends to elicit complex emotional energies, memories, and insights as individuals bear witness to formative or challenging experiences in their personal lives relating to gender and sexual conditioning. Silent witnessing brings forward an immense degree of mutual awareness and unusual kinds of information in a group—minus the specific details—about the reality of gender conditioning in human society.

Silent witnessing is an exercise in which a series of questions is put forward pertaining to the experience of being women and men. First we ask one sex group and then the other. After each question, individuals are invited to stand in silence if the answer to that question is "yes" in their personal history. The rest of the community remains seated in quiet acknowledgment of those standing, and everyone is asked to be sensitive and mindful of their own feelings and reactions. Those who are standing remain for a few seconds, until the facilitator says "Thank you," and they sit back down. Then follows the next question, and the process is repeated until the questions are complete. A key guideline for this exercise is that we stand not as victims, but rather to bear witness to the gender injustices present in our lives and in our world as a whole. Behind each person standing is a unique story, and we recognize the experience in that person's life without knowing the particular details. Moreover, when we stand, we do so not only for ourselves, but also for countless others who have similar stories but may never have an opportunity to be witnessed. Thus, each person standing is bearing witness for millions of others with the same or similar experience.

Sometimes in this process the women are asked questions first, at other times the men. The questions begin with the simplest forms of gender imbalance: "Have you ever felt your needs came second to a man's?" (for the women) or "Have you ever felt your needs came second to a woman's?" (for the men). Gradually, the questions become more challenging and pointed: The women are asked if they have ever been afraid to walk the streets alone because they are women. Similarly for the men. We ask about violence and sexuality, both from the point of view of the victim and of the perpetrator: "Have you ever feared for your life or your physical safety in your own home?" "Have you ever been hit or physically abused by a man—or by a woman?" "Have you ever hit or physically abused a man—or a woman?" As the process continues, the questions and responses become increasingly revealing.

At the conference in Croatia, when we asked the question, "Have you ever been forced sexually against your will?" nearly half the women stood, as well as three men. The emotion-laden silence intensified perceptibly in the room as the men sat in quiet acknowledgment, bearing witness to this profound violation of nearly one hundred women and three men standing before them. In our work throughout the United States and in several other countries, we have found that this stark reality is not unusual: generally one-third to one-half of the women present stand for this question, and not infrequently two-thirds or more. In Croatia, when we asked, "Have you ever feared that you might have to die fighting in the armed services for your country?" every single man stood, but only two women. And when we asked, "Have you ever fought in a war?" at least a dozen men stood, but none of the women.

The impact of witnessing so many people stand in response to these questions moved the group profoundly. Waves of grief and compassion were palpable in the hush that followed. We asked each person to turn to someone near them and share what they were experiencing—first within their own gender group. In general, both women and men are often surprised by the shared reality—across the gender divide—of pain and suffering. Women, for example, expect to revisit the familiar pain of women during this process, but they are often startled to witness the pain of men. Men are startled that it is the women actually present in the room, rather than some remote victims in a newspaper article or statistic, who have suffered violation. For everyone, the fact of violation shifts from the abstract to the concrete, and this very awareness is transformative in itself.

After the separate gender groups have had a chance to process the exercise among themselves, each group is given an opportunity to present their reflections to the whole community. The insights that came forward at the peace-building conference were similar to those that emerge in our other gender reconciliation programs. A sense of collective compassion was born in this community, and with it a very tender warmth. The women and the men were surprised by the degree of pain and victimization experienced in the room and were aroused to feelings of empathic solidarity—both within and across the gender divide.

As the last stage of the witnessing process, we asked participants to begin milling slowly about the room, mixing women and men back together again, and to pay particular attention to the subtle energies and feelings as the community reformed. Then we asked people to pair up with a partner of either sex, and each person was invited to share a personal story with their partner from their own background that represented one of the questions for which they had stood. Each partner spoke in turn, uninterrupted for several minutes, while the other listened. Speaking and hearing these stories further deepened the intimacy and compassionate presence in the community, and the dyad process concluded with mutual blessings and heartfelt affirmations between partners.

To close the morning, the entire group gathered into a large circle, joined hands, and sang a simple healing chant. There was a strong presence of interconnection in this community that was now awakened, at least a bit more deeply, to the profound need in our time for social healing and cultural transformation in relation to gender. We had experienced together a natural heart opening, and there was an uplifted sense that the needed changes in our society are actually feasible.

## Silent Witnessing in Small Groups

The same silent witnessing exercise is conducted in all our events as a standard part of the gender reconciliation process. In a group of fifteen to twenty-five people the process is also very powerful, and it becomes more intimate and personal. In small groups, the individuals who stand in response to each question are in much closer physical proximity to those who witness. People can see more clearly, and affectingly, one another's faces and nuances of body language. The responses to the questions comprise a kind of intimate revelation, and it can be shocking to see most or all of the other gender group stand for certain questions, as well as to see them all remain seated for other questions.

Participants take different lessons from this exercise. As one South African woman exclaimed after our gender reconciliation workshop in Cape Town, "The silent witnessing exercise was powerful, and it gave me an opportunity to acknowledge what I have been through, and also to 'stand up' against it. For me, it was to say, 'No More!'"

For others, silent witnessing serves as an opening to new levels of awareness and empathic awakening to the pain of the other gender. Women are often surprised to discover the degree of men's wounding and violation around gender conditioning, and men are frequently amazed to see how many women have suffered different forms of abuse or sexual violation.

At the same time, the exercise reveals striking differences in participants' behavior and life experience. People often comment that the exercise is a poignant reminder not to lump all men (or women) together into gender groups. Women are often surprised to see men standing for experiences which they believed applied only to women, such as sexual coercion and manipulation, or vulgar harassment on the streets. Similarly, men do not always stand for behaviors that women believe apply to all men—and the same holds for women. As one participant observed, "In seeing each other as individuals, we were reminded to not—indeed we really cannot!—write the other gender off as a collective group that all acts a certain way."

**Thousands of Years of Lived Experience**

In a typical workshop group of twenty to thirty adults of diverse ages there are somewhere between eight hundred and twelve hundred years of lived human experience—sitting right there in the room. From this perspective, every group has all the "data" it needs about gender conditioning and experience—firsthand. Collectively, the group knows very well what needs to be healed and transformed, and it also encompasses a depth of wisdom and healing potential to become a kind of alchemical universe unto itself. As gender reconciliation proceeds, every group unfurls its own unique dynamics and psychic energies, as well as its own "shadow" that gender work tends to discover and unveil. Of course, every group is different, particularly in terms of the precise content of what emerges, yet most groups of well-intentioned participants are similar in having the resources and wisdom within their own ranks to effectively navigate the collective healing process.

**Levels of Gender Conditioning: From Planetary to Personal**

The silent witnessing process described above asks participants to bear witness to how gender injustice affects them within their own communities and within the workshop community. To set the stage for this and other experiences that follow throughout the week, we first prepare the field by introducing participants to the larger social and historical context of gender injustice, raising awareness of what might be called the collective gender shadow (to borrow from Jungian terminology). This introductory phase generally lasts at least half a day in five-day workshops, and includes data on gender injustice suffered by both women and men. Some examples of these data include:

- A summary presentation of excerpts from the 1993 United Nations "Vienna Tribunal" on Human Rights, in which thousands of women from around the world testified for the first time to the United Nations about the widespread abuses suffered exclusively by women. The major theme of the tribunal was that women's rights are human rights, yet women's rights have been systematically violated or ignored across the globe. As organizer Charlotte

Bunch proclaimed in her concluding statement, "This is not an appeal by a special interest group, but a demand for basic human rights that have been systematically denied to half of humanity."

- Compelling analysis from Jean Kilbourne's book, *Deadly Persuasion*, and her documentary film series, *Killing Us Softly*, which demonstrates the powerful and damaging effects that corporate advertising has in promulgating negative images of women, including the crass portrayal of sexual exploitation and violence against women's bodies.

- Key ideas from the works of Robert Bly, Sam Keen, and other leaders in the men's movement. Of particular interest is the work of Alexander Mitscherlich, a German psychotherapist who asserts that in the traditional nuclear family, because the father is absent—i.e., away most of the time at a mysterious place of unseen work—a hole develops in the psyche of the young son. "This hole does not fill with little Bambis," Bly warns us; "It fills with demons."[1] These demons render a young boy's tender psyche highly vulnerable to the destructive images of macho masculinity that prevail in the mainstream culture around him.

- Clips from documentary films such as Jackson Katz's *Tough Guise*, which clearly portrays the artificial guise of toughness and pretensions to invincibility that men are conditioned to adopt as masks that cover their true vulnerability and sense of powerlessness.

- Descriptions and video clips of men's experience in fighting wars, and the disproportionate suffering men have historically endured in the military domain. One of the "benefits" of women's emancipation is that women are now allowed to participate in combat warfare.

These punchy multimedia presentations demonstrate the global dimensions of gender injustice and different ways in which both men and women are afflicted. As participants discuss among themselves their responses to these presentations, they naturally begin to examine the effects of such injustice in their own lives. After a short break and silent meditation, the process of silent witnessing described above flows naturally.

In the structure of our gender reconciliation work we begin the process of raising awareness around gender dynamics at a broad level by examining gender injustice in human culture and society. This is the "safest" and least threatening context in which to examine this material. From there, we gradually narrow the focus, first to the collective experience of the participants attending the event, through the silent witnessing exercise described above, and then further still to the more intimate and vulnerable domain of participants' personal histories.

For this last step of the process, we ask participants to share their own "gender biographies," usually in small groups. This provides an unusual opportunity for people to explore their particular life story in relation to being incarnated in either a male or female body and the unique experiences and struggles they encountered in relation to societal gender conditioning. Proceeding in guided stages from birth through childhood, adolescence, young adulthood, and onward to the present, people often discover certain recurring themes or patterns throughout their lives that are highlighted when viewed through the lens of gender. Participants are then invited to share their stories in small groups at whatever level of depth and intimacy feels appropriate. For many people, the details of their particular gender biography include some of the most intimate, humbling, or vulnerable aspects of their personal life experience, as will be clear from examples given in later chapters. We always caution participants to honor their own boundaries, and not to share any information that feels too personal or private. At the same time, we encourage people to use this opportunity for sharing in a substantive way that may stretch them beyond their usual comfort zones.

Not surprisingly, one of the powerful results of this process is that people with particularly challenging or painful personal histories often discover that others in the group have had similar or related difficulties in life. This stark recognition is often an enlightening moment that awakens tremendous compassion and empathy. It also ushers in strong feelings of relief, as well as a shared solidarity in wanting to collaborate to transform the damaging gender dynamics that remain so prevalent in society.

# CHAPTER 4

# Deepening in Women's and Men's Circles

*We see things not as they are, but as we are.*

—Talmud

Having experienced the intensity and vulnerability of the silent witnessing exercise described in the previous chapter, there is often a strong wish in a community of women and men to break into separate circles. Participants may be feeling sheepish or vulnerable in view of what they have silently revealed about their personal histories. Some of the men or women may be feeling unfairly lumped together, perhaps feeling falsely implicated for behaviors that do not apply to them personally. The intensity of what has just been witnessed, the commonality of women's pain and men's pain in relation to gender injustice, and the degree of personal and collective exposure all point to a need for restoring a greater sense of safety. Same-sex groups often provide this safety, where men (and women) can take refuge among themselves to explore the often raw and delicate emotions or experiences that can be difficult to address in mixed company.

Partitioning the group into separate women's and men's circles is therefore often a natural next step at this point in gender reconciliation work. Yet the nature and function of these groups in the context of gender reconciliation is generally quite different from what many people are used to from previous experience in either women's or men's groups. The reason is straightforward: the dynamic character of the women's group is shifted to a large degree by the presence of the men—and vice versa. Even though the women's and men's circles meet in separate spaces entirely out of earshot of each other, the two groups affect each other greatly.

To give some examples of the kind of difference this can make, in a conventional women's group the women may speak about their relationships with men—husbands, sons, fathers, lovers, and so forth—but there is no active engagement of the relational dynamics because no men are actually present. By contrast, in gender reconciliation work, when the women's circle meets the women have all experienced one another in the presence of men, and they will soon be moving back into community with those same men. Behavior speaks louder than words, and the women's dynamics in relation to men will tend to be reproduced right there with the men present in the workshop. And, of course, this same process will also be going on among the men in relation to the women in the workshop. So, in both cases, ingrained patterns of behavior in relation to the opposite sex will naturally arise, and these patterns will be observed by others within the same sex group.

All this creates grist for the mill of intragender work, which plays out in innumerable ways. Competitive dynamics often surface. In a group of men, when even one woman comes onto the scene, a whole new dynamic immediately comes into play—especially if she is regarded as attractive. Traditionally, the men begin to compete for her attention—often unconsciously attempting to outshine one another. In gender reconciliation work this competition may not be overt or play out along traditional macho masculine lines of physical prowess or brilliant intelligence. Some men might jostle and maneuver themselves so as to be seen as the most "sensitive," "compassionate," or "heroic" advocates of women's plight, thereby seeking to draw to themselves adoration and respect from the women.

A similar dynamic often emerges in a group of women when a man enters upon a scene where previously only women had been present. The resulting dynamics vary depending on the man, and are often influenced by where the different women's alliances lie. Women are socialized to create alliances with men in order to substantiate and advance their own positions. The more skilled a woman is at creating alliances with men, the better she is likely to fare in society at large. In a mixed group, women often seek to form alliances with men even at the expense of the other women in the group. It's another form of competition. Later, when the women gather back into the women's group and expect and ask for allegiance among the women, an interesting tension can arise. It often becomes quickly evident how much value each woman places on sisterly allegiance, and which women will readily sacrifice this allegiance to establish deeper alliances with men. And the true alliances become plainly visible for all to see.

In short, it is evident that gender reconciliation work sets in motion a complex process that interweaves both intergender and intragender dimensions of interaction and conditioning between women and men. By working both within and between the two (or more) gender groups, rich and revealing dynamics often surface rather quickly. Participants' individual behavior patterns are inevitably exposed on various levels, often unwittingly, which frequently brings invaluable insights and learnings. It is crucial to keep in mind that many ingrained patterns of behavior and interaction between women and men are socialized and culturally learned, and the only place to start unlearning unhealthy patterns is to see them with unflinching clarity—as they emerge in real time. This is where much of the richness and power of gender healing work is often found.

We now explore two specific examples of what transpires in same-sex circles—one anecdote each from a men's circle and a women's circle. These examples are drawn from two different events, and, in each case, the process that began in the same-sex circle became a pivotal element in the unfolding process and outcome for the entire event.

### The Men's Circle
The first example comes from a workshop (organized by Heart Phoenix and Jeffrey Weisberg with Harriet Rose Meiss, and co-facilitated by Will Keepin) that was held in a large ranch house and

the facilities lent a certain informality to the gathering. Participants found themselves in a cozy, intimate situation that left them feeling rather like housemates. Meals were catered, but participants did the dishes and helped keep the kitchen and house clean.

About two days into the retreat, the women's and men's lunch times were staggered to allow each gender group to meet for the entire day without encountering the other. As it happened, the men ate their lunch after the women on this day, and they decided afterward, as a service to the community, to do the dishes and clean up the kitchen.

When the men finished the cleanup, one of them—we'll call him Sam—wanted to leave a note for the women—"as a joke"—saying that since the men had cleaned up the kitchen, they expected sex from the women later on. Two of the other men began to laugh and hoot and chimed in their enthusiastic support for Sam's suggestion. But the proposed prank quickly met with resistance from several of the other men, who were concerned that the women would be offended by the note, especially in the context of a gender healing workshop. Sam protested that it was only a joke and would certainly be received as such by the women—all the more so *because* it was a gender workshop. He insisted on going forward with his idea.

The resulting rift in the men's group rapidly escalated into a crisis, polarizing the men into two camps: Sam and his two supporters on one side, and the rest of the men, to varying degrees, on the other. In an attempt at compromise, Sam and his team proposed they leave the note and sign only their three names to it, making it clear that it wasn't from all of the men. But several men objected. They felt the note would still affect the whole course of the workshop and would be seen by many women as a betrayal, typical of the ways in which women so often experience men. The men as a group would all be tainted with the same negative brush, they argued, even if they did not all sign the note—a reenactment of an age-old dynamic between the sexes.

It quickly became clear to me and the other male facilitator that we had to address this issue head on; indeed, to do so *was* the men's work in that moment, and it took precedence over our existing agenda. So we announced that the men's group was reconvening to address this issue among the men. Sam was visibly irritated; he just wanted to leave the note and get on with whatever was next on the agenda. His critics were equally irritated, and several of them groaned out loud as they realized the afternoon's program for the men's circle was now in jeopardy because of the need to address what seemed to them an inane issue coming from just a few individuals within the men's group. Despite almost unanimous resistance among the men, we insisted and reconvened the men's group to address this issue.

As we opened with a simple council process, there was a lot of energy and tension in the room. Several of the men began expressing serious concern about how some of the women in the group would likely react when they found this note. Meanwhile, Sam and his cohorts kept insisting the women would take it as a joke. "And if they don't," Sam exclaimed at one point, "they have a lot to learn!"

This remark outraged a couple of the men, who demanded, "What exactly are the women supposed to learn!?"

"About sex!" shot back Sam.

"And what is your note going to teach the women about sex?!" the opposing men persisted.

Witnessing this heated exchange and the rising tension it was generating, we conceived the idea of delving more deeply into this conflict and having the men act it out. So we proposed a spontaneous psychodrama process in which several men would play the various roles of the women reacting to the note. We explained the idea to the group: "Let Sam and his cohorts make their case and defend it however they see fit, and let the men who are expressing concerns about the reactions they think the women might have play the parts of those women in the psychodrama."

The men set up the imagined confrontation that would ensue after the women had found the note. Sam and his two supporters were playing themselves, and six other men were playing the women—with the rest of the group in witness. Each of the latter six chose a specific woman in the group whom he thought he could accurately portray, including a fourteen-year-old boy who played one of the young teenage girls. (This was an intergenerational workshop that included both teenagers and adults.) The fourteen-year-old boy did a masterful job of portraying a particularly tender, innocent ninth-grade girl in the group. He chose one of the girls he felt would be deeply offended by this note because, he said, this was the kind of nonsense she always got from her peers at school, and the workshop was supposed to be a place where she would not have to deal with this kind of disrespectful, adolescent male energy.

Another man played the part of an outraged feminist activist. "She'll be fit to be tied!" he exclaimed, and he dove into the role. Still another played one of the older women facilitators, a circumspect and loving matriarchal figure who could understand the joke from one perspective but also see its potential harm. He thought she would try to orchestrate all the conflicting views to create harmony. Three or four of the men played angry women who were basically saying, "Not again! We came here to do a new and different form of gender healing work, and what we get is the same old abuse and patriarchy all over again—right in our face!"

As the psychodrama proceeded, the facilitators supported both sides of the confrontation, encouraging full expression of all views and feelings. Sam and his team played their roles adamantly, insisting the note was harmless and just good fun, while the other side countered with how offended they felt by the note. The situation heated up, with passionate arguments on both sides. Sam insisted that if the women didn't find the note funny, then they needed to "loosen up" around sexual matters. This outraged many of the "women" [played by men], who called for a retraction and apology from Sam, pointing to centuries of sexual violation, rape, and other abuses committed against them by men.

As the arguments were hurled back and forth, the "women" portrayed a rich tapestry of reactions. Many were vocal in their outrage, and two demanded some form of retribution for this latest patriarchal abuse. One conceded that she found Sam's note amusing herself but was concerned for how her sisters were feeling. Some expressed total loss of hope in gender reconciliation because this incident had reenacted yet again what men always do to women. The circumspect, wise crone could see all sides of the conflict and sought to bring resolution and harmony back into the community.

Over time, Sam's cohorts slowly began to soften their position, as they realized the note actually *was* likely to elicit a strong reaction and sense of betrayal among at least some of the women. Deciding that this possibility was not worth the risk, one of Sam's cohorts switched camps about halfway through the psychodrama. Toward the end, Sam's other supporter followed suit, leaving Sam to argue his case alone. Sam eventually came around to the view that leaving the note was not such a good idea after all because it carried a significant risk of precipitating a crisis, which was not his intention. In the end, Sam not only withdrew his proposal, but expressed gratitude for what he learned in the process.

This feeling of gratitude and deep learning was mutual as the men debriefed the experience. They had become truly empathic as they delved deeply into their roles and began seeing things from the women's perspective. A number of the men were amazed at how strongly they identified with their roles as women, and at the passion for justice that inspired and energized them. In the end, all the men felt a sense of great achievement and grace at having handled a potential crisis internally among themselves, and at having come through it with deeper insights and compassion for the women.

The men were beaming as they came back into the mixed group that evening, and the feeling among them persisted throughout the rest of the workshop. The women could feel the men's positive energy and were eager to know what had happened in the men's group that had brought about the heightened intensity of the men's warmth and affection, attentiveness, and *presence*. But the men had made an agreement of confidentiality, in part to protect Sam and his cohorts but also to maintain the integrity of the process in the men's group and in the workshop itself.

On the last morning, to his credit, Sam elected to reveal what had happened, and his disclosure opened up the space for the rest of the men to share. The women were deeply moved by their story. The positive energy that arose from the men's group work had spread so tangibly out into the larger circle that the women had taken notice and were favorably impacted throughout the event. As the event came to a close, the women expressed their gratitude, and many felt deeply honored by the way the men had handled the situation and by their capacity to empathically identify with the women's concerns. To a large extent, the men's work had shaped the entire workshop, transforming what might have been a text-book replay of abrasive sexism into a powerful healing event that lifted the entire group to a high level of sensitivity, caring, and collective intimacy.

Before proceeding to the next case, an important reflection about what happened in the men's circle needs to be made. If, as in most men's groups, the circle of men in the above example had not been accountable to a larger mixed community—then a joke along the lines of Sam's proposed note would not likely have been processed by the men to any significant degree. Typically, when a crude or unconscious sexual joke is made among men, the response is that those who find it funny laugh out loud, while others who may find it offensive either feign a laugh, say nothing, or at most mutter something to themselves under their breath, eager to move beyond it. But rarely does any conversation or processing beyond this take place, and thus old patterns remain unexamined and thereby reinforced. This same response would probably have occurred in this men's circle had it not been for the gender reconciliation context. Indeed, neither Sam nor his adversaries wanted to delve into the issue, and both sides would have avoided it if they could have. But the need for accountability and integration with the women led them into it, and this in turn led to the unexpected power of what emerged and the discovery of a bit of alchemical gold in the process.

### The Women's Circle

"I almost died; I have to remember that!" Carolyn stammered. "And I know I'm not an isolated case. It sounds dramatic, but it has to be said: I almost died, and I know that if pornography hadn't been involved, I would not have gone off the deep end the way I did."

Carolyn was beginning to share her personal experience with pornography, following a group exercise that dealt with the effects of pornography (described in Chapter 6). A vibrant and keenly insightful professional woman around forty years old, Carolyn had never shared this part of her personal history with any group before. In fact, she had never told it to anyone.

"I was very armored around this. I don't know of any arena, other than this gender reconciliation work, that could have broken this open for me. Pornography is not some little thing we can just banter around. It's a gigantic thing that is having a huge impact—a hugely negative impact—on many people's lives. And I felt a need to say, *'Look people, we can talk about pornography up here [in our heads] all we want, but the bottom line is that people are dying from it.'* I know that sounds extreme, but I also know that was my experience."

After the pornography exercise, Carolyn had been listening to several women speaking about how they had come to terms with pornography. "They said they were using it for education. They were talking about pornography as a corporation, a big institution that somehow was not impacting us on a human level. As they spoke, I felt myself vibrating, literally vibrating, and I knew I had to speak, because I'm lucky to be alive. And I almost wasn't—and it was a long, slow process of killing myself that is *absolutely acceptable* in our society."

"If it had just been the men talking," she continued, "I could have felt like there was someplace for me to go, that I had some support. But when I come across women who support pornography, it's a double whammy for me. I get confused about how I'm supposed to feel about it, but when I heard the women, that's when I started to crack and I realized, *people need to understand how harmful this stuff really is.*"

So Carolyn took a deep breath and recounted the following story. When she was in her early twenties, she had married a young officer in the U.S. Air Force and moved with him to an airbase in the South where he was training as a fighter pilot. She had met her husband while working for a civilian company that ran the recreation center at a top-secret site where they were testing the stealth fighter bomber. "I knew what pilots were like. I knew what went on because I was the bartender there. There was plenty of stuff [pornography] around there," she said. "They would come to the bar; I would see it, but I wasn't affected by it. My husband didn't seem like that kind of guy. He was a nice guy. He was friendly, and he was funny. We played a lot. People who would see us together would say, 'Oh yeah, good match.' He was my best friend.

"So when he introduced pornography into our home, I said, 'Wait a minute, what is this? What is this about?' and I expected him to understand." Carolyn and her husband were young newly-weds and had only been at the base for about a month when, "All of a sudden, boom! He brought home all this stuff, and I was shocked. I was really firm. I said, *'No, this isn't coming into my house. I'm sorry, this is not okay.'* I put up a strong front. I thought, if he loves me, if he's a good husband, he's going to say, 'Okay, I get it.' He's going to see that this is wrong. Instead, just the opposite happened. He really jerked the rug out from under me. I can still pinpoint the moment—I can tell you exactly what I was wearing, exactly where I was standing, everything, because that's the moment I realized I didn't count, I didn't matter. This other thing [pornography] was much more important."

In fact, Carolyn's husband's interest in the pornography *was* more important to him than his wife or his marriage. It was part of an embedded, systemic behavior adhered to by all the pilots in training. "The reason we *needed* pornography in our house, he explained to me, was because he was in pilot training, and he was at the top of his class and wanted to stay at the top of his class. In order to do that, every week each of the guys would cut out the most disgusting picture they could find, laminate it onto a dollar bill, and turn it in. Whoever had the picture that was the most offensive—or as they thought of it, most titillating—would win extra flight time. And of course, if you got extra flight time, you would be the better pilot." The pornographic dollar bills were laminated and submitted every week by the young training pilots to their elder, higher ranking officers, who judged them and duly awarded extra flight training hours accordingly every week. Carolyn's husband often won, but the price of his winning was a growing preoccupation with pornography. "He'd go through the magazines all the time. He'd have to go through them several times just to figure out which pictures he liked. So we had magazines all over the house—not just *Playboy*, *Penthouse*, and *Hustler*, but all kinds of other obscure ones, too. He would drive off base to the next town to buy them, where they had a bigger selection."

All the training pilots would get together a couple of times a week in Carolyn's home and go through the magazines and laminate their dollar bills. "It was hard to hear him sit with his buddies around these magazines going, 'Ooh, look at this one! Ahh, look at that one!' All I could think about was, what can I do to look like them, so he will look at me the way he does at them? There was a lot of time spent on it.

"Everyone thought it was funny," Carolyn recalled, including the other wives. When Carolyn tried to discuss her objections with the other women, they told her, "Oh, just chill out, it's no big deal." The women were right in line. When Carolyn persisted, some of the women stopped being friends with her. In fact, one night when the men had gathered to make their dollar bills, the wives showed up at Carolyn's house carrying stacks of *Playgirl* magazine. "We thought we'd come over and lighten you up," they told her, "so we're going to make our own dollars."

"That was the hardest thing, I think, to have the women come over and tell me that I needed to lighten up, that it was no big deal." As time went on, Carolyn was admonished in no uncertain terms and told to step in line and be a team player. "The peer pressure was so great that even if my husband had realized it was hurtful to me and had stopped wanting to participate, he would have been dropped to the bottom of his class, which would have affected the rest of his career life in the Air Force. That was made clear to him again and again. They called him in to reprimand him about me. The message to him was very clear: *Tow the line, you're one of our top guys here, we want to keep you there. You could even make colonel early on. But you have to get your wife under control.*

Carolyn's husband hardened his position. "He just kind of shut me down," she said. "He wasn't mean about it, we didn't fight, he just left the magazines out everywhere and told me, 'You need to deal with it. You need to get over it. This is something I have to do.'

"So I shut up," Carolyn explained. "It was hard, though. We'd been buddy-buddy, hanging out and doing things together until we got married, but then after we got married I couldn't go out with him anymore because it wasn't okay for the wives to go. It was okay for me to go when I was his friend, but then everything shifted and all of a sudden I was on the back burner. That isn't the way he wanted things, that's just what was expected, and he wanted to be good. He wanted to be the best."

Carolyn was chastised not only for her objections to the pornography, but when the colonel's wife determined that the colonel was spending an inordinate amount of time at the swimming pool gawking at women in bathing suits, Carolyn's employment there as a lifeguard was suddenly deemed "inappropriate" for an officer's wife, and she was forced to quit through internal pressure on her husband. "I was confused," Carolyn explained. "There were so many things I seemed to be doing 'wrong,' yet there in front of me was what was right—because *it* [the pornography] was what got the extra time on the flight plan; *it* was what we spent all of our time on."

Carolyn became increasingly insecure. "I was so afraid that I was going to lose him, that I wasn't good enough, wasn't pretty enough, that I had nothing to offer." When her husband's training started to include more special assignments and temporary duty, the situation deteriorated further. "I knew that when they went on special assignments or on temporary duty they spent their time in the strip clubs, hitting on women. That's just what they do," and on one occasion she inadvertently found confirmatory photographs in his bag.

Gradually, Carolyn turned to the models in the pornographic magazines, believing they had what she needed in order to secure her husband's love. "I thought if my body could be that perfect, I wouldn't lose him, and it would be okay." She found a job teaching aerobics five times a day. "In between, I would bike or run. I started spending my whole day doing workouts. I knew the calorie and fat count of every single thing that went in my mouth, and how much exercise I needed in order to offset anything I ate. At first I was eating, but then I stopped and started living on four liters of Diet Dr. Pepper a day. That's all I would put in my body." By this time Carolyn was looking at herself constantly in the mirror "to see what was wrong, comparing myself to the pictures, picking myself apart, and never really seeing myself. Seeing only parts."

The pattern continued to develop over the ensuing months. "I remember pulling out the magazines and comparing myself to the pictures, even to the point of putting myself in different poses, to see what was so enticing in the magazines and to see if I was there yet. It got to where I would do that four or five times a day, at least. It's what I did during the day when he was gone, and on the weekends, too, if he was on travel. Then I would step on the scales and see how much I weighed and how much more I needed to lose."

By this point Carolyn was drinking so much caffeine that she couldn't feel her body anymore. "I couldn't feel a thing," she told us. "I remember praying one night that somehow I could be zero weight and just start over; then I could rebuild my body and make it perfect. That was informing everything I was doing. I know that's not a rational thought, but at the time it just seemed that if I could go all the way to zero, I could make it better."

When Carolyn, who is five feet, nine inches tall, got down to ninety-seven pounds, she had a split-second epiphany one day when she actually saw her true reflection in the mirror. "I could see every rib and every vertebra. Then when I blinked and looked again, I couldn't see it anymore." She had a moment of panic and called her mother, asking her to come get her and take her home. "Two minutes later I called her back and told her I was just kidding and not to worry about it." Fortunately, Carolyn's mother realized something was amiss and immediately booked an airplane ticket to visit her daughter.

Two days later Carolyn and her mother were back home. "When I checked into the hospital, I weighed ninety-four pounds. I had a heart murmur, one of my kidneys was operating at 30 percent, and the other at 70 percent. Between the two of them, I had only one kidney, and all sorts of other physical ailments were going on. The doctor told me that my body was literally shutting down, and if it continued I would die. He said it would continue to shut down until I started building it up. He said, 'That's how you die, not from starvation per se, but from the shutdown of all of your systems.' When I saw it on paper, I started to cry. I was thinking, *Oh my God, what have I done to myself? What am I doing to myself?*"

Carolyn was in the hospital the first time for four months. The staff tried to make her eat frequent, substantial meals, which was extremely difficult for her, which is why it took four months before she was ready to leave. "When I got out of the hospital, I made the mistake of going to the mall with a friend. It was like I was a huge walking bruise. We walked into the mall and—you know what a mall looks like—there were tons of pictures in every store telling me what I needed to look like to be beautiful and successful. I couldn't handle it. I couldn't deal with it. I got angry again, and I looked at all those pictures and I thought, *Damn it, I want to be beautiful! I have a right to be beautiful! I have a right to look like that. Who are these people trying to make me ugly, trying to make me unacceptable?* And I stepped right back into it—the anorexia—at that moment. Even now, there are times when that's still my knee-jerk reaction if I'm not on top of things. It's still a struggle," Carolyn explained. "I'm not talking about an isolated incident that occurred only once in my life."

Carolyn had to return to the hospital a second time for another month and a half. During both these hospital stays, her husband never once visited her, and Carolyn came to the realization that her marriage was finished. She filed for divorce and traveled to Germany, where she lived for four years. In Germany, where she found less emphasis on women's bodies, she came to feel stronger and more certain of her choices around her body and food. But, as she was quick to point out, anorexia changes the brain chemistry, and one has to confront an ongoing range of psychological symptoms. "I'm lucky," she told us, "because many women with anorexia don't make it, they don't kick it, they end up dying.

"There was discomfort in the group after I spoke," Carolyn reported, "because it does change things if we face rather than deny this kind of information" about pornography and anorexia. "There's so much at stake. There was so much at stake for my husband. For him to actually start looking at this he'd have to reevaluate himself as a human being, and I think that would be too much for him. He couldn't do it in that context. There would be no support for it. There's a lot of activity within that little cult, especially among the higher officers and pilots. They get in less trouble. The more elite they are, the less trouble they will get in, and the more deviant it seems they're allowed to be.

"When I was working at the test range, the base commander raped one of the maids," Carolyn continued. "There was nowhere she could turn for justice. She went to the military police and they basically told her, 'What do you want us to do about it? He's the base commander. He did it because he knew he could, and get away with it. He thought it was funny.' So she said, 'I'm going to go to the police down south,' which was what we called the city, and the police told her, 'If you do that, it's a breach of the oath that you swore to come up here to this top-secret base, and you will go to jail.' We were at a top-secret site. We all had top-secret clearances, and so we swore an oath. And part of the oath is agreeing never to reveal that it's there. So they told her that if she went down south to the city police, she would go to prison. So she could say nothing, and do nothing about it.

"My husband was one of the nicer guys. One time we drove up and dropped him off in Washington at a camp where they train officers how to deal with torture by an enemy without disclosing military secrets. When he came back, I was really upset because it took him so long to recover, especially when he was telling me what happened. I had never seen him cry, and there were a couple of times when he broke down and cried as he talked about it. I was so angry. I remember thinking about the kind of people that they train and hire to staff this camp. These men, their jobs—my tax dollars pay them—is to hurt, to torture somebody's mind. I was so angry, and there was nothing I could do."

A postscript to this story occurred about ten years later, when, after years of no contact, Carolyn had lunch one day with her ex-husband. It was early winter 2003, just weeks before the start of the Iraq War. As they sat down to lunch, Carolyn wondered how he had changed and grown over the years. They had a friendly social chat. With the country on the brink of war, Carolyn was surprised that he made no mention of it, and she wondered how he really felt about it, being an officer in the armed forces. She hesitated for a moment as a memory flashed through her mind of their early days as best friends, laughing together. She recalled the warmth and beauty of his youthful, innocent spirit. Then she lowered her voice and gingerly changed the subject, asking him how he felt about the current political situation and the impending possibility of war. He replied casually, "Oh, I'm glad all this is happening."

Carolyn was stunned. "Why?" she asked him.

"Because it means I get to fly more," he replied flatly.

From the "winning" pornographic dollar, to the loss of his best friend and later his marriage, to his nation going to war—these things were all good, if it meant that he got to fly more. He had not changed one bit, except perhaps for how much more he was prepared to sacrifice—in order to fly more.

# CHAPTER 5

# *Cure of Grace:*
# *The Alchemy of Reconciliation*

*Never through hatred does hatred cease, but through love alone.*
*This is an ancient and universal law.*

—Dhammapada

Things were getting off to a rough start for the men. For the first
several minutes all they could do was express their frustration—and, in some cases, anger—at the fact that they were sitting
in a circle talking to each other, while stationed all around them
were the women, silently listening in. Earlier the men had called an
emergency meeting to consider the strong resistance several of them
had to this whole idea of a "men's truth forum," as the facilitators
were calling this exercise. There were complex dynamics, including
secrets of different kinds, some involving particular individuals in
the community. Three men had specifically requested that what they
had shared earlier in the men's circle be kept strictly confidential,
not to be disclosed in this new context with the women witnessing.
The men were faced with the necessity of trusting one another not to
blow it—creating a vulnerability to mutual trust that was unnerving.
Adding to the tension, the facilitators had decided to let the women
(who had somehow known to ask) go second. This seemed like a
repetition of a familiar pattern—women and children first when the
ship is going down; otherwise, it's men who are supposed to test the
dangerous waters of the unknown.

For most of the men, it was unthinkable that they could speak in any way even remotely like they'd been doing all afternoon, when no women were present. Their instructions for the truth forum were to continue with their men's circle as if the women of the community were not sitting all around them, quietly listening in. The men were convinced the process would be utterly contrived. The stakes were high. Nothing real was likely to happen, and that too would be classic—the men would get nailed for being superficial. Obviously, doing the forum poorly would be more destructive to this gender reconciliation process than doing nothing at all. The men felt trapped.

As the talking stick went around the men's group, gradually some of the men who had less resistance began to model ways of sharing authentically. Building upon the cumulative courage of one another, several men gingerly entered into a discussion about sex and their attitudes toward women in general, continuing on a theme they had been discussing earlier in the men's circle. Their honesty deepened as they began to speak about lust and desire, acknowledging their preoccupation with female bodies and physical beauty. Yes, they imagined having sex with the pretty women they passed on the street or saw in a bar. Yes, they ranked women at parties and gatherings—from the one they most wanted to the one they would settle for if she was all they could get. Yes, they imagined larger breasts or smaller hips as "needed," or added a more elegant nose or wider-set eyes.

Several men acknowledged that they habitually sexualized their encounters with women, implicitly measuring the value of every interchange by its sexual charge. "Attraction is not a matter of rational choice," exclaimed Charles, a lanky, sharp-witted law student. "It's a matter of biology. Men are hardwired to respond sexually to attractive women," he concluded in passionate earnestness. "It's an incontrovertible fact of life." Expounding on similar themes, others spoke of how they inevitably compared the women in their lives to images in the media. Yet the media were not necessarily to blame, they explained, because the media were simply reflecting back what men instinctively already knew: perfect female bodies and youthful beauty were in fact what captured men's attention and motivated their desire. "In fact," intoned a reflective man with chagrin, "given how men are—that is, hardwired to pursue women merely on the basis of their sexual desirability—this attempt at 'gender reconciliation,' noble as it sounds, is probably a complete waste of time."

As several men seemed to nod in agreement, others began shifting in their seats, preparing for their chance to speak. The women watching outside the circle remained quiet, though hardly calm. They had been asked to listen deeply with their hearts, to bear witness in silence to whatever the men shared. Listening quietly was the women's only task during the men's truth forum, and the women had been advised that the more they were able to do this, the more their energetic presence would actually create the support to allow the men in the inner circle to go deeper. It was not an easy task: on the one hand, every woman in the room was deeply moved, gratified to be privy to such frank male honesty. Most would later report that they had never heard a group of men share so candidly. On the other hand, many of the women would also report that what the men were sharing was very difficult to hear—reinforcing their nightmare images of men. One woman later said that the only thing she heard in the men's truth forum that she completely agreed with was the remark that we might as well all give up and go home—that the gender divide was too wide, and true reconciliation was a hopeless chimera.

But then, as so often happens when honesty prevails, something remarkable occurred. John, the only gay man in the group, had become increasingly quiet as the conversation progressed. But suddenly he interjected, "I need to say something about my experience—as a gay man." He paused to collect himself, acutely aware that he was entering treacherous waters. "I get sized up all the time," he began cautiously, "by men who are awash in the same kind of sexual lust that you're talking about here in relation to women." John glanced around the circle of men, looking for silent permission to continue, and then proceeded to explore the ramifications of men who unconsciously indulge their sexual appetites. "In the gay culture," John explained, "men's sexual desirability is measured by a crude term known as the 'Fuckability Quotient.' Many gay men quickly assess the Fuckability Quotient of every man they meet as a means of determining who they will pursue for even the simplest exchange. In fact, there seldom are simple, honest exchanges— almost every nuance is a calculated invitation or measured rebuff.

"Furthermore," John continued, finally casting off all self-consciousness, "some very specific components determine the FQ (as it is known for short), none of which have anything whatever to do with a person's soul or true self. High ratings are conferred for good looks, for how well someone is dressed, for handsome bodily proportions—for how hard and muscled they are—or for how well they return a sexually suggestive stare." John explained that FQ also increases with evidence of apparent wealth or other emblems of social status and success. "The bottom line is that specific, unwritten 'standards' are operative in various domains of the gay culture. The more a man fits those standards, the higher is his FQ and, consequently, the more attention he commands, and hence the more potential he has for selecting lovers and for a host of other social and even professional opportunities."

A few of the men stiffened as John spoke, and the women inched forward, making sure not to miss a word. The attention of everyone in the room was riveted on this lone gay man as he challenged the heterosexual men in the circle and expressed disdain for the superficiality of unbridled forms of raw male sexual energy. "Whether we're heterosexual or gay," John continued, "it seems that such crass frameworks for pursuing sexual intimacy are utterly misguided, and they are demeaning and hurtful to all parties involved. For me personally, my deepest desire is to discover true intimacy, and I know for certain that the profundity of sexual intimacy transcends the mechanics of physical passion and the functional release of body fluids."

As John spoke the energy in the room began to shift. One could almost hear the women in the room wanting to shout "Yes!" in appreciation of the fact that this man was naming something they too experienced. His words somehow exposed the offensiveness of objectification—the trivializing it entails. That it was a gay man speaking to this experience was profound; it opened the space in a unique way. There was something in John's stance, in his acknowledgment—here was a man saying, I know, from experience, that exploitative male sexuality is hurtful, and it's a travesty of the true purpose and promise of authentic intimacy.

John's challenge opened the space for the men to drop inward to a deeper level of honesty and self-critical reflection. Some of the men conceded their own complicity in this kind of behavior. And rather than continuing with the shared rationalization that that's just the way men are and nothing can be done about it, the men began to examine and explore their sexuality and how they had grappled with it in different ways. Some spoke about how they were conditioned to think about male sexuality in the crude ways they had been describing. Others spoke of unacknowledged initiation processes that went on in school locker rooms—boyhood rituals in which they were taught what it is to "be a man."

A stocky, bright-eyed man named Jerry who had been quiet during much of the earlier discussion suddenly opened up with an insightful perspective. He explained that he had been very active in the "mythopoetic" men's movement in years past, from which he had benefited a great deal. Yet there were some aspects of the male experience, including sexuality, that were not adequately addressed in the men's movement, he said. Jerry then proceeded to offer a soliloquy of sorts on the effects of pornographic pictures passed around at school by adolescent boys. He spoke with conviction:

> There is a kind of false imprint on the young male psyche about the nature of sexuality that is crystallized in adolescent masturbation experiences with pornographic pictures and magazines. Those moments are devastatingly formative in his innocent psyche. As a result, the young boy then falsely believes that he knows what sex feels like, what women are supposed to look like and act like, and what it's all about— when actually he doesn't have a clue.
>
> And all this backlog of charged energy and expectation gets carried into his first sexual encounters with an actual girl or woman. Even as a young man falling in love for the first time, he is carrying all this pornographic conditioning without even realizing it's there. It's a kind of contamination, or

a deflowering of his innocence and purity that happens long before he ever gets to that first sexual experience as a young man. And of course it's constantly reinforced at school and in the media and TV, which he's been watching since before he could walk. So the impressionable young male coming of age never has a chance; there is a kind of toxic poisoning of his intimate heart in relation to sexuality that starts in childhood, and then gets strongly reinforced in adolescence. And there it stays stuck, for most men—it's rarely healed after that. I think many men in society are still frozen at that adolescent stage, and it explains the continual obsession so many of us men have with young, naked women throughout our entire lives.

Many of the men nodded in agreement, and the room grew silent. One of the facilitators rang a bell chime to respect and sustain the charged silence for a few moments. As the men began speaking again, they slowly started to examine their sexual histories more deeply through this new lens. The word "wounded" entered the conversation for the first time. The emotional energy shifted—softened, and became more tender—as several men shared experiences they'd had as boys that left them feeling devalued and damaged. Several spoke in hushed tones, others choked back tears.

Howard was a striking man in his mid-forties who was very active in men's work. He commanded a particular power and respect in the group, in part because he was a senior leader for a major national men's project. "When I was eight years old," he began slowly, "my mother was terrified of sexuality. Neither she nor my father ever talked about it with me or my sister. One day I was playing with some kids in our back yard, and after a while they all left except for a little girl named Janice. We kept on playing, and after a while we got into that game—you know, what's it called?—where you show me yours if I show you mine. It was exciting, and I remember we both knew we had to be careful not to be seen. So we went behind the bushes at the back of the yard, where we'd be all alone.

We hadn't been there very long when suddenly my mother appeared—like out of nowhere—towering above us in a raging fury.

She sent Janice off scurrying home, yelling at her never to do that again. And then she took me inside and really let me have it."

Howard's lip began to tremble as the painful memories bubbled back up. He lowered his voice. "She had spanked me before, but this time she made me take off my pants, and she went at me with my Dad's thick leather belt on the bare butt. She kept shouting over and over—driving in each word with every thwack of the belt—'*Don't -- you -- EVER -- do -- that -- again!!*'"

Howard sat silent for a moment, and large tears began rolling down his trembling face. The man next to him reached out, gently placing his hand on Howard's shoulder. This gesture gave silent permission for Howard's grief and he broke into sobbing, but then quickly pulled himself back together again, and blew his nose.

"I've done a lot of therapy around this," Howard continued, "but it's amazing how that pain is still right there. Just under the surface." He paused, and then looked down. "The whole episode had a major debilitating effect on my later relations with girls, and basically destroyed my first marriage. And never, to this day, has my mother been able to talk about it with me. She just can't face it. I eventually gave up trying to address it with her."

Howard's tale struck a nerve and further dissolved the men's fear and self-consciousness. Other stories started coming out as the men became more forthright. The women listened ever more intently, and several quietly sniffled or choked back tears. There was a baseball coach who had used dirty jokes as a way to separate "the men from the boys." One boy had been repeatedly shamed by his sister and both parents for liking to play with girls. Another had been sexually violated by his priest when he was in junior high school, something he had only come to terms with in recent years.

A vibrant, athletic man named Mark reached for the talking stick. "When I was in eighth grade, I started 'going steady' with my first girlfriend. My parents became concerned and sat me down for a serious talk. I was raised Catholic, and they spoke about religious values, using big words like 'concupiscence,' which I didn't understand at all. But the message was clear. My mother got all tied in knots trying to say that sex was dirty and demeaning; not appropriate behavior for Christians like us. But then my father was saying it's different when you're older, and you're in love with your wife. It was obvious that neither of my parents was the least bit comfortable with the conversation, or with each other on this one. It was totally weird, and I knew they weren't giving me the whole story."

Mark started shaking his head, and then began to chuckle. His face suddenly lit up. "The absurd double message," he said, with a gleeful twinkle in his eye, "was this." He ceremoniously mimicked the unveiling of a somber proclamation: "Sex is disgusting, nasty, and immoral. Therefore, save it for someone you truly love!!" Laughter filled the room, and with it came a wave of welcome relief to the intensity we had all been sharing.

As one man's revelation led to another, the power of each person's story was amplified by the others. The themes shifted beyond sexuality to include other issues. Many felt they were pushed to fulfill functional and disposable roles in society: as moneymakers, sperm donors, and child support providers (rather than fathers), as well as canon fodder for the military machine. The silences between the words were thick, filled with irony and mutual recognition. Taken together, what became conspicuously clear was the massive conditioning the men had been subjected to in their lives as boys and as men. One way or another, most of the men in the group felt they'd been used or manipulated by the culture, coming not only from their childhood and parental upbringing but also from peers and social influences in their adult lives.

When the time for the men's truth forum was completed, the women were given an opportunity to reflect on what had been said. They began by honoring the men. For many women this experience was a first, and they felt privileged to have witnessed the men speaking so frankly, authentically, and searchingly about these aspects of their sexuality and conditioning. The men were genuinely surprised and touched by the women's reflections. They had not expected the women to be so appreciative; they had been more prepared for judgment and criticism. As the women spoke, expressing their feeling that the men had given them a gift by being so open, everyone in the group began to understand something about the work that needs to be done between women and men. The men felt they had accomplished something significant in their forum, and we all knew that we had, collectively, begun an important piece of healing work.

The irony, however, was that for many of the women portions of the men's sharing represented a devastating confirmation of their concerns about male sexuality. This was doubly ironic because the confirmation had arisen precisely because the men had chosen to make themselves vulnerable by sharing candidly. An attractive, fiery woman in her mid-thirties named Julia spoke to this paradox. Carefully, but with determination, she said she feared the men were justifying their behavior to each other. "As a woman, I have to constantly compensate for the way my true being is trivialized by superficial lust. Men who desire me because they find my FQ sufficient are rarely available in any authentic way." She went on to explain that unbridled male sexual energy was ultimately assaulting. She was distressed that the men's truth forum seemed, even in the end, to have concluded that male sexuality is an unchallengeable reality—whether conditioned or biological—that women just have to accept. Her conclusion was abrupt and blunt: "I find it difficult to believe there isn't a more fundamental connection between men's hearts and their penises."

Others began to respond, but the hour was late, so the facilitators brought closure to the day with a silent meditation and honored the group for the unique and difficult nature of the work they were doing. As a way to respect the delicate place we were in as a group and to support deep integration of the work done so far, it was agreed that everyone in the group would maintain silence until we met again the next day.

### The Women's Truth Forum
In the morning, it was the women's turn to be in the inner circle while the men, seated around the outer edges of the room, listened in silent witness. The women's and men's roles were now reversed for the women's truth forum. As the talking stick went around, many of the women spoke about the power of the previous evening, and about the complex layers of gratitude, poignancy, and anger they

were feeling as a result. Then Susan, a self-confident woman in her late twenties, interjected her thoughts.

"I totally identified with some of the men. When they defended their appreciation of female beauty and of evaluating women on a purely physical basis—I think this is perfectly natural, and what's more, I do it all the time myself—with both men and women. I often see men or women on the street and wonder what it would be like to have sex with them. I think this is perfectly normal, basic human behavior—sizing up potential mates. I don't mind that men do it to me, and it doesn't feel wrong when I do it, either."

An elegant older woman named Harriet bristled, and angrily challenged the whole idea of either gender sexualizing the other. "I find it unhealthy and dehumanizing," she exclaimed, "and I don't buy the idea that it's for potential mate selection." Harriet explained that the Fuckability Quotient more accurately described a system by which both women and men are manipulated, and coerced into manipulating each other. "We are essentially turned into commodities, and we exchange our quotient of desirability for whatever else we want—sex, power, position, even cash!

"Desirability is a kind of currency, almost like money," she prickled. Then she turned to Susan, who had spoken earlier, "and you're feeding the system. You are complicit in your own exploitation. You're attractive now, so it's to your advantage to stay in the game. But that won't always be the case. Eventually your FQ will drop, from aging if nothing else. What will you do then?"

The mounting tension among the women was forceful, so much so that one of the facilitators briefly interjected and encouraged the women to take some deep breaths and join hands in order to stay present with the intensity. Silence settled back in, and then Sally, a thirty-something self-identified feminist, took the talking stick. She urgently implored us to look more carefully at the ramifications of a society obsessed with the selling power of sex. Referencing video footage we had watched on the first day—testimonies of rape and related gender violence presented during a U.N. tribunal on human rights—Sally became adamant. "Rape is born from precisely the kind of sexual objectification that the men were talking about and that some of us have been romanticizing. Men are habitually aroused, not by relating or by imagining an actual relationship with the personhood of a woman. What arouses them—habitually and obsessively—is looking at a woman's body as something to possess, as a thing."

There was silence for a few moments as Sally's words sunk in. Then Julia, the woman who had expressed her dismay at the end of the previous evening, reached out resolutely and practically seized the talking stick. "Nancy Raine wrote a book called *After Silence— Rape and My Journey Back*. She writes about living with fear the way others live with cancer." Julia's eyes dropped toward the floor. "I know exactly what she's talking about."

Julia then began to describe how, some years earlier, a man had broken into her apartment at night while she slept, grabbed a jacket from her closet, and used it to cover and hold down her head. Her first awareness, she said, was of struggling to awaken from a terrible nightmare. But then Julia realized that this was no dream: "Whatever I was trying to wake from was actually happening in reality. My head was in some kind of grip. I spit and hissed and fought my way up until I could feel the windowsill against my back. It was my first contact with substance, a point of reference: Yes, I was awake in my bed, in my apartment, in Oakland, California, in the United States, on planet Earth."

She managed to sit up, she said, but could not free her head. Until the man spoke—threatening her life—she wasn't sure what she was fighting, or why. "Stop fighting me, bitch!—or I'll kill you!" Julia's voice rose to a near scream as she repeated his threat. All attention was riveted upon her as she stopped herself, drew in a deep breath, and became almost unbearably calm.

"It wasn't until he spoke that I understood that a man was in my bedroom, holding me down with something that he'd put over my head, that it was his hands and arms that were forcing me down as I tried to fight my way free. I couldn't see. I was trapped in the dark. The whole sequence of events was so abrupt and unexpected, so wrenching and incomprehensible, so the way violence is—changing everything in a heartbeat—that the truth of my experience simply overwhelmed me. I collapsed inwardly. Like everything else about being raped, it's hard to describe the sensation of deadly surrender. It felt like the space between my vertebrae gave way, like my body simply crumpled into half its size. I became inexplicably compliant and cooperative. I went limp.

"The next few minutes and hours are there inside me. I know, because whenever something wakes me in the night—my heart pounds, my body goes rigid."

Julia paused and took a deep breath. "I always want to stop the story right here. I never want to say what happened next. I don't want to talk about his penis, or the way it felt to have my face forced into a pillow so I could barely breathe. I want to end the story with the relief I felt when I realized my attacker was human. But, in fact, the rest of what happened is there, the events I didn't tell the police, although they tried to get me to. Events I didn't tell my mother, my father, or my brother. Events I've never laid out for any of my close friends, not even for a therapist, because every time I get to this place in the telling, I feel the shame crawling up the side of my neck and I feel the difference between the fear, which I can talk about, and the degradation, which I cannot."

Julia was silent for a time. Then, using her hands to shield her face, as if it weren't enough that her eyes were closed, she slowly began to relate a full description of the rape and the psychological annihilation she had experienced. As she spoke, Julia's outrage grew. Rape, she told us, is an experience of utter obliteration. No words could convey the dehumanizing impact of such a total invasion of her physical being. How could she begin to communicate the shattering loss of selfhood? It was as if he was the only one there, the only real person, the only sentient consciousness. She opened her eyes and looked around fiercely.

"But I *was* there! I existed! I mattered! And he didn't know it. I actually tried to reach out to him psychically. It was kind of an instinctual thing, I guess. I thought if he could feel my existence, my beingness, that he might somehow be moved to kindness. I didn't understand how committed he was to penetrating, without being penetrated—you know, touched, reached, connected."

The rapist, it turned out, was not the only one who violated Julia that night. After he made his escape, she called the police. Two male officers from the Oakland Police Department came to Julia's apartment. While questioning her, the officers made jokes about sex and asked about the rape with thinly veiled voyeurism—insisting on knowing what seemed to her like pornographic details. The two officers encouraged one another in this inquisition, exchanging knowing winks and raised eyebrows. After completing their investigation of her apartment the police took Julia to a building she could not identify. It was not a police station—more likely the morgue. The only person she saw there was another man, who was identified as a "police physician." While the two officers stood at the stirruped end of an examining table, watching the "exam" and continuing with sexual banter and innuendoes, the "physician" probed Julia's vagina, looking for evidence of semen or physical injury. He chatted casually and joined the officers with laughter and jokes of his own. Eventually, he announced cheerily, "Yep, she's been raped!"

"I was never taken to a hospital, nor was it offered to me as an option," Julia continued. " I was never given the support of another woman, or consoled in any way. To my knowledge, there was no further investigation of the rape. No one was ever prosecuted. In fact, my middle-of-the-night rendezvous with the officers was my only contact with the police department. I felt like I'd been raped yet again. They were as putrid to me as the smell of semen that stained the sheets of my bed."

Pin-drop silence filled the room when Julia finished speaking. We all sat in this poignant stillness for several minutes, absorbing the impact of her story. Then the group took a break in silence before reconvening back in the full plenary circle.

As the men began reflecting back their experience of the women's truth forum, many acknowledged that they had never before heard a woman speak so candidly about being raped, especially not in a way that captured the physical and psychological dimensions of the experience so vividly. One by one the men spoke, several with tears or visible anguish.

Mark began, his face flush with new realizations. "Never will I hear the word 'rape,' or think about rape, in the same way again," he said. "I had no idea what the experience must be like, until today." Others resonated with this, saying they felt they'd experienced something of the shock and horror of rape.

"It feels like I came as close as possible to living through the experience of rape," reflected Howard, "without actually being a woman, or facing the violation directly."

An older, quieter man named Jim had been relatively quiet through much of the gathering, and had become visibly upset during the rape story. He spoke haltingly, choking back tears. "I have five daughters. My middle daughter was raped when she was nineteen," he said. "At least two of my daughters were physically or sexually abused by their husbands and boyfriends. I never realized, until this day, what they must have gone through." He paused to collect himself. "I always thought . . ." His voice trailed off and he sat in silence, looking devastated. One of the facilitators moved next to him and put an arm around him. Jim began crying and mumbling softly, and then raised his voice slightly. "I realize I can't speak about this now. But thank you, Julia, and thank you to all the women. I'm grateful beyond what I can express."

Charles, the young law student, said that he realized for the first time what it must be like for women to live with the constant threat of sexual assault. "It's a shattering realization. I never really got it before how women and girls are always having to be vigilant—alert every minute of their lives; how they have to go through their daily activities with the perpetual threat of attack—as if they were prey to some wild animal on the loose."

Another man, in his early forties, named Tom, had hardly been able to contain himself, hearing all this. He became increasingly distraught as the conversation progressed, and finally burst in. "I need to—I *have to* interject here!" he stammered. "I know exactly what Julia is talking about! I was raped when I was fourteen—by the priest at our church!" Tom was shaking as he spoke, and his face was glowering red. "Sodomized!! Do you have any idea what that's like?!" he thundered. "There is an assumption here—and in our society—that only women get violated! Only women suffer from the patriarchy. I'm sick of that lie! I've lived with it all my life. It's not just women who suffer from rape!" Tom's rage filled the air, and two facilitators moved next to him, offering containment as well as support for him to move deeper into emotional release. Tom looked around the room, making eye contact with each person, and then dissolved into tears as grief overtook him. Recomposing himself within a few moments, he continued, "My mother was a staunch feminist. She was a leader in the women's movement, and she raised me to feel like a total schmuck, just for being male. All my life, she and her friends constantly engaged in male bashing of one kind or another, and they always made sure I understood every detail about how terrible men are."

Tom explained that he developed a deep guilt and inferiority complex, and grew up feeling constantly apologetic for being male. "It wasn't until I was in my late twenties and started years of therapy that I began to reclaim my own manhood. And with that came all the memories with the priest. It was brutal."

Tom's story ushered in a deeper sense of openness and trust in the group. Several expressed gratitude to both Tom and Julia for their courage and vulnerability in sharing their stories. Then Julia stood up, walked over to Tom, and whispered something to him. The two of them hugged, and tears began to flow freely around the group. The entire room was transported into a space of empathic sorrow and compassionate healing presence, not only for Julia and Tom, but for women and men everywhere who have suffered the excruciating agony of rape or sexual violation.

Despite the unimaginable pain and agony that was being expressed, a growing sense of intimacy was emerging in the group. Each story that came forward, each step into further exposure and vulnerability, brought us closer together as a group. The very act of bringing conscious, compassionate attention to our pain—unraveling and giving voice to these challenging and humbling experiences—was loosening their grip on us. Meeting the need for these long-repressed aspects of our humanity to be unveiled and witnessed was beginning to awaken unique dimensions of mutuality, human forgiveness, and authentic intimacy. We became acutely aware of the profound healing that is needed in our species. We knew with conviction that what we were doing, as women and men together, was confronting the cultural dynamics that are killing us all—killing women and men, killing our children, killing the planet.

## The Heart of Reconciliation

The time had come to shift gears entirely. All the intensive work we'd been doing was profound and transformative, but also demanding emotionally—even draining. It was vital to shift into an altogether different experiential space together—one that would restore and rejuvenate us and consecrate our work. So the next afternoon the women's and men's circles convened separately to create rituals of mutual honoring and blessing for one another, which were presented on the last evening.

Rituals in gender reconciliation work are experiential offerings created and choreographed by the participating women and men— as a means to express gratitude and offer blessings of mutual appreciation and forgiveness. The focus and content of the ritual springs directly from the uniqueness of each group and the particular work that has transpired within it. A true ritual is never forced or staged. Both the design itself and its choreographed execution are spontaneously crafted through the power and process of the group that creates it.

An effective ritual serves as a kind of meta-narrative, helping us to structure our attitudes and behavior in daily life beyond the ritual space itself. It is not something we simply witness, but rather something we participate in together—a special time out of time—an experience invoked and orchestrated from within our deep selves. Through the ritual we glean new information, insights, guidance— similar to the way one receives information from a dream that can then be brought into waking life. In gender reconciliation work, the power and beauty of the rituals is directly proportional to the authenticity and depth of healing work and truth-telling that has preceded them. In this case, the group had done some extraordinary healing.

As the women's group and men's group embarked upon designing ritual offerings for each other, there was tremendous enthusiasm and spirited joy all around. Both groups entered into a rarefied environment of high energy, creativity, and playful tenderness—peppered with frequent outbursts of laughter. Because their hearts were so open, people were willing to risk and stretch themselves in ways that might have seemed unthinkable only days before. Everyone was aware that this was a rare privilege: to actually take the time and "trouble" to honor, acknowledge, and bless one other across the "gender gap."

The men presented their ritual first, but this time it was because they wanted to. They were pleased to be offering a ceremony of their own creation, weaving in unique references and vignettes from the foregoing week. The men ushered the women into a beautiful, sanctuary-like setting and seated them in a semicircle facing the men. The room was lit all around with candles. After an opening song and prayer, each man stepped forward, picked up a candle, and stood before the women. One at a time, the men spoke to their complicity in reinforcing the "patriarchy," which had been largely unconscious. Each man named a behavior or characteristic that he no longer found acceptable in himself, and committed himself to changing it. These declarations varied greatly according to each man's unique character, maturity, and personal growing edge. Charles, the lanky law student, said "I have learned so much about women's pain this week which I never realized before. I can see how insensitive I've been to some of the women I've been working with and dating at school this year. I am committing myself to listen to them more deeply, to open to them."

Each man had written his behaviors of complicity on a piece of paper beforehand, as the men had planned, and after all the men had spoken they put all these papers together into a ceremonial fire pot and burned them—dramatically symbolizing the release of these behaviors and ritualizing their commitment to personal transformation.

After the papers were burned, the men made personal vows of renewed alliance with the women, coupled with a symbolic offering of summer blossoms they had gathered. Each man stepped forward, spoke his vow, bowed deeply before the women, and then floated his blossom with his personal blessing in a basin of scented water.

When it came to be Howard's turn, he began to speak in halting tones, but his voice grew stronger and more confident as he spoke. "This week . . . has been a major breakthrough for me. I realized something very important: I have been spiritually asleep . . . while dreaming that I am spiritually awake . . ." He paused, allowing his words to sink in. "I have resisted waking up from this comforting slumber. As you know, I've done lots of men's work over the years, and I've been leading it for a long time. Until this week, I had believed that I'd pretty much healed my personal collusion with the patriarchy, and that I was taking full responsibility for it in the world through my men's work."

He paused, making eye contact with each woman individually, and then continued. "But what I've realized here is that there is another whole level of work to be done. Until now, I had believed I was free of patriarchal insensitivity, and that I never took male privilege for granted. Because of these cherished beliefs, I could not see that there was a deeper level of complicity and denial still operative within me. I have been blind to the ways that I am still perpetuating patriarchal dysfunction, on more subtle levels. And I don't think I'm the only 'sensitive, aware man' for whom this is true. There is a huge, uncharted territory here that needs to be explored . . . with great care and sensitivity. And it requires that men and women do this healing work together. I believe this is the next step that is needed in the men's movement. And I vow to find ways to bring this mutual healing work between women and men into the men's community."

Howard silently placed his blossom on his heart and then gently floated it alongside the others in the water. When each man had spoken, the men clustered around the basin and approached the women. They anointed each woman individually with the water, speaking her name, and offering specific reflections of her soul's depth and beauty. The men then stood together before the women, bowed, and prostrated themselves on the ground.

Many of the women wept. The men's ritual had been startling and beautiful. The women understood that the men were acknowledging the ways in which cultural conditioning creates difficult gender dynamics that women must grapple with, often on a daily basis. The men had expressed personal awareness of these realities in a ritualized manner. And they offered more than an apology; they expressed their commitment to transform personal complicity and become instruments of healing between the masculine and feminine in society.

Deeply moved, with their hearts wide open, the women began their ritual for the men. Each man was escorted, flanked by a woman on each side, into the community room, which the women had decorated with flowers and candles. The women seated the men in a circle and gave them flowers to hold. Then they began chanting a song of compassion and love, which they sustained throughout the ritual.

As the women chanted, they moved around the circle. Each woman stopped before each man and thanked him individually by quietly naming that man's virtues, gifts, and beauty, as she saw them. Each woman made her specific offerings to each man in whatever way felt appropriate to her: softly whispering appreciation, grasping hands, giving a warm hug or a sisterly kiss, bowing, massaging the man's face or feet, or simply looking fully and radiantly into his eyes—offering each man her respect, affection, and honor. Words and thoughts dissolved into a profound presence of nurturing harmony and reverence as the women's soft chanting and attentive ministering led the men into a gentle yet stirring ecstasy. The sweet rose fragrance of the burning incense was but a tiny semblance of the loving presence that filled the room and lifted the hearts of all in the spirit of cherished communion. Tears flowed freely on both sides.

The depth of the healing work we had done together was powerfully consecrated in these rituals. As Howard put it later, "The pinnacle of our work together in this workshop was, without a doubt, the group rituals. It felt like I saw God—or, actually, the Goddess!—in a new way."

In Jerry's words, "Our ritual for the women was highly charged. I found tears streaming from my eyes. I truly felt that this outpouring of intent was the least we could do to represent all men—those who are involved in gender reconciliation work, and those who aren't ready for it yet. And then, the ritual in which the women honored us men was sublime. Talk about an altered state of consciousness! The energy of the nurturing feminine was so thick in the room that I felt like each woman, thanking me in her own way, was a unique incarnation of the Goddess. My experience of the ritual was a magnificent, intensely beautiful evocation of the many facets of the Divine Feminine. It was truly a transcendental experience."

Harriet, who had earlier been so "triggered" during the workshop, later described her experience of the rituals: "I felt all those unresolved issues within myself. And then I saw all the contradictions break apart, and our hearts break open, when in ritual on the last day the men prostrated themselves in front of us. Many of us were left speechless; there was incredible power and sincerity in that silent, collective gesture. And later I saw tears in the men's eyes as we women circled in honor of them. Out of the ashes of our disagreements and confrontations rose the sacred masculine and the sacred feminine again."

The women and men in this workshop who so courageously attended to each other discovered—and embodied—the essence of gender reconciliation. They opened themselves to the "alchemical" nature of authentic healing and persevered through the agonizing pain buried deep in the collective human psyche until they reached the "gold" of ecstatic loving communion between masculine and feminine.

The Vietnamese monk Thich Nhat Hanh has observed, in reference to the ecological crisis, that "what we most need to do is to hear within ourselves the sounds of the Earth crying." The process of gender reconciliation works in an analogous way. When we feel not only our own pain and suffering but also experience within our own hearts the tears of the other gender(s), then the mysterious alchemy of gender reconciliation begins. It unfolds by means of an unfathomable wisdom that confounds the mind and exalts the heart. The results are described beautifully by the mystic poet Rumi:[1]

Hear from the heart wordless mysteries!
Understand what cannot be understood!
In the stone-dark heart there burns a fire
That burns all veils to their root and foundation.
When the veils are burned away,
the heart will understand completely—
Ancient love will unfold ever-fresh forms.

# CHAPTER 6

# *Embracing the Beloved: Transmuting Profane Sexuality into Sacred Communion*

*Doing our own will is usually what harms us.*

—Teresa of Avila, Interior Castle

In the sacred epic *Mahabharata* from India, there is a story of a noble young prince named Pandu who, while hunting, takes the lives of two mating deer. His five swift arrows pierce effortlessly to the heart of their unguarded pleasure. As the stag lies dying, he turns to Pandu and begins to speak. He is no ordinary stag, but is in fact the holy rishi *Kindama*, who transformed himself and his wife into wild deer so that they might couple in sublime innocence. The holy stag curses Pandu—not because the hunter has killed, but because he has defiled life's most precious union. "You have taken advantage of the hallowed union that perpetuates and delights all life—henceforth are you cursed. If ever you should lie with a woman again, that shall be the moment of your death!"

This story from the *Mahabharata* reminds us that the sexual act is something sacred, to be protected and honored—and that to take advantage of this most tender of human experiences can lead to our demise. And we don't have to look far in society to find striking examples of such demise. From the Catholic Church, to Capitol Hill, to multinational corporations and progressive social change organizations, symptoms of our troubled relationship with sex are everywhere manifest. We live in an environment in which sexuality is often trivialized and defiled, stripped of its emotional depth and divorced from its sacred root. This occurs in different ways throughout our society, and one particularly challenging arena is the complex domain of pornography, which we now examine a bit more closely.

## Grappling with Pornography

Issues related to pornography frequently arise in the course of our gender reconciliation work as an important element of participants' personal experience. Many participants have reported powerful impacts on their lives in relation to the pornography industry. As a result, we began looking for a way to explore this charged issue in a substantive and insightful manner.

The pornography industry today is growing by leaps and bounds. In the United States alone, it mushroomed from an estimated ten million dollars in the 1970s to some ten billion dollars today—a thousand-fold increase.[1] Greatly enhanced by the Internet, there are now more than ten thousand active Internet sites dedicated to pornography. Sexually provocative images are promulgated through cyberspace to ever wider, ever younger audiences, as well as to diverse peoples across the globe, most of whom had little or no prior exposure to pornography. Analysts and critics are divided in their assessment of the phenomenon, but no one doubts that the impact on society is huge.

At the 2003 meeting of the American Academy of Matrimonial Lawyers, two-thirds of attending lawyers said that online pornography is playing a significant role in contemporary divorces. Yet advocates such as Candida Royalle and Carly Milne maintain that pornography is a healthy force in people's lives, and Royalle received a lifetime achievement award for her work at the Feminist Porn Awards in Toronto in 2006.[2] Meanwhile, author Pamela Paul, in her 2005 book, *Pornified*, reports that obsessive porn surfing on the Internet is wreaking havoc on men's and boys' conceptions of women and sexuality—rendering them numb to conventional sex, and impatient with their real-life partners.[3]

During a series of exploratory workshops on gender reconciliation organized for leaders in the women's and men's movements and other social change professionals, we experimented with a controversial exercise developed by John Stoltenberg to explore pornography in groups. Stoltenberg is author of *Refusing to Be a Man* and *What Makes Pornography Sexy*, books that outline a practical exercise for working experientially with pornography.[4] Our purpose in introducing this exercise was to engage the group in an experiential process to explore how pornography is impacting our society and shaping unconscious attitudes about sexuality, physical beauty, intimacy, and socially acceptable behavior. We worked with this same exercise again in our yearlong professional training program for facilitators of gender reconciliation work.

In Stoltenberg's exercise, a few men are asked to be volunteers, and their task is to adopt the physical poses taken by women in photographic pornography magazines. Participants gather around each male volunteer and coach him into reproducing, as accurately as possible, the actual body position and precise facial expression of the model in a pornographic photograph. Although the volunteers perform this exercise with their clothes on, they often report that the experience of adopting the poses makes them feel emotionally vulnerable, and the experience is often described as demeaning and psychically disturbing. Adopting the physical poses evokes a kinesthetic understanding of the exploitative nature of pornography for the poser.

We entered cautiously into this experiment. After introducing the purpose and parameters of the exercise, we asked for volunteers among the men. We had modified Stoltenberg's design so that participants could freely choose their degree of participation, ranging from simply remaining in the room and witnessing at a distance, joining one of the coaching teams, or (for the men) volunteering to be one of the models. Three men volunteered. Each was given a photograph from *Playboy* or a similar magazine, and three teams of men and women formed to coach each volunteer in taking up his pose. A delicate atmosphere of vulnerability and hushed tones quickly emerged in the room as the three coaching groups worked with their volunteers.

Going through this exercise elicited a plethora of challenging issues and emotions surrounding the role of pornography in our personal lives and society. Responses in the group after the exercise brought forth multiple layers of tension, ambiguity, and feelings of betrayal or numbness, and highlighted stark differences between women and men in relation to pornography. Some women didn't look at the pictures and stood back, not wanting to have anything to do with the entire exercise. Others who were right in the middle of it noticed afterwards they felt disoriented or even betrayed by what they had participated in. And a few women who participated liked it and were not ashamed to say so.

The men had equally varied responses. Some male volunteers were shocked by the physical pain they experienced from trying to take the poses. Other men felt shame because of past or present involvement with pornography. Myriad private memories and images came up for people about their personal histories—men and women alike. The exercise revealed clearly to everyone that, in some way, we are all powerfully affected by pornography. It's not just the person who plunks money down in the store and walks away with the magazine that has a relationship with pornography—it's the entire culture.

As the group continued to process the exercise, the primary response among the women was a feeling of disorientation and vulnerability. Several reported feeling numbed by the exercise, especially those who had volunteered to work directly with the magazine images. Others felt knocked off center by a wave of agitating energy, and almost every woman in the group felt the exercise required her to struggle to stay in touch with her sense of personal power. One woman voiced the opinion that the entire exercise would only carry real meaning for the men if they had to actually undress and pose naked, like the women in the pictures. Many of the women fell into talking about "the men" as if all men in the world, and each man in the group, were identical. A few of the women defended the use of pornography in private relationships as part of the preliminaries to consensual sex; some defended the ever present cultural "need" of pornography, arguing that legality made it less harmful. Others objected strongly to any tolerance of pornography. One woman told us that she had been forced to share her partner with the women in the magazines, as if he were literally having an affair. He found her inadequate, she explained, when he compared her to the passive, no-fuss, airbrushed photographed models, who never talked back and never required any foreplay.

The conversation among the women was peppered with discord and conflict. Two general camps developed, one comprised of women with greater (self-proclaimed) sexual "sophistication" and another camp of women of strong moral principle. All the women, however, agreed that the exercise had thrust them into an environment that invited a mostly self-critical questioning of their sexual attractiveness. The images tended to trigger an inevitable, involuntary comparison in which each woman found herself privately measuring her body against the standards she either saw or assumed were portrayed in the pictures. It made little difference that the pictures were airbrushed and posed; they represented an "ideal" of beauty toward which every woman was presumed to aspire.

Furthermore, the presence of pornographic images led the women to measure themselves not only against the photographs but also against every other woman in the room. It wasn't until one of the women pointed out, through her tears, that she no longer felt safe in either the women's circle or the community as a whole that we began to see just how powerful the cultural dynamic unleashed by pornography is—regardless of the position one takes in relationship to it.

The men's reactions were also varied and complex. Some were left feeling unseen, others were deeply moved by new insights, and some were resistant to the whole exercise. Several shared candidly their experience of pornography and its relationship to their own sexuality. One man spoke about the profound manipulation of men by pornography and the advertising industry. "Men are vulnerable to the beauty and attractiveness of women, and this is used in very precise ways to manipulate and control us." He said he had to stop looking at pornography altogether because it was affecting how he looked at all women. "It's as if there are invisible handles on me, and they can be pulled against my will." Active nods of recognition and agreement emerged among the men as he spoke. "So I had to stop allowing myself the enjoyment of pornography images, because I found that when I went through regular life, I was being pulled by those handles against my will—all the time: in the street, in the grocery store, everywhere."

One man admitted to the power that pornography had been in his life, and how he had developed a tenacious habit of becoming glued to certain pornographic Internet sites, hiding it from his spouse and children. As another man characterized the situation, "Advertisers and the pornography industry know very well that men are easily manipulated by this energy. And very few of us are conscious of how deeply we can be manipulated. It's a profound disservice to a vulnerable young man growing up to have this happen to him, yet it's routine in our culture. We get hooked by it and don't even know it, and then we just end up following our dicks around."

This was not an easy conversation. Even in a group of sophisticated and well-informed individuals actively involved in gender issues and social change we found ourselves easily tripping over faulty stereotypes or risky generalizations. As the processing continued, tensions ebbed and flowed in the group, and there were moments when it felt like the men and the women were not going to reestablish trust of each other again.

At least one man defended pornography as a legitimate avenue of sexual expression, and felt the approach inherent in this exercise was an unfair representation of pornography that distorted its actual value in intimacy. Others found the exercise invasive, and still others did not wish to grapple with this dimension of human sexuality, either because it was too painful or simply irrelevant to them personally.

In the end, however, the group felt that they had successfully ventured into highly delicate terrain together and returned with some powerful learnings and much deeper compassion for one another. The group had come through an experience of collective healing that was bigger than we were. It left us all changed. Toward the end of the workshop we experienced the nourishing silence that comes when no words can express the poignancy of what has been witnessed. In the closing circle, one of the men quietly affirmed his intention never to indulge in pornography again. "The price," he said, "is simply too high."

## Passion and Poison

Given the rocky reception of the exercise, we have not pursued it further, nor do we normally include it in our five-day gender reconciliation programs conducted for the public. Yet, the learning from this exercise was invaluable, and some profound healing moments emerged from tackling pornography head on. In fact, two personal stories emerged during our professional training group that are among the more remarkable stories we have heard in relation to the impact of pornography on people's lives. These stories were recounted by a man and a woman, neither of whom had ever shared their story in any group before. It took great courage to recount these stories in the gender training community, and both stories moved the entire group toward a deeper level of honesty, vulnerability, and intimacy. The first was Carolyn's story, recounted in Chapter 5, and the second is recounted below.

## Jim's Story: From Betrayal to Beloved

"How did I end up with a picture?" Jim asked, as he tried to reconstruct his experience with the pornography exercise for our interview process.

"You volunteered," we reminded him.

"Oh, right," he was startled to recall. "I volunteered, and a picture was given to me, and as soon as I saw the picture, I blurted out, '*Oh, I know her!*' The words just came right out of my mouth. If I could have censored them, I would have. The minute I blurted that out, I knew I was screwed with the group, because I knew I'd been heard. And yet, it was true, she [the woman in the photo] represented thousands of naked women that I had had in my possession over thirty years. She was the generic centerfold, which is a highly disrespectful thing to say of her, but it was true—there she was, the typical centerfold. And I told myself, '*Oh my God!—you so need to be doing this exercise,*' although I didn't yet realize the obvious: I also needed to tell my story."

Jim's story emerged during the processing of the pornography exercise, and continued to come out over the course of the next several days and the next few training modules. Jim, a bright psychotherapist in his mid-forties, told the group he grew up in a "typical American household" where *Esquire*, *Gentleman's Quarterly*, and *Playboy* were commonly available in the living room of his house—his for the taking from his father's magazine rack. "By the time I was ten years old," he said, "I could sit in the living room and read *Playboy*."

Jim's father and uncles were upscale businessmen who thought of pornography as part of the sophisticated "man-of-the-world" package they admired and sought to emulate. They viewed it as "swank," Jim explained, a private "wink-wink" culture shared only among themselves in relation to sex and power. They were, he mused, preoccupied with "gathering and getting as much power, money and possessions as they could . . . and one of those possessions was women. The goal was to possess as many women as you could." Jim went on to say that looking at pornography was really the only sex education he ever received as a boy.

Before long, Jim was buying his own pornography. "This was the beginning of the setup. It was something I could buy. I could buy myself these pictures, and along with them came certain feelings, and that was great. I could masturbate with the pictures whenever I wanted to, and I developed intense fantasy relationships with these women: I knew them by name, and I would read what was printed about their lives and favorite activities and pretend they were somehow in my life. Of course I also loved cars, so I had magazines with cars, and I had magazines with girls, and it all seemed normal."

Jim's parents divorced when he was about thirteen, and the divorce was traumatic. "The pornography became an escape. The fantasy relationships were a comfort." He filled in some of the details of his confusion as a teen, going off to an expensive, high-profile college with a trunk filled with Brooks Brothers's clothing and a fancy sports car. But by Christmas of his freshman year he had sold his expensive clothes for drugs, grown a scraggly beard, and set out hitchhiking as he searched for meaning in a world that felt empty to him. Eventually he found a girlfriend, and they got married.

The marriage quickly failed. "It didn't work, and three-and-a-half years later it was over. I had created my own family, and what happened of course was that all the unprocessed material from my family of origin came right up. I created my new family, and then I destroyed it. I let it go. I divorced her. I left her house one cold October day in New Hampshire—freezing cold. It couldn't have been more depressing—gray, leaves were gone. I had a green army duffel bag with everything I owned in it. I got on a Greyhound bus and decided to go down to visit my mother in Miami. And that's where it all started. I was twenty-four years old. Did I process anything? No. Did I feel anything? Did I go to a therapist? Did I stop for a moment and reflect? No, and that's where the real problem was."

At twenty-four, rebounding from a failed relationship, Jim found himself "lonely, sad, and angry," but with an excess of cash in his pocket from a job as a valet at a "swank condo" where wealthy businessmen tipped him for parking their cars. He started buying pornography again, and then found his way into the nearby strip joints. "Naked women, here they were, right in front of my face." In retrospect, Jim realized the scene frightened him. He said he felt like "a kid" and started drinking in order to "fortify myself." He didn't ask the women to dance for him, he just wanted them to talk. He became a regular. He developed a crush on one of the girls and started bringing her flowers. He had a fantasy relationship. They talked, she accepted his flowers, but that was it. The relationship was limited to the club. They never went out. She had a boyfriend.

He discovered that in the background of the strip-club scene there were drugs and prostitution. He wasn't interested in the drugs, but became fascinated by the prostitution. "I was lonely and needy, and had money. I had cash money—I could never have done this otherwise."

One night at one of the clubs, the management decided to have a ladies' night with male strippers. The girls he'd been talking to asked Jim if he'd like to dance. Ladies' night brought a huge crowd: "Everybody was screaming and yelling. The women were totally enthusiastic." Jim found himself an object of desire, and with that came "a false sense of being wanted." Women were telling him how sexy he was, and asking him to have sex. A few days later he was approached by an older couple who ran an escort service who told him he was the perfect person for an easy, well-paying job.

"This is where I got into a whole other world," he said. "They told me all I had to do was go out with these women, be friendly, and have a good time with them. Nothing else was required." Jim was excited by the prospect of being sought after. It felt good to him. "This was more than I could ask for; it was the perfect way to make the pain go away." He bought nice clothes and started making even better money. As an escort, he said, "You didn't have to have sex, but the women all wanted to have sex. I was parking cars from eleven to five, and then I'd go run on the beach. I was tan and buff, not eating much, and I was drinking. I would drink and then go out. I was having varying degrees of sex for money. I was the male escort. I was the male prostitute. My social life revolved around strip clubs. I was twenty-four years old and I was lost. I was really out there, and just completely lost. Most of the women clients felt bad about what they were doing with me because they were mostly all married. A lot of it was about trying to make an unhappy wife happy. Everybody's unhappiness and pathology, all blending in together to create a business; it's the strangest thing.

"One day a Mercedes pulled up to the place where I was parking cars, and I reached for the door like I always did, and suddenly I froze in my tracks—it was my father!" Jim's father had flown in from two thousand miles away, unannounced. "What are you doing?" his father demanded to know. "Although he didn't know what was *really* going on, he knew he didn't want his son parking cars," Jim told us.

For Jim, his father's attention meant everything. Two days later, he moved back to his hometown and, for a while, his life began to normalize. He took up carpentry and was "relatively happy." The problem, he told us with a shake of the head, was that he repressed everything that had happened in Florida. "I just stepped right out of it and didn't look back. Again, I didn't process anything, I didn't tell anybody anything. It all went underground and I just walked away. The problem is, if you don't talk, if you don't face it directly, if you don't share it and process it—nothing changes."

One day his father announced, "I've got a deal for you," and offered Jim a job in the Dominican Republic, where he and three of his business buddies were building a shoe factory. Jim went down to do carpentry—to build benches and tables for the stitching and cutting machines in a twenty thousand-square-foot shoe factory. This was the early 1980s, and it was "too expensive" to make shoes in the United States. After Jim finished the carpentry job, his father suggested he stay for a while and help get the factory up and running.

"I was thinking, 'This is a way to stay connected to my Dad,' so I stayed, and was dealing with the manufacturing managers from all these big-time shoe manufacturers . . . I was running a factory with 250 Spanish-speaking employees. I did not speak Spanish at the time.

"We—all these white American business people—are practically at the top of the totem pole in that country: the politicians are at the very top, then there's the military generals, and then there's the American business people. Which means, *I'm God*, I can basically do whatever I want to do. Here I was again in this strange power dynamic where I'm a white male with money and I'm in a third-world country, and the local people are *desperate*. It's just utter desperation. Meanwhile, I have a nice place to live near the factory that I share with one other guy. We have a pool, and it comes with pool boys; it's across the street from the beach. It's an ex-general's house."

Each morning when Jim arrived at the factory, however, he was confronted with a very different reality: "To get out of my car and walk to the front door of the factory, I had to walk through between fifty and a hundred people standing there every morning at eight o'clock, begging me for anything—work, a job—imploring me: *'It's my mother, my sister's dying, I got a kid, I got this, I got that.'*"

Jim didn't know what to do. He was there with just a couple of other American businessmen, learning the trade. At first he gave the beggars whatever he could, but then he "hardened," he said, overwhelmed by the fact that he couldn't really meet the enormous needs that were confronting him. "I didn't know how to process this. I didn't know what to do. There was nobody there mentoring me in any of this. They [the other Americans] were all about just making money."

After about six months, Jim got his own apartment in Santa Domingo: "a penthouse on the twenty-fifth floor of an apartment building—four bedrooms, maid's quarters, marble floors, 360-degree views. It was 250 dollars a month. I got a new vehicle, and I had a house on the beach and a penthouse apartment in town." When the manufacturing managers came, Jim was expected to take them out to dinner and "show them a good time." "I didn't know what a good time was, I really didn't." But they did. They'd been having a "good time" for a while—in the Dominican Republic, in Brazil, wherever they had business interests in third-world countries. As Jim recounted, "These guys are fifty and up, they got bellies, gray hair; they've got families; they're showing me pictures of their kids. They're from back east and they're staying in Santa Domingo."

The first time he accompanied these men, they knew of a club they wanted to go to. They got Jim to take them to a strip club and pushed him up toward the front, right next to the stage. "The men are laughing, just having a raucous good time, and I'm trying to go along with it because I'm trying to be a *man*, a sophisticated man." After the strip club, they headed back into town, wanting to "get laid." They knew where there was a whorehouse, and insisted, laughing and winking, that Jim accompany them there. "It was a real bordello, with a madam at the door. You sat on a couch and the girls were all leaning against the wall. I couldn't believe it. The girls were young—they were all ages, but a lot of them were so young, just kids . . . It was desperate. It was horrible.

"This was a night of hell," Jim recalled. "Truly, this was hell." Each man had his own room, and they passed the girls from one room to the next when they finished having sex. "I could hear them in the rooms next to me. It was living hell."

The following day found Jim walking the beach, deeply disturbed and in pain. "I was miserable," he told us. "This was my father's world. This was the world he wanted me to be a part of, the world he was teaching me about, he and his trusted friends, his business associates. I didn't know what to do." Jim called his father and told him he wanted to come home. His father somewhat reluctantly agreed. Jim returned to the States, but was never able to emotionally connect

with his father in any way, and after several fruitless attempts at communication he abandoned the relationship altogether.

From that point on, however, Jim's use of pornography took a
more serious and compulsive turn, becoming a "steady and active
relationship." The magazines and the masturbation were powerfully
intertwined in his psyche, and he fell into a pattern of using pornography that continued until he was forty years old. He had an intimate relationship with a woman for several years that helped him let
go of the compulsion for a time, but when the relationship ended he
returned to using pornography.

"I knew all this was going to come up in the gender work. I knew
that part of my healing would be to tell this story out loud—and I
was scared. I was really scared to tell this story. I didn't know how it
would be received. But I knew I *needed* to tell this story and I knew
that it needed to be heard in the sense that pornography is damaging to men as well as women. Its effect on me was just like a drug
addiction."

Jim's journey out of addiction began with men's work, where he
was able to process his pain in relation to his father. He also went
into therapy, and eventually became a therapist himself. What created the most dramatic shift for Jim, however, was spending a month
in residence at a spiritual retreat center with a teacher he trusted
deeply. This teacher's practices "helped me get to what was beneath
the addiction, beneath the behavior. He was a master in the nondual
*advaita vedanta* tradition." Jim began intensive training in this tradition. "I began looking deeply at the *moment*, looking at *mind*. I had
to be with myself. There was no escape. It was very profound for me,
very revelatory. I started to become aware of a deeper and higher
meaning to what my longings were about, which brought me to the
awareness that I was longing for *something*—it was like longing for
home, a longing for a deep connection to Source that was playing
itself out around my sexuality."

Jim recounted that he gradually began to see that his longing was
for "a sacred inner mate, or for this thing we're calling The Beloved.
I realized I was reaching for it in the magazines and the women, and
in the dancers—but in a twisted way." He started to see the deeper,

underlying spiritual meaning of his addiction, and this helped him begin to make a shift. "This was the most important part of what I'll call my recovery—awakening to the deeper meaning and learning how to embrace that meaning. I'm still working with this. It's not a done deal. It's changing the way I experience women, and the way I experience women's bodies, but the imprint of pornography is still there. It's just there. I have such a long history with it. It's a relationship."

Jim explained that he has come to view pornography as "part of a ploy to continue to create dominance and separation, and to keep our sexuality separate from our hearts and our spirit." He emphasized that pornography fits into our "long-standing history of separation, disrespect, polarization, alienation, and making people into replaceable, usable commodities. But if you go beneath the cover of the magazines," he added, "and see what's behind it all—what fuels it, whose dollars, which people, what political, socioeconomic sources drive it—then it's a whole different story." And these underlying networks of monetary, social, and psychic forces "are all right there, every time you step up to the magazine rack, ready to suck you in."

Jim has been a practicing psychotherapist for over ten years now, and he collaborates with several colleagues to organize events on gender reconciliation. His story is one man's account of an addictive process in relation to pornography, from which he eventually recovered through intensive psychological and spiritual work.

We have explored pornography in this book because it arises repeatedly in the course of gender healing work. Again and again, participants in our events have described powerful impacts in their personal lives from pornographic influences. The majority of these accounts are reported as harmful, painful, or destructive. A smaller number of participants say that pornography was neutral or irrelevant in their lives, and a few individuals have considered pornography a beneficial influence.

Those who decry the "sex-negative" values of our culture have a legitimate point, as discussed in the previous chapter. Yet pornography is certainly no remedy—indeed, it seems more a symptom, based on what we have witnessed firsthand in gender reconciliation work. In any case, we now turn our attention to the domain where

Jim's story left off—a domain ripe for further inquiry: the sacred and spiritual dimensions of sexuality.

## Sacred Sexuality and Tantra

We hear much today in both mainstream and countercultural media about "tantra" and sacred sexuality, and there is a plethora of books, articles, and workshops about the relationship between sexuality and spirituality. In particular, the tantric traditions of Hinduism and Buddhism are frequently cited as the basis for uniting spirituality and sexuality, and these days there are all manner of seminars available that purport to teach the long-hidden practices. A thorough review or analysis of these offerings is far beyond the scope of this book. Nevertheless, a brief summary of basic information about spirituality and sexuality is important for several reasons. First, sexuality is clearly fundamental to gender healing work, and sexuality plays a major role in the experiences of many participants in Satyana's gender reconciliation workshops. Second, spiritual aspects of sexuality are particularly important in gender reconciliation as people strive to heal themselves and their intimate relationships from damaging sexual conditioning. Finally, there is tremendous confusion, exploitation, and rampant misinformation in relation to spirituality and "tantric sexuality," so it seems important to briefly present some basic information. As author(s), we by no means represent ourselves as experts or adept practitioners of these disciplines, and our treatment here barely scratches the surface. Our purpose is to offer a glimpse of the profundity of these disciplines, perhaps to dispel a few popular illusory notions, and to direct interested readers to informed sources for further information.

Sexual conditioning in the West has been extreme, and devastatingly effective. One consequence is that many Westerners blithely assume that their experiences and perceptions of sexuality are universally shared by all human beings. Not so. In particular, the West has so commercialized sexuality, and our Christian heritage has so oppressed sexuality and distorted its sacred nature, that it is difficult or impossible for most Westerners to conceive of the sexual act as a sacred, religious, or spiritual sacrament. The materialism of

our culture is not limited to corporations and the excesses of material affluence. It is also reflected in the desacralization of sexuality,
reducing it from a form of worship to the mechanical fulfillment of
bodily desires and fantasies. In various other cultures, both ancient
and contemporary, sexuality is held and experienced in utterly different conceptual and experiential frameworks; in some cases it is an
esteemed vehicle for spiritual purification and awakening.

Probably the most widely publicized traditions that honor the
spiritual dimensions of sexuality are the so-called tantric traditions
of Hinduism and Buddhism. Though widely popularized and commercialized in the West, the true nature of tantric traditions has
nothing to do with these mass-marketed misrepresentations. This is
not to deny all legitimacy or value of Western workshops and trainings focused on enhancing sexual experience and performance, but
rather to affirm that tantra is something entirely different. The tan-
tras actually refer to hundreds of specific scriptures and associated
complex systems of spiritual training and practices, only a handful of
which have anything to do with sexuality. As Daniel Odier describes
the tantric tradition of Kashmir Shaivism, "This is a path of incom-
parable depth and subtlety, and has nothing to do with the product
that the West has commercialized under the name 'Tantra.' It stands
in opposition to both the hedonistic sexual quest and the ascetic
spiritual quest, because it reunites the totality of the person."[5]

The goal of all tantric paths is spiritual liberation (*moksha*) or
enlightenment. The underlying philosophy of tantric practice is that
the manifest realm of the physical senses can be utilized as a vehicle
for spiritual realization. Tantra is by no means limited to the sexual
arena, and tantric traditions encompass a broad spectrum of sophisticated philosophy, science, and specific spiritual training integrating
all aspects of physical experience, visionary practices, meditative and
ritual disciplines. Sexuality is thus just one of many rich dimensions
of tantric tradition, and in many ("right hand") schools of tantra,
there is no actual practice of sexual union.

The essential philosophy of tantric sexual yoga is summarized
by Sahajayoginicintra, an ancient female tantric Buddhist master,
as follows:

Human pleasure,
with its identifiable characteristics,
Is the very thing that,
When its characteristics are removed,
Turns into spiritual ecstasy,
Free from conceptual thought,
The very essence of self-arising wisdom.[6]

She goes on to describe the practice of tantric sexual yoga as a loss of the sense of separate selfhood through a merging of identities in which "one ceases to know who is the other, and what has happened to oneself."

In Buddhist and Hindu tantra, the practice of sexual yoga entails the realization or manifestation of deities within the human body. Through intensive chanting and visualization disciplines, deities are experienced as entering and literally becoming or merging with the tantric practitioner. In the ritual sexual ceremony known as *maithuna*, a man and woman unite in sexual intercourse, and ideally they realize together enlightened states of consciousness. The woman realizes herself as the actual Goddess, in one of her particular manifest forms, and the male worships her as the living manifestation of the Divine Mother.

The goal of tantric practice is not to indulge sensual pleasures, nor is it even to manifest the presence of spiritual deities. Rather, the purpose of tantra is to serve as a means to attain enlightenment. The tantric adepts sought to manifest full Buddhahood in a single lifetime, something normally believed to happen only after innumerable lifetimes of spiritual practice. In tantric practice, the heart opens at a very profound level, thereby freeing all the knots, constrictions, and obsessions lodged there by false views, egocentric emotions, and self-regarding vanities. These energies and fears surface, are fully experienced, and then released—permanently relinquishing their hold on the practitioner.

The true purpose of entering into tantric practice is to support the other partner to reach enlightenment. In tantra, the experience of intense sexual pleasure or bliss is not the occasion to be swept away by ecstasy, but, instead, the ecstasy is to be "dissolved" in the very moment it arises, through realization of its inherent emptiness. There is nothing ultimately real about the bliss of sexual union; it has no source, no owner, no existence in itself. The tantric practitioner realizes this, and continues to realize this essential emptiness of sexual bliss as it continues to build in intensity. The practitioner eventually enters into a vast, sky-like experience of universal or cosmic awareness.

Of course, words cannot describe the experience. As Miranda Shaw summarizes it,

> In tantric practice, one goes beyond pleasure and follows the pleasure to its root, which is the core of the mind, which is made of pure bliss . . . When you're in this deep level of bliss, it's very easy to become attached to the object of the bliss, or source of the bliss—which is your partner—and also to the experience of bliss itself, and to turn the bliss into yet another experience of entanglement. That is why the experience of bliss is combined with meditation upon emptiness.[7]

Tantric practice is not something that can be learned through books, and certainly not in a weekend workshop. It is considered to be one of the highest, most advanced practices, requiring years of preparation, purification, and intensive meditative practice. Prerequisites include extensive spiritual practice and realization of emptiness, a purified motivation, and breaking through the illusion of the separate, isolated self. Only after such preparation does the student embark upon the tantric path, for the sole purpose of attaining enlightenment and supporting the tantric partner to attain enlightenment. Even the Dalai Lama has stated that he has not personally achieved the requisite level of spiritual attainment to perform the Tibetan sexual yoga practices with a consort. Nor have, by their own account, some of the popular Western teachers of tantra.

In tantra, the avenue for a man to realize his innate divinity is to honor and worship the divinity of his female consort. The woman is the channel for enlightened energies of transformation, and the man honors and worships her as the Goddess. Men are devotees or servants who are advised to "take refuge in the vulva of an esteemed woman." The actual details of tantric practice are kept secret, and only shared with appropriate students under highly controlled circumstances. As Miranda Shaw describes her experience after years of personal research and study of tantric disciplines in India and Nepal:[8]

> I changed profoundly on every level from my research and study . . . even on a cellular level. I was completely transformed physically. People who knew me before I started my research and then saw me towards the end of that period did not recognize me.

> I discovered a whole form of male celebration of women that I did not know existed. I was also surrounded by images of divinity in female form, and seeing the unclothed female body in a religious context rather than in a commercial, secular context as it is in the West was profoundly affirming for me as a woman. My understanding of what is possible in male/female relationships changed and my understanding of myself as a woman completely changed. I had internalized a lot of the shame-based attitudes of the West, not only the general attitudes of the culture at large but also specific forms of shaming that had been inflicted upon me in my own personal trajectory from which I was able finally to be healed.

> I encountered the power and full sacredness of being female, because the tantric teaching is that women are pure and sacred in the essence of their being . . . their very cells, their energy, not simply something that they can attain, but an ontological fact.

According to Sufi teacher Llewellyn Vaughan-Lee, this innate spiritual purity of women has to do with the creative power women have to bring life into the world. This feminine power is far more profound than what is generally recognized as the physiological capacity to give birth. It is the spiritual power to incarnate a human soul into living flesh, for which purpose a woman's physical and spiritual energy centers are inherently, at their core, utterly pure and directly connected to the divine Source.

In the course of psychospiritual transformation associated with tantric practice, there are different elements and stages to the esoteric process which entail the activation and purification of spiritual energy centers in the body, called *chakras* in the Asian traditions, of which seven are most commonly mentioned: the perineum, sexual center, navel (or solar plexus), heart center, throat center, the "third eye" (between the eyebrows), and the crown chakra (top of the head). The process is described differently in various spiritual traditions, each one using different names and conceptual frameworks to depict the process.

In the articulation given by the Tibetan Djwhal Khul, three key elements to this process are described. First is an "upward trend" of energy moving from the lower chakras upward, a process called *transmutation* that purifies and refines the energy of the lower energy centers. This generally begins with the activation of the Kundalini, the spiritual "serpent" energy that is normally dormant, seated at the base of the spine. Second is a "downward trend" from the higher to the lower chakras in a process called *transformation* that energizes and aligns the upper and lower energy centers. When all the chakras and subtle energy channels are consciously and simultaneously aligned, then a third process, called *transfiguration*, can take place: a form of initiation in which the person's being and consciousness are utterly transformed to an altogether higher level and energetic frequency of consciousness.

The intricacies of this process are complex and precise, guided by a deep wisdom that is generally hidden and entirely beyond the understanding of the aspirant. It is thus usually futile if not counterproductive for aspirants to try to map out which stage of this process they might be in at any given time.

Some of the better writings on tantric sexuality include works by authors such as Daniel Odier, Miranda Shaw, Georg Feuerstein,

Lee Lozowick, Mantak and Maneewan Chia, Barry Long, Robert
Svoboda, and Alice Bailey (Djwhal Khul).

### Teachings from Tantric Kali Worship

A remarkable autobiographical account of a tantric sexual initiation
in South India is recounted in a recent book entitled *Kali's Odiyya* by
Amarananda Bhairavan.[9] The author and his partner were instructed
and guided by the author's aunt, a tantric adept or *odiyya*, named
Preema. We close this chapter with a brief distillation of some of
Preema's teachings on the essence of spiritual sexuality and devotion
to the Divine Mother. The information and short quotations below
are drawn from in-depth dialogues between Preema and Bhairavan
presented in *Kali's Odiyya*. This summary can only convey a glimpse
of the full richness and depth of these teachings, and the interested
reader is encouraged to read the full account presented in *Kali's Odiyya*.
Bhairavan also has a new book out entitled *Medicine of Light*.

Preema explains that sexual energy is not something to be
eschewed or rejected, as has been done in many spiritual traditions
of both East and West. She affirms that sexuality is a manifestation
of the Divine Mother, and therefore it makes no sense for sincere
aspirants to negate the very divine they seek. As she puts it:

> Sexual energy is pure divine energy. If humility and love
> for the Divine Mother are not felt, then this energy will
> fuel lust. But if the heart is filled with love and a sense of
> surrender, then even lust will be dismantled, and its energies
> transformed into worship. (*Kali's Odiyya*, p. 167)

Preema describes in detail the nature of sexual energy and the
process by which the practice of tantric sexuality transforms the body
and inner energy centers of adepts. She explains that sexuality resides
in the *moola* chakra—the lowest of the higher human chakras—at
the juncture of the lower animal realm of largely preconscious mind,
and the intermediate human realm of conscious mind. Preconscious
mind is comprised of essentially instinctual behavior patterns that are
somewhat evolved beyond unconsciousness, but are not especially

amenable to reason or the higher mind. Because the moola chakra is located at the interface of lower and intermediate worlds, it is subject to opposing forces from below and above. In cases where the lower demonic forces have greater influence, sexuality is tainted with lust and violence, whereas if the angelic energies have a stronger hold on the moola chakra, then sexuality is suffused with love and worship. The attitude with which sexuality is approached is therefore all important. As Preema emphasizes:

> Utmost, worshipful humility toward each other . . . is the only way sex can be used to awaken the divine Kundalini. Used any other way, sex will only power the base emotions, giving the dark forces a foothold. (*Kali's Odiyya*, p. 160)

The moola chakra is the seat of the Kundalini, a sacred spiritual energy that is feminine in both men and women. The Kundalini normally lies dormant at the base of the spine, often symbolized by a coiled serpent. When the Kundalini ascends through the chakras, consciousness rises with it and the awareness of the physical mind is gradually dissolved into the subtle dream mind or the astral mind. The aspirant does not arouse his or her own Kundalini during ritual sex. Rather, each partner does it for the other.

The rise of Kundalini can free a person from sexual thoughts and needs, and when the ascent is complete, the person becomes entirely free of sexuality. When the Kundalini has completed its ascent, well above the moola chakra, there are no demons to degrade the energy, but only angels who exalt the Kundalini. The influences of the lower realms are thereby nullified, and karmas are readily dismantled. Preema describes what happens next:

> Kundalini, in most cases, will descend back to the moola chakra and there are no more demons to pull her down. Now the upward path is clear and her energies are drawn up into the angelic realm. But her light shines all the way to the 'bottom' of the erstwhile underworld, thus unifying the unconscious with the higher realms, to form a single,

massive superconscious mind. Now we have a mystic, or an odiyya, who has no more divisions in the mind. It is one, single, superconscious awareness . . . The awakening is actually preceded by the opening and purification of the *ida*, or female, lunar astral channel and the *pingala* or male, solar astral channel. (*Kali's Odiyya*, p. 171)

The spirit's androgeny must be experienced in order to perform sex with the proper attitude. The unification of male and female energies takes place in both women and men, but happens in different ways. In the male, the Kundalini awakening is associated with the unification of his expressed maleness with the repressed female within him. His physical conscious mind becomes androgynous, which unifies the dualism of sexual identity, thereby preparing him for mental ascension into the higher realms while purifying the instinctual levels. In a woman, the same basic events happen, but in addition to androgyny, *odiyyas* recognize a "completed female" in which "the expressed female has joined with her repressed male." (*Kali's Odiyya*, p. 171) The *ida* and *pingala* channels are opened and purified, and when Kundalini awakens, the awakened woman becomes the living goddess, Kundalini herself.

As one of my own spiritual teachers emphasized, the esoteric mystery of masculine and feminine is something so sacred and so secret it cannot even be whispered. Preema upholds a similar admonition, explaining that the process of ritual sexuality is a carefully guarded secret that can be intimately guided and protected only by truly realized and selfless masters. Otherwise there is a strong propensity for corruption or misappropriation of these profound energies to serve egotistical purposes.

One of the crucial distinguishing characteristics of authentic tantra is that the practitioners engage in sexual practice for the benefit of their tantric partners or consorts, rather than for themselves. This contrasts sharply with much of normal human sexuality. As Preema describes the remarkable purity of tantric adepts:

Their selflessness is so supreme that they are ready to activate each other's sexual energy to mutual liberation. Under the constant guidance of their teacher, they put themselves through rigorous practices to cleanse their psyches so that they are fitting agents to awaken their partners to freedom. All the hardship and perils involved in preparing for this ritual are undertaken only to activate the partner to freedom! (*Kali's Odiyya*, p. 172)

The most crucial factor in tantric practice is deep surrender and devotion to the Divine. This is what enables the entire mysterious process to take place. In Preema's words,

. . . devotion to the Divine Mother acts as the lynchpin. It is devotion that enables the safe release of this awesome energy, and its focusing into awareness of pure intent. Without devotion, these energies are horrendous. (*Kali's Odiyya*, p. 188)

According to Preema, peace of mind comes from surrender to the Divine Mother. All actions in life are to be carried out with this sense of surrender. In this way, new karmas are prevented from taking form, while existing karmas play themselves out and are eliminated. The aspirant then becomes free. Such a freedom is incomprehensible to a person whose mind is fragmented by desires and ego drives. Through surrender to the Divine is born a capacity for worship.

Worship flows from surrender. Only surrender can manifest worship. Acts of passion, if sanctified, can be transformed into articles of worship. Desire, passion, attachment, and so on, are unrefined forms of love, the highest expression of which is worship. (*Kali's Odiyya*, p. 190)

One of the crucial guidelines for tantric sexuality is that it can be practiced successfully only under the guidance of an authentic master or teacher. This holds for many spiritual disciplines, but is perhaps all the more true of the tantric path, because of the inherent potential for self-deception, ego gratification, or sexual degradation. The master manifests a vast spiritual love and expanded consciousness. The student or disciple need only drop all resistance and merge his or her intent into that of the master's. This has nothing to do with the master taking control of the student's life, or conditioning the student with laws and rules. Rather, the love between master and disciple is profound and often extends over multiple incarnations:

> It is only through lifetimes of struggle and ardent search that the disciple and the teacher find each other, having been separated by currents of desire in the great stream of existence. There is no reason for pretense, rules, and mandates. There is only love. (*Kali's Odiyya*, p. 187)

Not only having the right teacher, but also having the right partner is critically important in tantra. Otherwise, engaging in tantric sexual practices can drag down both partners, rather than exalt them. Tantric aspirants must be deeply committed to rigorous self-purification before engaging in practices to raise the Kundalini. Otherwise, one or both partners could be plunged into bondage from the powerful energies and impressions exchanged during the ritual.

Inspiring as these teachings are, their demanding nature and exacting conditions may render the authentic tantric disciplines beyond the reach of many people. Yet this is no cause for chagrin, because the beauty and richness of sexual lovemaking as most people experience it is in no way denied by these teachings. On the contrary, study of the tantric tradition can help us to illuminate and exalt the spiritual and sacred dimensions of sexuality. Beyond this, if our deepest longing is for divine love, then in one way or another, it will be realized. In resonance with the teachings of the Hindu mystical tradition, Preema asserts that desire for divine love will eventually transform all other desires into divine ones.

We need not be tantric practitioners or adepts to reclaim sacred sexuality in our own lives. We can all play a role in lifting and cleansing the erotic from the clutches of a culture that has long degraded and repressed sexuality on the one hand, and lauded it in outwardly trivial and obsessive ways on the other. There are multiple levels to sacred sexuality, and myriad trainings and workshops available that cover these various levels, all of which have their place. Even a brief study of the tantric traditions can help us to reenter the erotic domain with renewed respect and deep sensitivity to its sacred dimensions, and to cultivate the divine in every aspect of our lives, including the sexual.

# CHAPTER 7

# *Harvesting the Alchemical Gold*

*Do not store up for yourselves treasures
on earth, where moth and rust consume,
and thieves break in and steal; but store up
for yourselves treasures in heaven. . . .
For where your treasure is,
there shall your heart be also.*

—Matthew 6:19-21

Gender healing work is not quite what it first appears to be. Delving deeply into this work inevitably takes people on an inner journey, and, if they follow it far enough, they are ultimately led into an awakening of an expansive, all-encompassing love. This is called in some traditions an encounter with the Beloved—a mystical form of love. It is where gender reconciliation work ultimately leads, but it's rarely what people are seeking when they enter into it. Gender reconciliation work could thus be likened to certain spiritual or mystical paths in which novices are coaxed onto the path by "veils of attraction" that draw them in through a kind of divine seduction, and only later do they discover what the path is really about.

In our experience, people come to gender reconciliation work with many different motivations. Some are seeking to heal from past wounds, others are hoping to deepen their professional work as clinical therapists or clergy or educators, and still others hope to become trained as facilitators themselves. Whatever their initial motivation, if people remain engaged in gender reconciliation work over time, their relationship to the work evolves as they discover its deeper layers.

The spiritual process behind gender reconciliation work bears some similarity to the trickster tradition of Sufi mystical lore. Unsuspecting wayfarers are lured onto the path by whatever their own attachments or "hooks" happen to be. The "Beloved" catches them by these hooks and drags them along, and then proceeds to remove the hooks one by one. As the journey continues, the Beloved pursues the dismantling process quite beyond mere hooks, and begins to take the person apart—deconstructing their ego and very sense of self. Carried through to its fullest extent, all that remains of the person in the end is a radiant heart of love, with no blocks or impediments. Pursued over extended time, gender reconciliation work bears a resemblance to this process. In its highest manifestation it becomes a path whereby the self is gradually deconstructed—disabused of false desires and identifications—and what eventually emerges is a profound capacity for universal love.

There are moments in the course of gender healing work when the veils obscuring its deeper mystery are suddenly parted and the underlying omniscient presence of the Beloved, or Spirit, or Love—the force and radiance at the core of the work—is subtly revealed. In such moments there is an inexplicable energetic shift that touches everyone present, and people are moved beyond their usual selfish attachments into a selfless, universal compassion. Each time this happens something new is given to the work, and the people involved are uplifted and changed in some way—bonded together in a shared experience of divine love.

This may sound a bit dramatic, but the experience of it is very real, and is actually quite natural and inevitable under the right conditions. There are times when the reality of a *collective alchemy* is palpably operative, far beyond mere New Age jargon, and the community touches into collective mystery and transformation. When this happens, the uncanny presence of Spirit or Love works through the group or community. The love is reflected in each person in the group or community, and there are particular moments when everyone present becomes aware of and inwardly connected to this love at the same time. We call these moments "diamond points"—times when there is a conspicuous Presence, an awe, a magic that everyone participates in and which moves the entire group into a shared experience of the universal heart of love. Such experiences are part of the birthright of the collective human family—when the veil is lifted and we catch a glimpse of the spiritual fire that fuels this work from "behind the scenes" and pours forth warmth and healing and radiance into everyone present. It is the fire of a love that consumes the barriers and illusions that separate us, a love that transcends all the diverse personality interactions between specific individuals. It is a deep, universal love—transcendent and immanent, refined and substantive, nurturing and numinous.

In this chapter we attempt to capture a few of these radical and transformative moments in hopes of communicating something of the power and validity of the experience. Because these moments are actually accomplished in the collective, they are shared experiences that serve as a profound inspiration for what is possible in human community and society—a bright beacon for our troubled time. These are diamond points, moments of special grace or power that no one can claim responsibility for, yet in which the Divine is most apparent, the synchronicities most baffling, and the magic most dramatically afoot.

## Meltdowns: The Power of the Collective Unconscious

One of the most challenging situations that arises in gender healing work is a particular type of crisis that precipitates a systemic breakdown in the entire group process. We dub these situations "meltdowns" because in those moments there is a complete deconstruction of the group process, which morphs spontaneously from one situation or context into an entirely different one. This shift can take place quite suddenly, often within less than a couple of minutes. The scene can transform from a warm and friendly circle of people sitting listening attentively to one another to a highly charged emotional cauldron of collective grieving and anguish. Although unpredictable and often cathartic, meltdowns are frequently junctures of exceptional healing potential and spiritual power. These moments constitute auspicious opportunities for a kind of collective metamorphosis around complex gender issues that can reach archetypal proportions.

The character of meltdown experiences is virtually impossible to describe in words. They are usually intense in the moment, lasting anywhere from a quarter hour to half a day or more. Afterwards there is often a transcendent or numinous quality that leaves everyone present feeling humbled and grateful, with a palpable sense of sacred integration between human and spiritual planes of consciousness. Meltdowns are never planned or orchestrated beforehand—they cannot be; rather, they emerge from spontaneous crises. They present a significant challenge to facilitators, who must respond in the moment to the unfolding situation with intrinsic courage, trust, and respect for what emerges—coupled with a triage approach to handling the practical needs that arise in the group. The process demands a high degree of faith, skill, and sensitivity on the part of the facilitators.

## Feminine and Masculine Agony

One such meltdown happened early in the morning on the fourth day of a five-day event. One of the women, Anna, shared with the group a journal entry she had written upon waking up that morning in tears from a disturbing dream. Her journal entry took the form of a "letter" she had written to the group in response to her dream and to the work we had been doing over the preceding four days.

> *To Whom It May Concern*: I know it is unreasonable to expect others to be more healed than myself and to be less needy. I know how difficult it is to come out of myself and reach toward another. I know I need a miracle. I know I can't heal my sense of destroyed self-image alone. I cannot look into the mirror and see beauty. I've been trained to see myself as an ugly, unwantable female. I've been trained to see myself as an empty shell of a woman who holds value only as one who can articulate ideas and hold forth as an intellect. My woman's body feels dead and empty. I've been without sexual touch, without profound intimate touch, for years on end.

My husband exited our relationship for reasons that spoke to me of my profound inadequacy as a woman. I felt humiliated, emptied of my last hope to be found beautiful. I lived for all those years with a man who had essentially lied to himself about his capacity to find me attractive and alluring.

I notice that when I find myself "outside the conversation," so to speak, it all caves in, and I become the woman in my dream who wants to jump off the building. I'm left with the anxiety that I might jump, instead of patiently climbing down. I'm left with the fear that I might be too old before I get down, or too *something*—too unattractive anyway, too overbearing, too intense, too needy, too much, just plain too much. I'm so very frightened for myself, for the part of myself that wants out so badly that I'll jump.

I'm hyper-vigilant, not just to the thought of physical attack, but to the thought of emotional attack, to humiliation, to the frustration of rejection time and time again. I'm afraid of the shattering lack of presence in the eyes of any man, the moment when I see him move inside and say, "Oh, oh, she's for real. She wants something here. She wants contact . . ." And then the lies begin. What I've learned in the last four days is how clearly I speak my truth. When I said I never wanted to hear lies again, when I said I need male allies who can be courageously intimate, I was saying things that are true for me. I'm relieved to see that I still have integrity.

I believe that most of the violence in my life has been emotional, the violence of nonpresence and of rejection. I've wondered why I was so angry at my mother, why she was the one who earned my rage over the fact that I nearly drowned as a child. I know now. It was because she was my last hope in that moment, my last chance to be seen. But she was checked out in her own delight at being inside the beauty loop. When you're inside it's pretty easy to be indifferent to or impatient or afraid of the outsider. When you're outside—there's nothing. I understand why all of my writing is about being outside. I understand why I'm desperate. I understand why

I woke up this morning in tears. I feel like I need someone as irreverent as Zorba the Greek, who loved the old village woman because he thought it was a shame for a woman to sleep alone.

If I could have what I really wanted out of this healing opportunity, out of this kind of workshop, I'd ask for sexual healing. I'd ask for someone to help me through by loving my body and caressing me. My estrangement is specific: I feel like a monster and I'm overwhelmed by my status, afraid I'm going to jump to my death before I find my way down, knowing that, given the choice, it's better to jump than to burn—with desire or in flames. I live in awe of my own capacity to survive emotionally in the isolation I've experienced.

I say my story: I was adopted. My birth mother was nineteen and in absolute terror and shame. I was unnamed for the first three weeks of my life and then placed in a family that was unprepared. I was jerked around emotionally all through my childhood, shamed for my precocious nature. My mother believed my need to experience sexuality was her failure. She campaigned to keep that from happening. It wasn't arbitrary. It wasn't accidental. It was a strategy under which I grew up and was imprinted. It was worse than sexual abuse.

I don't know if the "memories" I see in these altered states are "real." What I do know is real is that when I was six I was abused by a pimply, weird, teenaged boy who couldn't get girls his own age to pay attention to him, so he forced my hand over his penis. What I do know is I was twice violated in the cold light of a doctor's office. I don't need to know more because I know my brother told me if he looked like me, he'd hide under a bed; that my mother said if I didn't lose weight my life would be a failure; and that my father nicknamed my first boyfriend "Horrible." Those pieces are enough. The damage is real. The sense that I belong outside the dialogue is overwhelming, and each time a man pointedly pushes me outside that dialogue for fear that he might have to deal with my desire for connection in ways he can't easily do, I am repatterned to believe the messages of my family are true.

I know I have incredible gifts to offer. I know I have courage and wisdom and the capacity to provide healing, to provide inspiration, to provide insight. I know I am talented, articulate and insightful. I know my soul is visionary and intent on participating in the leadership of this moment, but I am dislodged from that power all too often. Too often I am reduced to the rabbit, the inadequate, the womanless woman. I cannot do my work alone. Without the constant courage of my brothers and sisters, I'll starve. I need all of you to come in from the conversation you leave me out of and see how you do it—and not just for me, but for every woman who isn't beautiful in ways that fit your picture. Or you'll lose me. I'll lose myself. The planet will lose me, and my piece of the work, which is elegantly beautiful, exquisitely special, will be lost to us all. I will perish.

I thought I was writing this to my friends, but I don't know if that's really where it belongs. I think it belongs with you, God. I think that's where I want to put this—at your feet. I am your child. I am the fruit of your vine, the branch of your tree.

A deep, pregnant silence filled the room as Anna unveiled the truth of her long-hidden pain. Many were wiping tears from their eyes as she spoke. A woman in the group began to respond slowly to Anna's story, but as she spoke her voice became shaky and she collapsed into sobbing. Her sobs touched off several other women in the group, who, one by one, began to wail, or quietly weep. A wave of anguish began to spread through the group, and within a minute or two, the entire group crossed over an invisible threshold and entered into a powerful cathartic release process. Various participants entered into states of deep grieving, while others offered them support, and a few assisted the facilitators in tending to what felt like a highly charged cauldron of purging and archetypal fire.

Anna's pain was not simply her own. Her story, although personal in detail, was at its emotional core so fundamentally and broadly recognizable that it was archetypal. It articulated what Eckhart Tolle has called the collective female pain-body. Anna's words carried tremendous power because they captured the flavor of oppression and pain that women have experienced for thousands of years.

The response to Anna was by no means limited to the women in the room. The men were deeply moved, many to tears. Some were filled with grief at the painful revelations, others were distressed by personal guilt or shame, still others felt anger at being trapped in the role of oppressor. Some had experienced similar oppression themselves. The men's tears expressed their solidarity and compassion in the face of this deep pain, borne for thousands of years by all human beings living in the shadow of gender oppression.

As the energies of this collective catharsis wended their way through the community, surges of emotion rose and fell in the room like huge waves at sea, breaking now in this person, next in that person—carrying the entire group on a wild and dramatic emotional ride. Small groups were huddled around the room tending to those most affected, and as one person would come out of their deep grieving process, another would start in. The energy seemed to rise up through one or more individuals, reach a peak, and then, as it was slowly subsiding, the energy would shift and rise up again to express itself through other individuals, repeating this same process of gut-wrenching ebb and flow. In this manner the energy seemed to visit itself upon almost everyone in the group.

It was well over an hour before these waves began to decrease in intensity and then slowly dissipate. Eventually, a remarkable peace settled into the room, and people reached out to one another in compassionate kindness and loving embrace. The presence in the room became one of exquisite peacefulness and safety—deeply nourishing, richly intimate.

It was into this profound tenderness that one of the men, Doug, began, haltingly, to speak. At first we could barely hear him. Doug was a Vietnam veteran, and as he began to tell his story he grew agitated and started to sob uncontrollably, tears rolling down his

cheeks and choking off his words. Doug's communication was punc-
tuated by long stretches of shaking silence. The authenticity of his
struggle drew us together as a group. Whereas only minutes before
there had been a number of centers around which the group energy
swirled, now this man became the focus of all attention, and the
group became a focused chalice for this man caught in the wrenching grip of his pain. The facilitators moved closer to him, offering
nonintrusive physical support.

Doug's story came out in bits and pieces. He had been on patrol
with his platoon. They had raided a village looking for nests of Viet
Cong, but the men of the village were nowhere to be seen. Only
women, children, and a few of the elderly men were there. The platoon had orders to push on across a rice field that they were afraid
was covered with hidden land mines. They had taken a number of
the village women as prisoners. It wasn't clear why.

As they headed out of the village, their lieutenant suddenly
ordered the women to walk out ahead of the soldiers through the
field. His logic for this decision was simple: there were likely mines
in the field. If the women walked first, they would either step on
a mine and trigger it, or they would walk between the mines and
mark a safe path. Either way, if the platoon followed precisely in the
women's footsteps, they would be safe. It was a reasonable choice
from the lieutenant's perspective; his first responsibility, after all, was
to his men, not to the Vietnamese women, who were suspected, in
any event, to be aiding and abetting the enemy.

Doug had only been a private, a boy of nineteen, yet he held himself responsible for what had happened that day. He told us over and
over, as he began to writhe in his pain, that he should have challenged
his lieutenant, he should have stopped the action, disobeyed the
order—done something. Instead, he and the rest of his platoon had
watched as the women one by one began making their way through
the rice field. After several tense minutes, the lead woman misstepped
and was suddenly blown to pieces in front of his eyes. Shortly thereafter, the second woman went down, and then the third, and the fourth,
until every woman was dead, their bloody, dismembered carcasses
marking the path of safe haven for these American soldiers.

This was a story Doug had never told before, and the wrenching grief and anger that accompanied his telling were chilling. He retched and writhed and gasped for breath. He appeared to be in physical as well as psychological pain, his hands grabbing at his head and his chest as if his heart was literally breaking from the horror of the memory.

One of the male facilitators moved in and grasped Doug in a loose bear hug as he thrashed about the floor. Doug was exploding with excruciating agony. The two men locked together in a sort of radically charged wrestling match that provided Doug with some degree of restraint, thus assuring he would not hurt himself yet giving him freedom to literally writhe in his pain.

There is a scene in D. H. Lawrence's novel, *Women in Love*, where two main male characters wrestle with one another in a match that is part aggressive challenge and part tender affection. This incident was not unlike what Lawrence was conveying about men, and the ways in which men understand and deal with the raw edges of masculine intensity. We were witnessing here the counterpart to the women's anguish that we had just shared: the parallel or opposite archetypal energy of masculine grief. Here was the personal pain of one man, whose story was unique to himself and yet was, at its core, so fundamentally universal that it resonated with mythical proportions. Doug's suffering seared all of our hearts precisely because it captured the flavor of the oppression men have faced for thousands of years, the oppression that accompanies the organized and strategic annihilation of one's own species.

As before, the grief in this moment moved everyone in the room. Tears flowed down every face as, gradually, the wrestling men began to wear down the energy, letting exhaustion play its healing role, letting silence and emptiness prevail. As the catharsis waned and was released, Doug eventually sat on the floor with his back against the wall, tears still running down his face, but now in silence except for the heavy sounds of catching his breath. No one spoke. There was nothing anyone knew to say.

We continued sitting together in the weighty stillness, waiting and feeling fragile and sorrowful, wanting somehow to bring the power of self-forgiveness to this man. It came in the form of an angel. A graceful young woman, who happened to be of Asian descent, rose from her place on the floor and walked quietly over to where Doug was sitting in his humbled exhaustion. She knelt down beside him and, with a delicate embrace, cradled him and brushed the tears from his cheek with her hand. She looked exactly like a Vietnamese woman as she held him. The poignancy of that moment defies description. It was something we all experienced in silence and shared gratitude, later realizing that we had touched into the archetypal pain of our species and come through it together. Each of us knew that we had taken part in a healing moment that was bigger than any of us, bigger than all of us who felt so fortunate to be present.

## A Healing Bow

Another example of a meltdown involves a young woman who remained rather quiet throughout most of the workshop she attended. She was afflicted by an acute awareness of the long-standing violence that has been perpetrated against women by men. She took special care not to project her personal rage and sorrow onto the particular men in the workshop, nor did she hold any of them personally responsible. Nevertheless, this awareness was very present for her, and although she spoke to it from time to time, she remained relatively detached, silent, and soft-spoken. On the last morning of the workshop, one of the men attempted to draw her out by gently asking if there was anything he could do or say to establish a connection with her. She responded to this man, speaking softly, as was her pattern, but then slowly opening up enough to finally share some of her personal story with the group.

Her words were circumspect and insightful as she told of various ways in which she had been deeply hurt by men in her life. She spoke with a clarity and authority that had not been present in her earlier participation. Everyone was moved by her vulnerability and authenticity, and, afterward, several in the group spoke up passionately, honoring this woman for her honesty and courage. Then one of the men took the talking stick and said to her, "I don't just want to honor you, I want to pay homage." At which point he folded his body forward until his forehead rested upon the ground, in a deep bow, before her. He made this gesture with utmost sincerity and integrity. The woman was stunned, and speechless. Her heart broke open as she vacillated between doubting what was happening—it was too good to be true—and seeing it take place before her very eyes. The man maintained the bow for a full two minutes, during which the woman's eyes softened and opened in a cycle of disbelief and gratitude.

This act led to a yet deeper sharing from the same woman, who made a passing reference to being raped—the first mention she had made of it during the workshop. Hearing this, another woman in the group let out an involuntary howl, and began to cry. Her sobs soon deepened into wails, and then further into wrenching screams of grief. Others too began to weep, and then to bellow and scream. Within one or two minutes the entire group was plunged into a deep collective grieving process—many crying or sobbing uncontrollably in one another's arms. The situation became a full-on meltdown which continued for an hour and a half as people accessed deep grief and rage, mutually supporting one another to go through dark caverns of personal and archetypal pain. The facilitators operated in a triage mode, assisted by several participants, supporting those who were in deepest grieving and emotional release. Eventually, the powerful energies began to exhaust themselves, and one by one the participants emerged from their inner realms, tender and delicate, all huddled close together in loving support and surrender. The experience left everyone moved beyond words, far beyond what can be conveyed here.

As mentioned earlier, such moments call forth an uncanny sense that a higher intelligence is orchestrating the entire process, because each person's internal issues are triggered in a manner that precisely suits his or her particular character. Such a synergistic, multilayered experience—in which several people simultaneously get precisely what they need for their own unique healing process—cannot be planned or organized. Something deeper and distinctly numinous is present and guides the process.

The man who bowed, a young pastor who had recently graduated from Harvard Divinity School, described his experience of the workshop: "What happened to me has given me more faith, hope, and love than any other single experience in my life. [Given] the epiphanies I've had over the past eleven years, and my mixed experience with group work, this is no small notice."

## Synchronicities in the Collective

An example of a different kind of diamond point entails a man and woman whose personal histories contained striking parallels in a way that became highly significant as the workshop unfolded. Their separate personal stories, each unbeknownst to the other, were intertwined in a way that was potentially explosive, although, happily, they were resolved in a powerful healing event.

The synchronicities began when two participants, David and Kathy, were paired at random in an afternoon exercise of experiential breathwork. The two had never met prior to the workshop, and both were health professionals in their fifties. During the breathwork, Kathy experienced a powerful revisitation of the trauma surrounding her sexual violation by several teenaged boys who had been friends of her brothers. Kathy was particularly troubled by the role her two older brothers had played in this attack, which was a kind of gang molestation. Her brothers had not engaged directly in the sexual assault, but they had done nothing to stop the attack. This had happened when Kathy was ten years old.

David was Kathy's sitter for her breathwork session, and he attended to her process with great sensitivity as she moved through several waves of intensive grief and emotional release in revisiting her childhood trauma. David happened to be a body-centered psychotherapist with many years of experience, and he "held the space" for Kathy skillfully throughout, providing a field of compassionate presence and nurturing support. This interaction led to a strong bond of mutual respect and affection between the two of them, which ultimately proved indispensable for working through what later emerged.

As the workshop progressed over the next couple of days, Kathy shared her story with the group, and subsequently two more women,

Ruth and Susan, came forth with their own stories of incest and childhood sexual abuse. Things shifted radically, however, when, during the men's truth forum, David brought forth a startling revelation from his own past, admitting that he had, some twenty-five years earlier, molested his own ten-year-old stepdaughter. A shock wave went through the group, eliciting especially strong reactions from Kathy and the other two women. Kathy was so distraught she was virtually unable to speak. The emotional volatility in the group rapidly escalated and became so explosive that Kathy stormed out of the room in a state of intense turmoil, determined to leave the workshop altogether.

The group plunged into mayhem and confusion. Expressions of unabashed outrage, grief, and misprojections flew around the room. One of the women facilitators followed Kathy out of the room and worked with her individually as she struggled to deal with feelings of betrayal and mistrust that threatened to overwhelm her. Kathy was beside herself with anger and despair. She felt betrayed by David. She sensed duplicity and hypocrisy in his offerings of support for her healing process. She challenged the integrity of a gender reconciliation workshop format that allowed people to attend without first being required to go through some kind of preliminary screening that would ensure that no perpetrators—past or present—were allowed to enter the work.

Meanwhile, the other facilitators continued to work with the group, processing the volatile dynamics. Ruth and Susan shared many of Kathy's feelings, although neither had become as close to David. They demanded to know from David why he had brought this story forth into the group when and how he did. He explained that his intention was not to hurt, but to help to heal. He felt a moral obligation, he explained, to disclose his own past complicity in the painful abuses that had been suffered by others in the group. David explained how very difficult it was for him to reveal this incident from his past, and added that this was the first time he had ever done so in a mixed group. Not to do so, he felt, would make a mockery of the unique and courageous work we were doing together. The men's truth forum had seemed the obvious and appropriate moment for this to come forward. He had actually shared his story first in the men's circle the day before, where he felt safer, but he felt that the women in the group, and perhaps especially Kathy, Susan, and Ruth, deserved to know. He was ready, he said, to "stand in the fire" if that would serve to heal the wounds of such abuses within the group, and perhaps help prevent them in the future.

Kathy finally returned to the group after a lengthy absence. She had decided to articulate her feelings of outrage and betrayal directly to David, with support from the group. She was very nervous as she began to speak, but once the words started to come, she poured out strong, passionate feelings about the incidents of her childhood, the betrayal by her own brothers, and the way in which such betrayals undermine a person's life. She talked about the fragility of the work we were doing together, the necessity of respecting one another completely. She then addressed her confusion about David, acknowledging that he had treated her kindly and respectfully. As she continued speaking, her demeanor shifted, and she came to a place of affirming that in the present moment, she could find no fault in his behavior, and she acknowledged that it was important for her to know about his history and that he had given her that opportunity by volunteering it courageously. During her sharing, Kathy cried and yelled and laughed and sat silent as she struggled with contradictory feelings and perceptions. Ultimately, she articulated her recognition that David's intention was not to harm anyone, and that he had a right to bring his own wounds and complicity into the work we were doing.

The workshop continued into the evening and the next day, with frequent reverberations around these issues. On the last evening, the women's and men's rituals were conducted to honor one another. During the ritual, Ruth, the elder of the two sexual abuse survivors, stood up and picked up a potted plant someone had contributed as a healing presence. She walked slowly across the room to David, kneeled in front of him, and placed the plant before him, then reached out and took his hand. She explained that while she was deeply grieved by what he had done—an act that she herself had suffered at the hands of another—she also honored his courage in bringing this out into the group and seeking to heal from it. She told him it was clear he had done much personal work to heal this past injustice, and that she admired this about him.

Then Susan came forward, and then Kathy. Each of them reached out to David, extending forgiveness and understanding. Each noted his courage and honored the healing impact of that courage on their own lives, not just on his. David was in tears, as they all were, and then, with tears running down their cheeks, David and Kathy gently embraced. The energy of this interchange was magical. It was clear that deep healing had become possible precisely because the victimizer had sat down with the victimized, and together they had grieved and borne witness and forgiven the other for their pain.

The entire group was moved deeply as these four human beings— three "survivors" and one "perpetrator"—continued to share and commune quietly with one another, with occasional spurts of tears or laughter punctuating their soft whispers. By this point much of what was said between them could not be heard by the rest of us in the group, but the healing energy radiating outward from them was intensely radiant and nourishing for all. Eventually, the rest of us moved into a closer circle around the four of them, and we all began to sing and chant songs of healing and forgiveness.

Three years later, in a subsequent event, Ruth told us that this gender workshop had changed her life in a profound way, and that it was one of the most important things she had done in her life. Kathy has made similar remarks to us over the years, and she has attended several gender reconciliation events since. David was also deeply grateful and expressed strong interest in working more closely with gender reconciliation.

**Spontaneous Forgiveness**
The final example in this chapter illustrates a similar synchronicity that led to a remarkable healing experience. It began when a woman in the workshop named Sharon shared a traumatic personal account of being forcibly date raped by her boyfriend. Shortly thereafter, another woman, Brenda, followed suit and shared her own story of a date-rape experience. The details in the two cases

were different, but the general pattern was the same—both women had been raped by men who were supposedly their special beloved partners, and both had been traumatized not only by the rape experiences themselves but also by the sense of profound betrayal and confusion afterward.

Meanwhile, there was a man in the group, Mike, who had become increasingly quiet and sullen as the workshop progressed. Finally, one afternoon following a breathwork session, Mike disclosed in the men's circle that he realized that what had happened to Sharon and Brenda was also part of his own life experience. Speaking with deep sorrow, in halting tones, he explained that he had forced himself upon his wife, as well as his former girlfriend, in the exact same manner. "In short," Mike announced quietly, "I have committed date rape, but I never considered it that until I heard these women in the group tell their stories." For the first time in his life, Mike faced the reality that he had date-raped two women.

Over the next several hours, the magnitude of Mike's realization came upon him with full force, and he sank into deep grief and anguish. Several women in the group noticed a difference in his behavior that evening, and began asking what was happening for him, but Mike turned his eyes away and did not respond.

The next day, after a fitful night's sleep, Mike took the plunge and shared his realization with the full community during the truth forum. A silent shock wave coursed through the women as Mike disclosed his story. He added ruefully that he had always regarded these experiences as macho sex acts with "his" women, and thus he had never been able to take seriously his wife's or girlfriend's protests about the harmful nature of his actions. When he finished, Mike collapsed into deep, grieving tears.

As the day progressed, Mike's anguish and shame became increasingly evident and extreme. He would not meet the eyes of the women, and he feared strong reprisals, especially from Sharon and Brenda. Many in the group extended themselves to him, particularly among the men's group. It was remarkable to witness Mike's process of healing and awakening, and many were moved by the depth of his remorse.

Toward the end of the workshop, something remarkable happened when Sharon spontaneously went over to Mike at one point and offered him consolation for his grief. Mike was shocked at first and totally disbelieving, because he had especially been avoiding contact with Sharon and Brenda. He continued to carry deep culpability and shame for his past. Sharon took his hand and explained that even though it was painful to be in the group with a man who had perpetrated the same harm that had been done to her, his coming to grips with his own culpability was something that her boyfriend had never been able to do. And so, despite herself, she said it was healing for her to witness a man confront his violent past so genuinely. She said she had never seen a man do this, and she was grateful for it. Brenda followed with a similar gesture a few minutes afterward.

Mike was moved to yet another level of surrender and humility as he melted into sobs of simultaneous grief and gratitude. The two women sat down next to Mike, crying and holding each other while gently holding Mike's hand. The three of them embraced each other softly, creating a spontaneous "forgiveness" ritual among themselves. Witnessing their process, the entire group was transported, and copious open-hearted tears flowed forth in response to the beauty of this remarkable healing moment.

Exquisite moments of deep healing such as these are a natural and integral part of the gender healing process. People sometimes mistakenly suppose that such jewels of collective healing could only emerge in a group after first completing the task of purifying and healing each participant's personal wounds. But this is not the case. Rather, these diamond points of healing emerge naturally when even a few individuals are willing to step into the fire and become the instruments for a larger wisdom and love to work through them. And these healing moments serve both to inspire the larger group or community and to deepen the requisite trust and integrity that is necessary for the next unfolding stage of healing to take place. Thus, the gender healing process advances by a kind of unlayering, in stages, of ever deeper material—like peeling the proverbial onion. And at each step the group trust and bonding is deepened, which creates the conditions for the next step to be taken. The growing intimacy and communion is thus an intrinsic part of the process of gender reconciliation and not merely a "gift" or reward that comes at the "end."

What is startling about gender healing work is that its true foundation and inner motivation is the yearning in each of our hearts for mystical love and union. Such yearning, however, is veiled to a great degree, and therefore appears in various guises: as masculine and feminine polarities, or as relationship dilemmas, or as the dynamics of oppression, power, and desire. All these veils and convolutions take place in the world, and we often experience them as "problems" that need to be addressed and healed. And so we pursue healing work hoping to resolve them, and, yes, healing does take place.

Yet, at the same time, something else quite beyond what we set out for also takes place, because gender work at its core seeks to unravel a radical, convoluted knot which, when unraveled, reveals the profound mystical impulse underlying human desire. What makes gender so powerful to work with is the fact that this knot is a conglomeration of multiple primordial forces that are all bound up and intertwined together. These forces include (a) the patriarchal dynamics of repression and injustice, which are ancient and deeply ingrained in the human psyche, (b) the intimate yearning of the human heart for love, (c) the desire for sexual passion and expression, and (d) the human longing for the deepest forms of intimacy, both with other human beings and with the Divine. This complex knot distinguishes gender diversity work from all other forms of diversity work because it interweaves millennia of structural violence and gender injustice together with the intensity of sexual passion and with the heart's burning need for deep intimacy.

Gender work is unique in bringing the most subtle and vulnerable yearnings of the human heart right into the center of the complex issues of power, survival, governance, culture, justice and morality. For this reason, it is our conviction that to unravel the gender knot would greatly facilitate the unraveling of many other structural injustices in our society. Gender disharmony is at the core of much human and societal injustice; therefore, gender healing is foundational to healing our society on multiple levels and to revealing and transforming the deepest truths of the human condition.

# CHAPTER 8

# *Beyond Words: Transformational Healing in Community*

*All things true are given and received in silence.*

—Meher Baba

Gender reconciliation work elicits challenging emotional, interpersonal, and group dynamics that have long-standing and tenacious psychological and cultural roots. Effective and safe navigation of this sometimes delicate, sometimes volatile terrain requires skillful modalities for group process work that go well beyond verbal communication and dialogue. Authentic healing and reconciliation between women and men rarely takes place through mere cognitive exchange and dialogue alone. Verbal communication, though vitally important, is fundamentally limited as a vehicle to foster lasting healing and transformation. Other dimensions of consciousness and sensitive awareness must also be engaged, and for this purpose experiential, transpersonal, and contemplative methods are invaluable for facilitating deep healing between the sexes. Several of these specialized skills and practices used in Satyana's gender reconciliation work are outlined in this chapter.

Modern consciousness research has opened up new doorways for exploring and understanding the deeper realms of human consciousness, many of which were hitherto largely neglected in Western psychology. The emerging field of transpersonal psychology and the burgeoning interest today in spiritual practices, alternative healing modalities, and ritual practices from diverse cultural traditions are creating a fertile field of new possibilities for working skillfully with the challenges of gender healing and reconciliation. Psychiatrist Stanislav Grof, a leading pioneer in transpersonal psychology, emphasizes that modern Western society is the only culture in the world that seems to believe that people can transform their psychological and spiritual dilemmas by merely talking about them; for example, in cognitively oriented psychotherapy. All other cultures across the globe—both ancient and contemporary—recognize that some form of contemplative or nonordinary consciousness is vital to the process of healing and transformation.

This chapter explores three different classes of such modalities utilized in gender healing work: experiential breathwork, contemplative techniques, and ritual processes.

## Experiential Breathwork

Breathing practices of various kinds have a vast, time-honored history in many spiritual traditions of the world. Specific exercises to intensify, control, or withhold the breath have been utilized in many cultures to awaken deeper levels of consciousness and spiritual awareness. Traditions that incorporate breathing practices include Kundalini yoga and Siddha yoga (*bastrika*), Raja yoga and Kriya yoga (*pranayama*), Tibetan Vajrayana Buddhism, Sufism, Burmese Buddhism (*tummo*), Taoism, and many others. More subtle forms of breathing disciplines are also found in Theravadan Buddhism (*Vipassana*), Zen, and certain Taoist and Christian practices.

In all these cases, focused breathing exercises (or "breathwork") serve to awaken interior levels of conscious awareness in the practitioner. Some breathwork practices activate powerful healing energies in the body/mind/psyche and shift consciousness to deeper levels where healing and transformation may occur. Breathwork therefore has a powerful application in gender healing and reconciliation work. Yogic forms of breathwork allow participants to stay present and work skillfully in the midst of intense emotions that gender work can trigger. It also allows participants to shift and stabilize their own consciousness and access their own inner wisdom.

In Satyana's gender reconciliation work we have utilized several breathwork modalities, including Holotropic Breathwork, rebirthing, BRETH, and tummo breathing, as well as more contemplative forms of meditative breathing. We have applied Holotropic Breathwork extensively, in which the author was certified (1990) following three years of intensive training with Stanislav and Christina Grof. The Grofs and their colleagues experimented for several years at Esalen Institute with many different kinds of breathing practices—drawn from both spiritual traditions and the experiential modalities of humanistic psychology. From this background, the Grofs developed the Holotropic methodology outlined below.

For readers unfamiliar with breathwork, it may be difficult to imagine that merely working with the breath could have significant effects of any kind whatsoever. However, breathing practices are capable of awakening deeper dimensions of consciousness and awareness in remarkable ways, which is why they are employed so extensively in spiritual traditions. As Grof remarks, "Unless one has witnessed or experienced this process personally, it is difficult to believe on theoretical grounds alone the power and efficacy of this technique."[1]

## Holotropic Breathwork

A full presentation of the principles and practice of Holotropic Breathwork is presented in several of Grof's books, and thus we give only a brief summary here.[2] The Holotropic technique combines sustained rhythmic breathing with evocative music and focused bodywork. The process provides a safe, protected environment that enables participants to explore a broad range of experiences and spaces within their inner consciousness. The practice typically activates an "inner journey" or introspective exploration in which breathers become aware of deeper dimensions of their own consciousness, often with pointed relevance or significance for their lives. In practice, the Holotropic process is usually done in pairs within the group, so that each person doing the intensified breathing has a designated "sitter" who attends to him or her throughout the session. Thus, breathwork is generally done in two consecutive sessions, where half the group are "breathers" and half are "sitters" in the first session and these roles are reversed in the subsequent session.

Breathwork serves to bond and catalyze the group of practitioners in several important ways. First, it supports deep interior work within each individual, which is often accompanied by new insights or healing experiences. Second, the breathwork process cultivates a unique form of bonding and intimacy between the breather and sitter, which often is a powerful aspect of the experience. Third, breathwork creates a subtle field of collective awareness and "healing energy" in the group—often quite palpable—that enables all participants in the group to bear compassionate witness to the inner work of one another. Finally, in a significant departure from traditional practice of Holotropic Breathwork, we sometimes ask the entire group to take a collective intention into the breathing process; for example, the intention that the breathwork process will support the larger healing and reconciliation between the sexes. Throughout the breathwork process these different levels of experience and interconnection operate simultaneously, interweaving and overlapping in intricate ways—often creating a powerful, transformative healing experience in the group.

One of the most crucial characteristics of breathwork is that each person's experience is unique and emerges from his or her own inner wisdom. Thus, the inner expanse of each participant's psyche is inwardly available for free and unhindered self-exploration. Especially important, even when there is a collective, stated intention, is that the facilitators or group leaders do not steer or shape the participants' experiences in any way, nor do they direct or decide what "should" happen in breathwork. Each person's particular experience is honored and received as the appropriate experience for that person at that time. Psychological interpretations of breathwork experiences by facilitators or other participants are discouraged, since each person's experience speaks for itself from within the breather's own wisdom.

The range of experiences that occur in breathwork has been mapped out in detail by Grof in what he calls a "cartography of the psyche." Breathwork experiences are classified into three broad domains of qualitative characteristics, called the *biographical, perinatal,* and *transpersonal.* The biographical realm refers to the person's personal life history; the perinatal domain refers to experiences relating to birth and death; and the transpersonal realm relates to experiences that go beyond one's personal identity, including mythological and spiritual experiences. The experiential terrain that arises in breathwork is thus vast and rich—analogous to the range of experiences that occurs in dreams, meditation, prayer, and other contemplative or spiritual disciplines.

Skeptical readers may question the value or relevance of such techniques, and particularly their application for gender reconciliation and related healing work. Such skepticism is understandable, especially given that Western science and the disciplines of psychology and psychiatry have not always embraced the profound spiritual and psychological experiences that arise in consciousness practices such as breathwork, meditation, and other contemplative disciplines. In fact, these experiences have often been dismissed, or even pathologized clinically—especially those of a transcendent or spiritual character. As Grof points out ironically,

> Psychiatric literature contains numerous articles and books that discuss what would be the most appropriate clinical diagnoses for many of the great figures of spiritual history. St. John of the Cross has been called an "hereditary degenerate," St. Teresa of Avila dismissed as a severe hysterical psychotic, and Muhammad's mystical experiences have been attributed to epilepsy . . . Many other religious and spiritual personages, such as the Buddha, Jesus, Ramakrishna, and Sri Ramana Maharshi, have been seen as suffering from psychoses, because of their visionary experiences and "delusions" . . . By pathologizing Holotropic states of consciousness, Western science has pathologized the entire spiritual history of humanity.[3]

However, this situation is now beginning to change significantly in many arenas of the mainstream health professions. The legitimacy and value of spiritual and contemplative disciplines is becoming ever more widely recognized. Meditation and other contemplative practices have been introduced into numerous secular organizations in the legal, academic, and service professions with excellent results and a growing demand for wider application.[4] Experiential modalities, including methods such as Holotropic Breathwork, are increasingly recognized as indispensable tools for fostering a deep level of self-inquiry, healing, and psychological integration that is difficult to achieve by other means.

**Application of Breathwork to Gender Reconciliation**
Perhaps the best way to illustrate the value of breathwork in gender healing work is to give several illustrative examples. The anecdotes recounted below all took place in the context of Satyana Institute's gender workshops.

The first example describes a participant's first experience with breathwork, in which she went through a birth experience, followed by a powerful opening into universal love. Such a strong "heart opening" experience, although perhaps dramatic, is not uncommon in breathwork.

> It felt like I was on a very intense ride of some kind, as I twisted and turned, always pushing forward. I heard the music but did not feel connected to the group or the room. It began to feel like birth. I pushed through this small narrow tunnel with much effort. After what seemed like a long time I pushed through this place, and exploded out into the most love I have ever felt. I cried in love and profound gratitude. It felt very sacred. Here I relaxed into expansiveness and love. There was no sense of body, only love.
>
> Suddenly I became aware that the music in the room had stopped and I wondered why that was. It seemed only a few minutes had gone by, when actually two and a half hours had gone by. As I opened my eyes I asked, "Am I done?" The room seemed so dark compared to the brilliant place I had been in. My sitter was there and had covered me to keep me warm.

It was truly a wonderful experience. As I meditate on this experience in the days that have followed I have a sense that it was a piercing of the heart . . . I now find myself to be a little stronger somehow. I am a little lighter, and the conflicts of life do not overwhelm me. I feel grateful for whatever happened.

The next example involves a woman whose father had died when she was six years old. This childhood trauma had colored her relationships with men throughout her life, and she had done extensive psychotherapeutic work to begin uncovering the enormous grief associated with her father's absence in her life. This paved the way for her powerful experience in breathwork.

The experience unfolded for me as a journey to the underworld. First I was falling down a long tunnel, like Alice in Wonderland. Then I found myself running through a dark underground world with the massive roots of mountains reaching down from above me, and the ground below me writhing with thousands of big black snakes.

With the help of a young man who I recognized as my Guide (someone I have encountered before in dreams and active imagination), I made my way through this ominous landscape to a place deep in the heart of the world. It was a large underground cave with a clear pool in the center. Here I met a dear friend of mine named Dino who died ten years ago, someone who I still miss very much. Dino and my Guide prepared me for the meeting with my father. First, without saying why, Dino suggested that I reach out to my sitter, because I was going to need his support. I was reluctant to do this, but as soon as I did, my father appeared. I think this is really crucial, because that reaching out was the first opening for me, the first sign that I was willing to allow my vulnerability to show, to acknowledge that I needed—and could rely on—a man's support.

The meeting with my father was incredibly healing and cathartic. He encouraged me in the work I am doing now, gave me the sense that he has been watching over and caring for me all these years with great attentiveness, and even gave me advice about my future and some of the relationships I am in right now. After speaking for some time, there was a laying on of hands, with my father, my friend Dino, the Guide, and another male friend of mine laying their hands on my abdomen and my heart in order to heal many old wounds . . . [This] was incredibly powerful and evoked an enormous emotional release. So much grief came pouring out, and I accessed a level of actively missing my father that I had never experienced before.

When the laying on of hands was completed, my father began to pour a red and golden liquid directly into my heart from a beautiful ornate vase. It seemed like an endless flow of compassion and healing was filling up my entire being, giving me the strength to do healing work for myself and also to share it with others. In the midst of this inundation with love, I had the sense of being a little girl again, lying in my father's embrace . . . It felt like the dispelling of years of pain and longing and sadness.

The journey ended in a place which I know only from a painting, but which I have always felt drawn to as some kind of "perfect" place of peace and tranquility. It is a beautiful lake surrounded by trees and dramatic mountains on all sides, with wonderfully expressive clouds filling the deep blue sky . . . I rested there feeling safe and loved.

Later, as this woman integrated the personal insights that emerged from this experience of reconciliation with her father, she found that this visionary encounter also helped her to heal some long-standing emotional and sexual patterns with men.

The incredible heart opening which I experienced with my father—my "open heart surgery"—gave birth to a whole new kind of openness and vulnerability which I have been able to access in my relationships with men. I suddenly realized how much of my emotional self I was hiding from men because I was afraid of being hurt, disappointed, or left . . . For years I have been using this "tough chick" persona (to varying degrees) in my relationships with men, and wondering why they wouldn't open up to me emotionally! Now I have to laugh; how could they feel safe opening up to a woman who was herself so well defended? . . . I realized that this persona I have been carrying around for so long, the "tough chick" who hides her emotions behind a sexually provocative, nonchalant exterior, was now obsolete. This is not the way I want to interact with men anymore.

I can honestly say that something important has shifted. I still feel my father's presence every day. He didn't leave me. He's still here, and he's always been here. I just never knew. The more I connect with my spiritual self, the more "real" his presence in my life becomes, and the more I feel I am connecting with some archetypal Father (God?) from whom I draw strength, compassion and understanding.

We have witnessed many other examples of powerful healing experiences that were precipitated in breathwork. Although the content and specific details of these experiences vary greatly, what they share is that the breather is opened to a new level of awareness in a way that is unique to his or her life experience, and this catalyzes a specific healing and integration process.

The next example illustrates one possibility for relational intimacy beyond romantic connection, which the breathwork often facilitates in a natural way between breather and sitter. This experience is described by a man in his sixties named Stuart:

During my breathwork I had an experience that continues to bring reflection and wonder. About midway through the session, my sitter, Mary, was moving her hand through the energy field near the top of my head. I could feel the warmth of her hand and was just experiencing the sensation when I was suddenly seized by a powerful desire to feel her touch. My back arched automatically and I thrust my face in the direction of her hand. I urgently said, "Touch my face, touch my face!"

She began to stroke my forehead and face, and I began to weep. There was no sadness in the weeping; the touch felt so good and so right. I had such a longing for it and felt such a release.

At the end of the session I shared my experience with Mary. I said it had a very different quality than my usual romantic desire for relationship with a woman. This longing seemed to come from a deeper, more archetypal level, from deep down in my physical being, in my bones. . . . As I was sharing with Mary I often wept. At some point, a last tear began to roll down the side of my nose. Mary gently reached up with a tissue and wiped it away. This act of tenderness caused another tear to roll, and she wiped that away, which caused another to roll, which she also wiped. I laughed, "Every time you wipe away a tear, it causes another to come."

Such tenderness and intimacy is not uncommon in the inter-action between sitters and breathers in breathwork. The process enables participants to enter a unique domain of intimacy and heal-ing with one another in full safety and mutual protection. In this context—which is so rare in our modern technological society, yet utterly natural and uncontrived when experienced—an unimpeded exchange of compassionate expression and tender presence natu-rally flows in people from the wellsprings of unconditional love that dwell within every human being.

In this touching vignette of each tear wiped causing yet another to flow, a deep truth of spiritual love is represented symbolically: The pain of the heart is the very medicine by which a broken heart is healed. This mystical healing process is described beautifully by St. John of the Cross (quoted on page 239 in the last chapter).

Reflecting on his experience, Stuart observed:

Later I thought, what a good symbol for gender healing! Every time the feminine wipes away a tear from the masculine, it causes another tear to flow. The tenderness of the feminine causes a successive softening of the masculine, the empowering of the feminine, and their mutual growing together. This experience has caused me to reflect upon the deep suspicion, mistrust and misunderstanding with which men and women often approach one another. We need one another at such a basic level, yet we often hold ourselves apart, almost intentionally, against our deep desire to be together.

Not only can women "be there" for men, as the foregoing example illustrates, but men can also "be there" for women. Here is one woman's account during a gender workshop:

The most powerful part of the breathwork day for me . . . was observing how most of the men were there for their partners. In my life experience, whenever the going gets tough, especially emotionally, men check out. Today I saw men cry, and hold women while they cried. The men's tenderness, gentleness, and love just blew me away. I absorbed beautiful new memories today, which in turn helped me close powerful gates to the belief system that "all men are bad," or "no man can be trusted."

A final example illustrates another level of breathwork experience that taps into mythological or archetypal dimensions catalyzed by the gender healing process. In this case, after the group had been intensively processing challenging gender dynamics in society, one woman participant had this breathwork experience:

Our focus on gender seems to have set in motion some powerful archetypal energies which emerged in my breathwork. As I cut loose in the breathwork session, my body focused on the release over and over again of fierce, fighting energy. As I cut through my own bonds, and the bonds of women over time, I became the fierce aspect of the goddess. The different polarities of Kali—the Hindu goddess of creation and destruction, the demon-slaying, sexual, independent goddess who seems to stand outside all social bounds in India—manifested in me. The all-compassionate mother and the fierce fighter for justice surfaced, and were all one.

But there was more. All of this intensity, all of this fury, all of this loving, compassionate energy, even sexual at times, could be held and witnessed by men. This had never happened to me before. And maybe this has seldom happened to women in the last four thousand years . . . I was in tears with the power of it—the new resources of masculine and feminine within me.

The foregoing examples summarize a few ways in which breathwork contributes to gender healing work. Breathwork makes a key contribution by providing a natural vehicle for training the group to remain present with powerful emotional energies and to embrace these challenging dynamics skillfully rather than run away from them, deny them, or otherwise allow them to derail the group process. This creates safety and security in the face of emotional upsets, both at the individual and group level, and it allows the group to move through challenging material which many other groups would not try to navigate.

Further examples of the impact of breathwork in gender healing are presented later in this book, particularly in Chapter 10 on recent work in South Africa.

### Contemplative Practices

"Silence speaks with unceasing eloquence." This aphorism from the Indian sage Ramana Maharshi encapsulates in a single phrase the remarkable gift of contemplative practices and meditation. A related injunction sometimes heard in Quaker prayer meetings is: "Don't speak, unless you can improve upon the silence."

Conscious use of silence serves to facilitate and deepen the delicate process of gender healing work. First and foremost, silence invites people to listen more deeply within themselves, which helps connect them with their own inner wisdom. Learning to listen deeply within oneself is probably the most universal spiritual practice, found in all traditions. Silence also helps participants to integrate complex or conflicting levels of experience, which often characterizes gender work because it combines intensive outer exploration and inner awareness simultaneously.

## Meditation and Prayer

The practice of meditation is becoming increasingly widespread as a powerful means to explore and transform the deeper realms of consciousness. There is a plethora of excellent books on meditation in various traditions, so rather than repeat what is beautifully presented elsewhere, we recount a simple teaching story that captures something essential about the nature of meditative practice:

Student: What is the essence of meditation?
Master:　Have you ever noticed that between one thought
　　　　　and the next thought, there is a gap?
Student: Yes . . .
Master:　Prolong the gap.

Of course, this technique of silencing the mind is just one of many different approaches to meditation, but meditation practice generally entails the need to stop chasing after the incessant waves of thought on the surface of the mind and plunge down into the underlying ocean of consciousness. Numerous forms of meditation are practiced in various traditions; some methods focus on a chosen object of meditation, or on dissolving thoughts in the ocean of love within the heart, whereas other practices entail being fully present and open to whatever arises in consciousness (without identifying with it). The power of meditative practice is profound, far beyond what can be summarized briefly here. For our purposes, suffice it to say that the practice of meditation over time cultivates a deep moment-to-moment awareness, sensitivity, and inner silence within the practitioner, and gradually awakens innate qualities of wisdom and compassion.

In the group context, silent meditation serves to convene and bond the collective community in an intimate, nonverbal way, similar to what is frequently experienced in spiritual or contemplative retreats. Silence also helps to create an atmosphere of authenticity and integrity, which in turn supports each person to connect more deeply inwardly before they express themselves. The judicious use of silence or group meditation can be especially important at times of broaching sensitive or tricky topics, or when an unusually poignant truth or personal story emerges. A related practice is the "mindfulness bell" utilized extensively by Vietnamese monk Thich Nhat Hanh. At certain moments, a bell or chime is rung in the group, at which point everyone stops whatever they are doing and enters into silent meditation for the duration of three breaths. This grounds people in the present moment before continuing again with whatever they had been doing before the chime was rung. We have found the mindfulness bell to be an especially useful tool in gender work.

The term "prayer" is often construed to carry a strong religious connotation. Because the gender work attracts people of many different religious persuasions, including some who have a deep practice of prayer and others who don't identify with any religion in particular, we generally work with silence in the form of meditation or simple contemplative practices, and participants are encouraged to utilize whatever inner practices suit their individual needs. The spiritual context for gender reconciliation work is nonsectarian and embraces the full range of authentic spiritual traditions.

That said, however, if we define "prayer" in a broad spiritual context as the yearning for or invocation of a larger universal wisdom or compassion—then prayer is definitely a key aspect of gender reconciliation work. Not only are various individuals within any given group engaged in internal prayers of their own during the work, but there are times when the entire group enters collectively into states of delicate sensitivity, vulnerability, intensive emotional processing, or exquisite communion with the "Beloved." At these times the hearts of everyone present are completely aligned and subtly intertwined in what can only be described as a deep collective prayer. This creates a field of "heart energy" that is extremely powerful and that serves to catalyze remarkable possibilities for healing and transformation. Seen from this context, both meditation and prayer are fundamental to Satyana's gender reconciliation work, and they play different roles at different times.

An advanced form of meditation or awareness practice in various traditions entails "just sitting" with what is. The Indian sage Krishnamurti coined the term "choiceless awareness" to refer to this broad category of practice. Notwithstanding the differences among specific approaches in different traditions, such as *shikantaza* in Zen, *jnana* in Vedanta, or *dzogchen* in Tibetan Buddhism, these practices all have something in common. The essence of this practice is to sit in open, receptive awareness and to remain consciously centered in whatever arises. Of course, as with all meditation practice, this is not as easy as it sounds. It requires a degree of sensitivity, presence, and disciplined attention that generally requires years of regular practice to develop. It also requires that no arena of consciousness be explicitly shunned, or preferentially pursued. Painful or challenging insights sometimes arise, which can require great discipline and courage not to push away. At other times extremely subtle levels of awareness emerge which would be missed altogether were it not for the fine-tuned sensitivity of the awareness practice.

## Collective Witnessing
Gender reconciliation work could be viewed as a particular form of choiceless awareness practice, carried out in a group setting. If the meditative practice described above is a form of *individual* witnessing in choiceless awareness, then gender reconciliation work can be viewed as a form of *collective* witnessing in choiceless awareness. The major difference is that instead of being a silent individual witnessing practice, the process is conducted in a group setting, which requires a form of witnessing communication within the group.

When a group of women and men gather to embark upon gender healing work, a powerful process begins of unraveling into group awareness what was formerly privately held in individual or unconscious awareness. When painful or challenging material arises, the task of the group is generally to face it and go into it, rather than

politely avoid it as we do routinely (and appropriately so!) in our public settings of everyday life. For example, in one intensive workshop, a
husband chose to disclose to his wife—in front of the entire group—
that he had had an affair in the not so distant past. His confession
created an intense dynamic that involved not only the couple themselves but the entire group. In another workshop, a woman confided
tearfully to the group that she had physically abused her son when he
was young. In both cases, these significant disclosures were presented
to the group as a whole, and the community was called upon to somehow engage the material with those involved, and to do so from a
place of compassionate witnessing and wisdom. In essence, what is
essential in these moments is for the community to sit in open and
receptive awareness, remaining consciously centered in whatever is
arising. This is not as easy as it sounds. It is not uncommon for one
or more participants in the group to become emotionally triggered by
what emerges and to respond from a place of projection, judgment,
fear, or personal need. Yet, a key to the work—the "work" of the
work, so to speak—is for those who can do so to remain in a space
of compassionate, focused witness. Their conscious presence helps to
hold the space for those who have brought forward painful material
in order to work through it to whatever insights and resolution may
emerge. The group process thus closely mirrors what happens in individual meditation as one confronts personal shadow material.

Zen master Bernie Glassman calls this kind of group practice
"bearing witness," and the associated communication practice he
dubs "talking meditation," which emerged within the Peacemaker
Order that he founded. As Glassman describes the practice,[5]

> We start from the unknown, we bear witness, and healing
> arises.
> When we bear witness, we become the situation . . .
> Once we listen with our entire body and mind, loving action
> arises. And it begins with the state of unknowing, with the
> vow to let go of our conditioned responses and penetrate the
> unknown. The broader the bearing witness, the broader and
> more powerful the healing that will take place.

Certain silences don't help, they hurt. It's important to tell your story, to tell where it hurts. In the Peacemaker order, we call it talking meditation. Without speaking the hurt, the healing won't come.

In the domain of gender and sexuality, the "silences that don't help" are legion. In gender reconciliation work, these silences have a chance at last to be voiced and witnessed—in a safe, skillfully supported and respectful group environment. As this unmasking process unfolds, deeper and more hidden personal stories and experiences begin to emerge, which catalyze the alchemy of collective healing. This process of unveiling helps the group shift into increasingly authentic and sensitive levels of communication, which in turn engenders more spacious silence. Collective engagement in contemplative practices helps to create an invisible field of "heart energy" that catalyzes the healing process and elevates group interactions to higher levels of meaning, intimacy, and subtlety.

## Ritual and Celebration

Ritual and celebration are a third essential component of gender reconciliation work. Ritual entails the intentional cultivation of creative interplay between archetypal or spiritual realms and the everyday material realm. Effective ritual combines spontaneous creativity with a deep invocation of universal ideals and symbolism applied to a particular theme or situation in a group. In gender reconciliation work, the men and women each create a ritual offering for the other as a way to bless and honor "the other," as well as the masculine and feminine.

In the West we have largely lost connection with the richness and power associated with ritualized or sacred ceremonies, which form an integral part of many cultures around the globe. Western ideals of rugged individualism coupled with a plethora of mind-numbing distractions in our society have exacted a huge toll, and we moderns have relatively few ways to connect creatively with the larger universal mysteries of life. Gender healing and reconciliation work provides one avenue for reclaiming some of this rich and fertile ground in a relatively natural, nonthreatening way. An example of how ritual process works in gender reconciliation was given in Chapter 5.

Ritual is sometimes defined as the invocation and embrace of the spiritual domain in the manifest world. It entails the meeting of different realms, where spirit, soul, and world weave creatively together. Western practitioners are increasingly turning to masterful ritualists from other cultures, such as Malidoma Somé or Sobunfu Somé from Africa, to learn how to skillfully integrate ritual into intensive group process work.

To be meaningful, a ritual must somehow invoke the presence or symbolism of a higher ideal, "archetype," or spiritual energy, and bring it into practical, real-world manifestation. Effective ritual combines elements of spontaneity and freshness with openhearted engagement of the participants. The ritual design need not be complicated. In fact, the essential ingredients of an effective ritual are neither an elaborate setting nor intricate choreography but, rather, sincere intention and enthusiasm on the part of participants. Some of the most powerful rituals we have witnessed in gender healing work have also been some of the most simple in structure. Ritual confers an authentic inner meaning or enables it to emerge in the context of a ceremonial process.

Rituals allow the community, as a whole, to move beyond cognitive and dialogical modes of communication and to engage intuitive or creative faculties, as well as the body's kinesthetic wisdom. In practice, a typical ritual might include a simple circle dance, chanting, singing, or rhythmic drumming. It might be enhanced by candles or scented with sage and sandalwood. It might inspire offerings such as footwashing, anointing, or blindfolded "trust walks" in the spirit of sacred friendship.

Ritual process in gender reconciliation occurs sometimes spontaneously, and other times it is planned intentionally. In both cases, rituals are generally orchestrated by the participants themselves. As an example, it sometimes happens that one person in the group brings something forward that is so challenging, pertinent, or painful that there is an immediate need to create a unique process to address the particular issue at hand. In such a case, a spontaneous healing process or group activity of some kind emerges that is, in effect, a creative ritual to fit the occasion. An example of this is the men's circle discussed in Chapter 4.

The most common use of ritual in gender reconciliation work takes place toward the end of the events, when the men gather to create an offering or gift to honor the women and the women gather to create a similar offering for the men. This form of "self-generated" ritual provides a vehicle for spontaneous creativity and group collaboration. The men and the women are each given a unique opportunity to bestow a kind of "blessing" upon one another—a process that often confers as much upon the givers as the receivers.

**Intimacy within a Community**
Transpersonal healing and collective ritual processes have a profound capacity to deepen intimacy within a community and cultivate new levels of mutual respect, empathy, and understanding. Once experienced or awakened, these processes often invoke a spontaneous wisdom and power that transcends the group's original vision and mysteriously transforms the emotional and even physical well-being of all the individuals involved. Such powerful phenomena are an integral element of gender reconciliation and collective healing in community. They serve to evoke wonder and restore an innate reverence for life, a phenomenon well known in other cultures that routinely engage in collective spiritual and ritual ceremony. Gender reconciliation work provides a natural doorway for such rich, nurturing experiences to come back into Western societies.

# CHAPTER 9

# *Maher-Bharata: Gender Reconciliation in India*

*Truth is one. Sages call it by many names.*

—Rig Veda

It was a peaceful, sunny afternoon in 1991 in Pune, India. Sister Lucy Kurien answered an insistent doorbell at her convent. In the doorway stood a woman from the neighboring apartment building. Visibly distraught, the woman introduced herself as Renuka and asked to come in to speak with some of the nuns. Sister Lucy explained that she was the only one home in that moment, and she invited Renuka in for a cup of tea. Renuka was grateful for the gesture, and began to unveil her story.

Renuka's husband had become increasingly violent toward her in recent months, and with each repeated episode his rage and abuse grew more intense. Renuka showed Sister Lucy several bruises and cuts, some of which were fresh from the previous evening. She was seven-months pregnant, and some of the bruises were across her expanding belly. Renuka asked Lucy if she could provide haven for her, explaining that she had nowhere else to turn, and that she was now fearing for her life.

Lucy was in a quandary about what to do. She listened very intently and became deeply silent and increasingly distressed within as she felt her compassion for this woman growing. Renuka's story touched a deep nerve in Lucy's heart, as she had long been aware of the unconscionable suffering endured by so many women in India. Lucy is Indian herself, and, like the other sisters in her convent, she had been born and raised in an Indian Catholic family in Kerala. Lucy wanted to offer shelter to Renuka, but such a request was unprecedented, and Lucy had no authority to take such a step. Her mother superior was gone until the next day, and Lucy needed to make an appeal to her and get her permission before acting in this case. So she simply listened, and when Renuka completed her story, Lucy asked how long she had been married. Renuka said three years, and then Lucy asked if she had lived with her husband that whole time. Renuka said yes. Based on this information, Lucy felt that it would be no problem to wait one more day, and she told Renuka to come back the next afternoon, by which time she would have a chance to take up the request with her mother superior. In the meantime, Lucy offered her condolences and assured Renuka that she would keep her in her prayers. There was a long, warm hug, and Renuka departed.

Later that evening, as Sister Lucy was doing her evening prayers, her reveries were suddenly interrupted by a blood-curdling scream from somewhere nearby. The screams continued as Lucy rushed outside to see what was happening. She followed the sounds into the adjacent apartment building complex. Turning a corner, Lucy beheld a horrifying sight: about twenty meters from her was a woman engulfed in flames—head to foot. Seeing Lucy, the woman started running toward her, screaming "Save me! Save me!" Lucy suddenly realized this was none other than Renuka, the woman who had sought her help earlier that afternoon. Renuka's husband had just doused her with kerosene, set her aflame, and fled.

Renuka fell to the ground, writhing and screaming in the blaze. Lucy ran and grabbed some blankets from an open apartment door and smothered the fire. She carefully wrapped Renuka's severely burned body. Renuka was still breathing, but went unconscious. A small group of onlookers had gathered by this time, and Lucy asked for their help. Renuka was still breathing, and Lucy was determined to get her to immediate medical help. Together they carried Renuka's body into an autorickshaw, as there was no car available. They drove Renuka to the emergency room at the hospital.

The doctors examined Renuka and told Lucy that she was burned over 90 percent of her body and there was not much they could do for her. They did not expect her to live. Lucy implored them to save the baby. The doctors rushed Renuka into the operating room, and a few minutes later emerged with the fetus. "What I received in my hand," recalled Lucy, "was—to put it bluntly—a cooked baby." Both mother and baby died that night.

Renuka met the same hideous fate that befalls thousands of women in India every year—murder by immolation. Many of these women are set ablaze by their husband or mother-in-law because they have not complied with the husband's family's demand for ongoing dowry payments, or else the wife is deemed to have fallen short of the husband's family's expectations.

Though prohibited by law in 1961, a dowry from the bride's family prior to marriage is still widely practiced in India. When the dowry amount is not considered sufficient or is not forthcoming, the bride is often harassed and abused. This can escalate to the point where the husband or his family burns the bride alive, usually by pouring kerosene on her and setting her ablaze. The official records of these incidents are low because they are usually reported as accidents or suicides by the family.

Accurate statistics on "dowry deaths" in India are difficult to obtain. Estimates vary widely, but there is general agreement that dowry murders have risen dramatically in recent years. In Delhi, a woman is burned to death almost every twelve hours. In 1988, 2,209 women were reported killed in dowry-related incidents, and in 1990, 4,835 were killed. In 1995, the National Crime Bureau of the government of India reported about 6,000 dowry deaths every year. But these are official figures, which are widely regarded as gross understatements of the real situation. Unofficial estimates cited in a 1999 article by Himendra Thakur place the number of deaths around 25,000 women a year, with many more women left maimed and scarred as a result of attempts on their lives.

The typical explanation given by the family in these cases is that the gruesome death was caused by a kitchen accident, or a stove that burst. To make this scenario plausible, the victim is doused in kerosene and set ablaze—an exceedingly horrific way to die. If the pretext of an accident seems too implausible, then the case is attributed to suicide. Either way, it is a relatively simple matter to murder a woman in this grotesque manner in India without legal retribution.

Police and criminal justice authorities typically do not probe deeply into these cases. The lack of official registration of this crime is apparent in Delhi, where 90 percent of cases of women burnt were recorded as accidents, 5 percent as suicide. Only the remaining 5 percent were shown as murder. Similarly, in Bangalore in 1997, there were 1,133 cases of "unnatural deaths" of women. Of these, 38 percent were categorized as "accidents," 48 percent as "suicides," and just 14 percent were treated as murder. As activist Vimochana V. Gowramma explained: "We found that of 550 cases reported between January and September 1997, 71 percent were closed as 'kitchen/cooking accidents' and 'stove-bursts' after brief investigations under section 174 of the Code of Criminal Procedures." The fact that a large proportion of the victims were daughters-in-law was either ignored or treated as coincidence by police.

The grotesque brutality of murder by immolation is hard to fathom, particularly in a culture steeped in such a profound spiritual heritage. India is the nation that produced Mahatma Gandhi, and people all across the land revere their beloved Gandhiji and his venerated teachings of *ahimsa* (nonviolence) and *satyagraha* (clinging to truth). It is difficult to decide which aspect of dowry murder more blatantly violates *ahimsa*: the widespread practice of burning Indian women, or the society's complicit willingness to turn a blind eye to this horrendous practice.

Sister Lucy was beside herself. Renuka had come to her with an earnest plea for help and Lucy had not been able to provide refuge. Now Renuka was gone. Lucy felt a heavy heart and tremendous responsibility for Renuka's death, even though rationally she realized it was not her fault. She felt a growing conviction that she could no longer be content to live a sheltered existence behind the cloistered walls of the convent while such horrific violence and abuse was rampant in the society all around her. She consulted her friend and confidant, Father Francis D'Sa, a Jesuit priest and professor in the nearby Di Nobli College. He supported Lucy in taking action and offered to help her.

Lucy spent the next few years actively promoting her dream to create a center that would provide refuge and rehabilitation for abused and destitute women. She met with strong resistance to the idea from many quarters—from Hindu community leaders who were convinced that she was out to convert their people to Christianity, and from her own Catholic congregation and the local bishop because she was determined to found the project as an interfaith spiritual project, rather than as a Catholic mission. Eventually, she found a European investor who helped her to buy a small piece of land and build a single building to house the shelter. Thus was the Maher ashram, born in 1997.

*Maher* is the word for mother in the local language of Marati. There are now about eighty women and three hundred children living at Maher and its seven satellite homes in surrounding villages. Extensive programs have been established to counsel and rehabilitate the women, to help them find employment, and to provide quality schooling for the children on site. In addition, the project has created support programs to interface with the larger community and to provide assistance, counseling, and rehabilitation programs to the men and the families from whom the women at Maher were forced to flee.

A key aspect of the Maher ashram project is that the staff and board of trustees come from many different religious backgrounds. Hindus, Muslims, Christians, Buddhists, Jains and others all work together, both on the board and the staff of the Maher ashram. The staff are all given ten days off paid leave each year to attend a Vipassana meditation retreat in the tradition established by Goenka, who has a major retreat center near Pune. Vipassana meditation is also taught to all the children over eight years of age, and the children have a regular meditation period for ten minutes each day. Vipassana meditation is viewed as a basic mindfulness practice that is consistent with the religious beliefs and practices of all traditions. This commitment to practical interfaith collaboration makes the Maher home for battered women highly unusual in contemporary

Indian society, where religious differences are a traditional source of strife and violence. To our knowledge, the project is utterly unique throughout all of India in this regard.

The Maher community has also developed a supportive relationship with local communities of *dalits* (untouchables) and indigenous "tribals," who are totally unrecognized by the Indian government and have lower social standing even than *dalits*. In the surrounding villages, Maher sponsors various "awareness training" programs to counteract certain widely held "superstitions," especially among the illiterate and uneducated. One such superstition, for example, holds that when a girl or woman has her menstrual period, she is unclean. Consequently, she is not allowed to enter her own home. For three or four days every month, during her period, she cannot be touched, must never enter the house, and has to sleep outside regardless of the weather. Food is given to her only at a distance. The person preparing the food cannot hand her a plate directly; it must be left for her, or pushed across the table or ground to her. This belief causes much needless suffering and contributes to the general misogyny in the society.

Maher faces daily challenges and conflicts, including the ongoing need to protect the women and children from sometimes angry men whose wives and children have left their abusive homes for the sanctuary that Maher provides. Sister Lucy's life has been threatened on more than one occasion. In one instance, an outraged husband appeared at Maher's door and threatened Lucy, shouting at her, "I can have you 'disappeared' in less than thirty minutes' time!" Without missing a beat, Lucy replied to him, "Yes, I know you can, and if you do, three things will happen. First, your wife will continue to receive refuge at Maher, so it will not bring her back to you. Second, I will die a peaceful death, knowing that I have lived a worthwhile and meaningful life. And third, you will continue to live on in even greater misery than you are already in right now!" The man was flabbergasted and speechless, unaccustomed to his threats and intimidation failing so utterly. He slinked away and never bothered Lucy again.

India is the home to some of the most gruesome manifestations of gender violence and abuse on the planet. A sobering example was recently summarized in an article published in the *New Yorker* magazine (Jan. 10, 2000). A thirteen-year-old girl was married off to a boy the same age in an arranged marriage and moved into her husband's family's home shortly after the wedding. After living there a mere three weeks, she was brutally raped by her new father-in-law. Traumatized and devastated, the girl turned to her own parents and family for help. But her father's response was a vehement demand that she commit suicide, in order to save his honor and that of his family. Fortunately for the girl, some local women activists got wind of what had happened and intervened just in time to save her life. Many other girls in similar situations are not so lucky.

Other manifestations of violence against women and girls in India are legion. Female infanticide has reached such epidemic proportions in several areas of India that many young men are simply unable to find brides nowadays.[1] The ancient tradition of *sati* is still practiced in some rural areas. *Sati* requires that when a man dies, his wife must throw herself upon his funeral pyre and be cremated—alive!—alongside her dead husband. If she refuses, the widow is often forcibly thrown into the fire. Such egregious practices are illegal and admittedly not commonplace, in part due to increasing public pressure and global attention focused on them. Nevertheless, such unspeakable practices are the product of a culture that has been flagrantly oppressive to women for centuries, and only recently has the situation begun to change—through the work of many courageous pioneers such as Lucy Kurien.

### Gender Reconciliation Work in India

Satyana Institute was invited in 2002 to conduct a program in gender reconciliation for a group of forty-two Catholic nuns and priests at the Sadhana Institute, near Mumbai, India. Given the patriarchal realities of Indian society hinted at above, coupled with the emerging revelations of widespread sexual abuse within the Catholic Church, the prospect of introducing gender healing work to Indian Catholic clergy was at once both auspicious and daunting, to say the least.

In an ironic juxtaposition, the profound spiritual heritage of India is probably more consonant with the archetypal and mystical dimensions of gender than any other culture on earth. The rich application of the spiritual dimensions of Indian mythology and culture to our work in gender reconciliation is enormous, and has indeed been a major emphasis underlying this work for some years. God does not exist in India without the Goddess; the two are intimately intertwined in mythology and religion. Janeneswar's famous soliloquy to the beloved communion of the God and Goddess is perhaps the most profound and poetic embrace ever penned of "gender reconciliation" on the spiritual plane. The divine consorts of Shiva/Shakti, Krishna/Radha, and Rama/Sita profoundly symbolize the power, goal, and mystical depths of gender reconciliation, and these dynamic deities are worshipped with as much fervor in India today as they have been for millennia.[2] Furthermore, they have inspired the spiritual hearts of people the world over. Nowhere has the divine communion and balance between feminine and masculine been more widely worshipped and celebrated than in the spiritual traditions of India. Hence, for many, many reasons, bringing gender reconciliation work to India felt like a powerful privilege indeed.

Our group consisted of twenty-one women and twenty-one men, all Catholic nuns and priests. Many came from the south of India, where the practice of Christianity is traced all the way back to Jesus' disciple, Thomas, who, according to tradition, is buried in Indian soil. Sadhana Institute, which hosted our visit, is a pastoral education and retreat facility for Catholic clergy near Pune (and Mumbai) that was founded by Jesuit priest and acclaimed author Anthony de Mello.

The nuns and priests who sojourn at Sadhana come from all across India, where they are engaged primarily in social service and charity work. They spend anywhere from a week to a few months at Sadhana pursuing a self-reflective, transpersonal course of contemplation and study that encourages them to explore new dimensions of themselves. It is one of the very few places where Indian nuns and priests can work together in a relaxed, coeducational environment. For most who come it represents an unusual opportunity to be in close community with the opposite sex. Our offering of gender reconciliation was part of a larger, two-month training that focused on deepening self-awareness, and included a week of experiential breathwork.

Our hosts, Francis Padinjarekara and Selma Nalloor, were incredibly gracious and welcoming to us during our two-week stay. The experience was unique and beautiful, not only because of the exotic nature of India itself, but also because of the strong commitment to spirit that permeates the Sadhana community. We began every morning by attending a simple, intimate mass, Indian style, offered by a different priest each day. We sat on cushions on the floor in a small, unassuming but elegant chapel. The service was earnest but relaxed, and many of the hymns, accompanied by guitar, were sung in Hindi.

In view of the recent sexual abuse scandals in the American Catholic Church, it is instructive to examine the dynamics within this Catholic community in India in some detail. Despite the vast cultural and geographical gulf between this context and our work here in the United States, the issues of gender that this community brought forward were, nonetheless, remarkably similar to what we typically find among U.S. participants, including some painful parallels within the Catholic clergy. The insecurities, angers, past woundings and confusion around sexuality and intimacy, as well as the difficulties inherent in creating meaningful, equitable and authentic relationships, seem to be universal. We heard stories of abuse and trauma that came from within the Catholic community and also from the larger cultural experiences that the nuns and priests were grappling with in their service and community work with Indian, Japanese, and Filipino nationals. The nuns, especially, are almost all charity workers: teachers, nurses, social workers and caregivers. They shared their grief over the many tragedies that punctuate their efforts to bring healing and comfort to the individuals, especially women and children, in the various villages where they work.

To speak about gender injustice was not altogether foreign to these people, but to do so in mixed company was virtually unheard of, especially addressing personal traumatic experiences and violation. Many of the priests were unaware of the abuse their sisters and some of their brothers had experienced, and some of the priests were quite incredulous as many stories began to come forward. This reflects a pattern not uncommon in our workshops in the United States. The discovery that it is the women sitting right there in the room who have been victimized—rather than some abstract victims in a newspaper story—is almost always disconcerting and unsettling. The weeklong workshop uncovered classic hidden pain and associated group dynamics, including the inevitable rise of tension between the women and the men as they delved into previously unexplored areas of vulnerability.

## The Priests' Circle

Communication in the men's circle was limited by a curious and telling phenomenon: many of the priests were unwilling to speak freely in the presence of other priests from their own religious order. Several different religious orders were represented in the group, including Franciscans, Jesuits, Benedictines, Salatians, Cistercians, and Dominicans, each of which carries a unique character and emphasis within the larger Catholic community. In general, the priests tended to have the least trust for other priests from their same order. Most of the priests were more forthcoming in smaller groups, especially if the others in the group were all from different orders. This revealed a sobering insight about the communication among priests within their own communities: many feel a relative lack of safety to speak openly about delicate issues among their peers. It seems that there is a significant degree of rigid control, accountability, and retribution in several of these monastic communities.

A major concern for nearly all the priests was how to be in proper relationship with women—nuns as well as laywomen in their parishes. Several reported that they simply limited these relationships, never allowing them to develop very far. A number of priests shared their conflicting feelings in relation to sexuality, guilt feelings around masturbation, and so forth. A few of them seemed to be fixated in early or adolescent development with regard to sexuality. Two or three spoke of bouts of indulgence in pornography, with generally unsatisfactory results as they discovered the addictive aspect of it.

One priest opened up and shared earnestly about a woman he had developed a very close relationship with over a seven-year period. He said this experience completely transformed him—both as a man and a priest—helping him to become much more compassionate, loving, sensitive, and mature. He indicated that they became very close, and were rather intimate, including physical affection, but he seemed to imply that his celibacy was maintained throughout. When asked about the emotional and physical/erotic aspects of the relationship, he was reluctant to go into detail, and he never recounted how or why the relationship ended. Our host, Francis, explained to us later that this man had taken a huge risk to share this story at all, especially because he presented his experience in such a positive light, with other members of his order present.

Another priest related a story about his best friend, a priest who had been deeply involved in a love affair with a nun for the past ten years. Their first four years had been a courtship, and for the past six years they had been having sexual relations. This created major tension within their communities, which in turn placed great stress on their relationship. The nun was ready to give up the sex, but not the relationship, because she was under considerable pressure of shame and guilt from the sisters in her order for having a sexual love affair. The priest did not want to give up the sexual aspect of their relationship, and the two had been going back and forth like this for some time. The situation was creating a significant dilemma for everyone involved.

Finally, there was a priest who privately revealed to Will that he was contemplating sleeping with a woman who was actively pursuing him. She was married to a husband who beat her, and the priest was a longtime friend of the family and a prominent figure in his community. He was clearly smitten by her and appeared to be very naive about the destructive potential of the situation. Will gingerly underscored some of the inherent dangers, emphasizing how vulnerable he was, and pointed him to some relevant passages in Proverbs. A few weeks after the event the priest sent an e-mail of appreciation and thanks, but he never told us what transpired, and he did not answer the return e-mail.

## The Nuns' Circle

When the nuns first met together, there was a reluctance to delve into any personal material. The conversation centered on the collective fate of Indian women and on the terrible things that they witnessed in the villages, things that happened to women at the hands of the culture. Eventually, one of the nuns, who was born not in India but in the Philippines, expanded on this theme by speaking of her efforts with young women in the college where she had been an instructor for many years. She was incensed by a pattern of exploitation in which young college girls were preyed upon by senior college administrators and businessmen from the outside, who found them particularly attractive because of their innocent, unpracticed form of prostitution. The college authorities were well aware that their institution's policies were effectively forcing many girls into prostitution because the girls were required to pay off all outstanding debts in full before they could take their final exams each semester. The fact that a Catholic college was choosing to uphold such policies greatly distressed the sister.

Not only were the college authorities aware of the situation, but other men in the region and growing numbers of businessmen, including many foreign businessmen, became increasingly involved in perpetuating it. Near the close of each semester, when the girls were under the most pressure to complete their coursework, an informal open hunting "season" was declared upon these young, vulnerable women. However, the sister explained that what pained her the most was the role the college authorities were playing in it. She and several other sisters had been trying to get the college to change their policies for some years now, without success. Her efforts were openly thwarted, and she finally lost her post at the college when she sought to expose some of the priests involved, some of whom were directly connected to the college.

This poignant story gave others in the group more permission to open up. Similar stories of abuse began to come forward. One nun shared that when she was a very young girl, during her first confession, her priest had fondled her sexually. She told her mother, who sought to expose the priest, but her mother was silenced. Tears flowed freely as she spoke, and her story was followed by long, uninterrupted silence. Then another sister began to speak, saying she had recently turned down the affections of a priest who had invited her to work at a prestigious youth camp. During the course of her time at the camp she had invested substantial monies from her own small savings to buy the girls things they needed for various projects, always with the priest's promise that the monies would be reimbursed. As the days went by, however, and their close contact made her the focus of the priest's attention, he became more and more blatant in his affection and demands until finally one day he simply cornered her and began to touch her breasts and kiss her. She pushed him away forcefully, saying, "Shame on you, Father!" But this only escalated the encounter into a highly unpleasant conversation in which he effectively told her that his unwanted affections were the price she must pay for her very coveted position at the camp. She was soon forced to leave the camp, and afterward her efforts to get the promised reimbursement were completely ignored, first by the priest and later by those above him whose help she had solicited. She now found herself being ostracized.

This story in turn elicited several more stories in the women's circle. At one point, one of the facilitators asked for each woman who had been sexually or physically abused to raise her hand, and about three-quarters of the hands went up. In some cases, entire convents were being punished for preventing their priest from pursuing sexual favors within their walls. After the offensive behavior was challenged, it seemed, there would suddenly be no priest available for confession or even for mass. There were convents where mass was never performed anymore, as an expression of retaliation from certain priests. In one case, a priest was incensed by the sisters' unwillingness to look the other way when he had forced himself on one of the villagers who was working in the convent.

Then one of the women who had been quiet for most of the circle began speaking quietly, with intense emotion. She related how she was engaged to marry before she decided to become a nun. Shortly after her decision to break off the engagement with the boy, he tried to kill himself. She found herself accosted by the villagers for this, and she had taken refuge in the convent, but the villagers came after her with rocks and sticks. They came to the convent in the middle of the night screaming that the sisters turn her out so they could kill her. She wept as she told her story, about how she had thought that the nuns should let the crowd have her, and she had been so ashamed hiding inside the walls as a rioting crowd outside called for her death.

As she related her story, the women's circle came closer together in deeper connection and compassion—holding hands and putting arms around each other. The women were sharing a common pain that grew from the confusing demands that the culture puts on women—aware of just how much they held in common, regardless of their diverse origins and ways of being in the world. It was a time of collective grieving that ended in prayer and song and camaraderie and, finally, in laughter that arose spontaneously from the joy of trust and shared secrets.

## Women's and Men's Truth Forums

In the beginning, both the nuns and priests found it particularly challenging to break their silence and speak to real issues affecting their lives and congregations. However, as the workshop progressed some of the nuns began to gingerly confront some entrenched sexist assumptions and attitudes prevalent in the priesthood. For many (both women and men), this was uncomfortable and unfamiliar terrain. To facilitate skillful communication and listening, we used the truth forum process (introduced in Chapter 5 and described in detail in Appendix A). First the men listened in silence while the women held a circle and shared with each other, and then the women listened while the men shared. The nuns came forward with many poignant stories, most of which had surfaced earlier in the women's circle. One nun recounted being molested as a child by a priest at age seven during her first confession. Several spoke about being mistreated and retaliated against when they refused unwanted advances of priests in their professional association. Numerous tales emerged of sexual overtures or abuses by priests when giving private confessions or spiritual direction to nuns, a context in which the females are particularly vulnerable. As facilitators we had the sense that, for many of the sisters, this was the first time they had shared such raw, emotional truths in the presence of men.

Systemic concerns emerged that are painful parallels to recent revelations in the American Catholic Church. For example, when a nun becomes pregnant by a priest, she is generally excommunicated and turned out on the street to fend for herself and her forthcoming newborn. Meanwhile, the priest involved is generally transferred to a new archdiocese, where the pattern often repeats itself. This was a source of deep outrage among several senior nuns, who over the years had witnessed cases of individual priests getting several nuns pregnant without retribution, while the nuns were each time stripped of their dignity and ignominiously expelled from religious life. The worst offending priests, we were told, are sent to the United States—though we did not verify this or learn of any specific cases.

In the men's truth forum, further powerful stories emerged, including several stories of sexual abuse. When the men were asked how many had been sexually or physically abused, over half of them raised their hands. This was a surprise to many of the nuns, who had assumed that such abuse was much more prevalent among women than men. The men's abuse was divided roughly evenly in terms of being perpetrated by women or men. Several stories of sexual abuse from older priests emerged, and one priest acknowledged being molested by a trusted adult friend as a boy. One of the older priests conceded that in his priesthood he had felt the temptation to become an abuser, particularly in his powerful role of giving confessions and spiritual direction to young women, but that he had never crossed the line. At one point, the facilitators encouraged the men to examine their roles and responsibility as priests for redressing gender imbalances and abuses of power within the Church—about which we had heard much during the women's truth forum. But this nudge did not seem to lead anywhere, and the men remained focused on sharing their tales of personal wounding and abuse.

## Disgruntled Men and a Backlash

With each new poignant story that came forth, a deepening sense of safety and intimacy emerged in the group, accompanied by a growing tension in the background among a few in the group who were challenged or disturbed by the entire process, especially the candid truth-telling involved. A number of the priests began tapping into deeper layers of feeling, including fear and anger about what was being said. As this anger found expression, there were some who began to question the wisdom of priests and nuns gathering and disclosing their dark secrets. Was it really necessary, they asked, for these things to be aired, especially in mixed company? Did the revelation of past wounds truly enable reconciliation, or merely deepen the shame?

On the last morning, we separated into the women's and men's circles to prepare the ritual offerings for one another. Several priests took a bold and creative step in devising some remarkable role-reversal processes to enable the nuns to experience themselves in the role of priests, giving communion and taking confessions. The priests placed themselves in the roles that nuns would normally be in, making confessions and receiving communion. This was a clear sign that many of the priests had no personal objection to women taking the role of priests in the future. There was a heartfelt enthusiasm and joyful generosity of spirit as the priests began rehearsing their ritual.

As the men continued their ritual planning, there was a knock on the door and a request for Will to come out. Will encouraged the priests to keep up their good work and stepped out of the room. He then learned that the women's circle had plunged into crisis.

On the previous evening, two of the nuns had overheard a few of the priests making strong, disparaging remarks about the women and about the entire workshop process. The nuns who overheard this had been upset but kept it to themselves that evening, but could contain themselves no longer as the women began planning their ritual. They disclosed what they overheard to the women, and it stopped the women's ritual planning dead in its tracks. The nuns were distressed and outraged to learn that one of the priests complained that the women were priest bashing in the truth forum, blaming all priests for the actions of a few. Another priest had accused the women of washing their dirty laundry in public, while a third priest had angrily exclaimed that during the truth forum process the nuns had handed them a "plate of shit." Before long, the entire women's group felt betrayed, and in an unusual move they demanded an immediate, full council process to openly confront the priests with this festering undercurrent that had been quietly brewing under the surface of the community all week.

Will returned to the joyous men's circle with the unhappy news that plans had radically changed. He explained that there was a crisis in the women's circle and the nuns were calling for a full community council, which meant among other things that the rituals would have to be postponed and most likely cancelled. The men were dismayed and disappointed and began to prepare themselves as best they could, not knowing what was coming next.

As the women entered the community room, the facilitators seated them in a semicircle facing the men—who were also sitting in a semicircle—with a few feet separating the two groups. The atmosphere was tense as the facilitators opened with silence and a community prayer to invoke the collective intention for gender healing and reconciliation, reiterating the common purpose. A simple communication technique was introduced to carefully balance each side's contributions to the process. The women would be given five minutes to speak while the men listened, and then the men would be given five minutes to speak while the women listened. The process would continue like this, back and forth, until there was some clear movement or resolution of some kind.

The women began quickly. Several challenged the men with the rumors they had heard and asked for honesty and forthrightness in the plenary gathering. They lamented the sense of hypocrisy these rumors carried and that some men were saying one thing in front of the facilitators during the "formal" gatherings and quite another among themselves when only close confidants were listening. This, the nuns insisted, was a replay of precisely what took place routinely in their larger orders—for both nuns and the priests—which made their religious lives so unsafe, and necessarily superficial. No one ever spoke the truth directly; rather, it was generally whispered behind people's backs. How could the men be continuing this behavior when we had gathered to confront and dismantle these negative patterns? Furthermore, how could it be that the priests had so little understanding of what the nuns had shared? How could they label the heartfelt vulnerability that had characterized the women's sharing "priest bashing" and "shit"? The women were particularly incensed by the use of this foul language and the disdain it represented.

The men responded slowly at first, but became increasingly forthcoming. Several expressed shock and dismay that this had happened and empathized with the women. A few explained that they were merely expressing their feelings and perceptions about what had happened and had no intention to hurt anyone, and that they were entitled to their perspective. One man opined that we were all making "too much fuss" out of nothing. Another priest was indignant and felt that the entire workshop had been an unfair attack on the men and that the women had planned this confrontation in advance. He suggested that the facilitators had probably put the women up to it, and pointed to times in the process where it seemed the facilitators had been heavy-handed in establishing the direction of things.

The tension in the room mounted as the first round of exchange drew to a close. As the nuns began their second round, they presented further confrontations from their own experience. Several soundly refuted the suggestion that this confrontation had been pre-planned or orchestrated by the facilitators, and explained how it had arisen spontaneously and justifiably from the painful revelations of the sisters who had been privy to the men's side talk. Some emphasized in earnest that their intention in the women's truth forum sharing had not been to blame anyone at all, but rather to bear witness to the injustices they had personally experienced, which, after all, was the purpose of the exercise. One woman suggested that the disparaging "humorous" remarks that men sometimes make in reaction to women's pain were perhaps a way to avoid having to feel the plate of shit within themselves. Two others emphasized that the men had yet to address the women's basic complaint.

The bell rang, and, after a pause in silence, it was the priests' turn again. They opened up with ever more candid sharings, expressing strong feelings with articulate eloquence. Several expressed solidarity with the women, and a few apologized on behalf of their fellow priests who had said hurtful things. The room became increasingly charged with emotion as this mixed group of forty-two clerics continued the exchange for several rounds back and forth—courageously and cooperatively.

As so often happens in gender work, we found ourselves immersed in a complex conglomeration of personal, social, institutional, and historical pain. The frustrations being aired had roots that reached deep into the personal histories and cultural dynamics that operated in these people's lives. There was a strong fear that we might never find our way through all this "gender muck." We had reached the point of no return, however, and it was clear that the only way out of the situation was by going through it to its natural conclusion. The resolution had to be real; it could not be artificial or "nice" for the sake of "niceness," which would only perpetuate the already damaging situation.

As the dialogue continued and challenging feelings were aired, tempers slowly began to cool. A spirit of love and generosity began to find its way back into the dialogue. It was a remarkable process to witness, and most everyone in the room was committed to finding a genuine and authentic resolution. The community was unwilling to gloss over the painful issues, and they continued sitting in the fire with the issues and with each other—sometimes in silence, sometimes in the form of one person's rage or humiliation, but increasingly without accusation and blame.

## Transmutation into Grace

The turning point came when Joseph, a priest who had been silent thus far, quietly revealed that he was the one who had made the remark about the "plate of shit" which had been so hurtful to many of the women. He went on to say that he was feeling extremely vulnerable, and that he had only meant to express his feelings authentically, but he never intended to hurt anyone. He offered a moving and tearful apology for the pain he had caused. He finished by saying that he now had a lot of pain inside himself. Several of the men expressed their gratitude to Joseph, some thanking him profusely for his honesty and courage. The women followed suit, thanking Joseph for his courage in openly acknowledging his role and expressing compassion for the difficulty of what we were all attempting to do together.

Joseph was visibly shaken, and quietly got up and left the room. One of the facilitators followed him out the door as the group took a tea break in silence. The situation felt dire to some, and many wondered if we would be able to find our way to the joy that we so hoped would mark the closing of our week together. Our tea in silence provided a welcome time for individual reflection and an opening for the miraculous powers of those larger loving forces to soften hearts.

Joseph was in considerable distress. His heavy armoring had cracked open, and the facilitators worked with him. His heart had been pierced by what had transpired, and in that moment he was feeling very vulnerable. Gradually, he began to recollect himself, and when the group reconvened, he was the last to return to the room. The wave of relief among everyone as Joseph entered the room was palpable. He sat down and quietly confided to the group, "It took all I could do to come back here, but I'm here. I may not be able to do anything other than just be here."

The anger in the room was now broken, and a new energy was present. Continuing the facilitated communication process between the women and men, compassion and understanding began to grow stronger until the energy and tone in the group shifted away from accusation toward gratitude and mutual appreciation. The storm had passed, and the sun was breaking through the clouds of fear and betrayal. As the positive feelings grew, the process flowed seamlessly into a healing ritual process that included a Sufi partner dance in which every man and woman had the opportunity to offer a blessing to the other. Tears of tenderness and joy flowed as people shared moments of intimacy in pairs as they moved through the dance. We closed with several group songs and chants, interrupted by eruptions of laughter and an atmosphere of celebration.

## The Spirit of the Christ

Later that afternoon, in a follow-up meeting with the facilitators, Joseph shared beautifully the deeper learnings from his experience. His eyes were shining as he spoke, and he explained that it had been his turn that morning to give mass. For the mass he had chosen the theme of deep healing, and he quoted the Biblical story of Jesus sending his disciples out to heal. "My whole purpose and prayer for mass this morning was healing," Joseph exclaimed in irony. "Healing, healing, healing! And then this happened!" At first he had felt betrayed by the process, but he explained that he came to see that a powerful healing had indeed taken place, in which he had been the (unwitting) sacrificial lamb. We confirmed that this was the case and that he had been used as an instrument for healing in the sense that his ego had been "sacrificed" for the sake of the community's healing process. Joseph noted that in this way his earnest prayers from earlier that morning had been answered, but certainly not in the way he would have imagined or chosen.

## Closing Reflections

What took place in this workshop is a microcosm of what often happens in society when painful gender issues are brought forward for healing. A backlash frequently ensues directed against those who speak up—be they women or men. There exist long-standing psychological, societal, and institutional forces that are determined to keep the structures of gender injustice intact. Measures to undermine the reconciliation work are therefore often taken by people and institutions who actively profess to support the healing work. As evidenced in this workshop, this undermining process takes place in interpersonal interactions and in small group processes, as well as in the larger society in relation to attempts at gender healing. Yet, given sufficient integrity, good will, and alignment of intention among the participants, these adverse forces can be overcome to produce a breakthrough in healing and reconciliation. We witnessed this in microcosm in the India workshop.

All in all, this initial experiment of bringing gender reconciliation work to India was deemed highly successful. We received several e-mails in the months afterward from a number of the participants, thanking us for the work. The process worked much as it does elsewhere, with suitable adaptations. Several weeks after the workshop, the newsletter from the Sadhana Institute had this to say about the work:

> The group of 21 men and 21 women religious who participated in the course bore witness both to the wounds of their lives from culture, religion and personal history. They also testified to the healing experienced . . . that included an awareness of the partiality and incompleteness of their perceptions of each other, owning the deep hurts of their lives, and opening them to the healing light of compassion for one another.
>
> Beyond the personal and social dimensions of the course, there are also signs of a major shift that is happening in the consciousness of many of the participants. There is a deepening awareness of the need to include this excluded dimension in religious formation. There is a better understanding that the repudiation of the feminine has afflicted the [Catholic] Church in major ways . . . This course has deepened the awareness of our participants both for the need for healing, as well as the wonderful richness of this holistic approach.
> —Sadhana Institute, *News and Updates*, August, 2002

Gender reconciliation work is ultimately driven by the spiritual momentum of the collective heart, and the resulting alchemy eventually produces its gold—provided there is sufficient time, integrity of intention, and surrender to the process among most of the people in the group. The nuggets harvested in this instance were hard won in a culture that embodies some of the most severe symptoms of gender injustice on earth, and they were all the more precious for this reason.

# CHAPTER 10

# *Gender Reconciliation in the Rainbow Republic*

*I have been looking for a long time*
*to find a way to bring healing and reconciliation*
*between women and men here in South Africa.*

*This work is the answer.*
*We need much more of this work in South Africa.*

—Nozizwe Madlala Routledge
Deputy Minister of Health, South Africa

"We have not even begun to deal with the gender issue here in South Africa!" exclaimed Nomfundo Walaza passionately. Nomfundo was our co-facilitator in a gender reconciliation workshop we were conducting in Cape Town. "We've made significant strides forward in terms of racial integration since apartheid ended," she continued, "especially through the work of the Truth and Reconciliation Commission, despite its inevitable flaws. But we've barely scratched the surface on the massive issues between women and men in this country."

Nomfundo is the director of the Desmond Tutu Peace Center in Cape Town, and her words echo what we have heard from other colleagues and friends in South Africa, most notably our host, Deputy Minister of Health, Nozizwe Madlala Routledge. Will Keepin first met Nozizwe in 2003, when she was Deputy Minister of Defense for South Africa. The two were introduced by Bernedette Muthien, an activist from South Africa who had trained in Satyana Institute's gender reconciliation program. At the end of a deep and inspiring meeting, Nozizwe invited Satyana Institute to present our gender reconciliation work to an invited group of Members of Parliament (MPs) in South Africa. Nozizwe explained that unexamined gender dynamics between male and female MPs in the parliament were significantly undermining the efficacy of their government service work. Despite the fact that women had come into parliament in much greater numbers after apartheid ended, women still had comparatively little voice there. Men largely ran the show, more out of cultural habit than by intentional exclusion. By inviting in Satyana's gender reconciliation process, Nozizwe sought to begin transforming gender relations in the Parliament, which she hopes will in turn serve to foster a similar transformation in the government, and eventually in the larger South African society.

Since apartheid ended in 1994, South Africa has been reconstituted—literally—and its Constitution is now arguably one of the most advanced and progressive of any nation on earth. Having lived through the horror of apartheid, the Rainbow Republic's new constitution is founded upon exalted principles of justice and equality for all human beings in society and provides extensive measures to overcome racial as well as gender discrimination.

This chapter describes the pilot project conducted by the Satyana Institute to introduce gender reconciliation work in South Africa. We convened two gatherings in November 2006. The first was a six-day workshop in Cape Town for a group of twenty-five leaders from the South African Parliament, faith communities, and non-governmental organizations. The second was a two-day workshop for a group of sixteen participants hosted by Ela Gandhi, granddaughter of Mahatma Gandhi. The project was funded by a seed grant from the Kalliopeia Foundation, based in San Rafael, California.

This pilot project was a major success and led to an invitation for Satyana Institute to lead a new initiative on gender reconciliation in South Africa, including a two-year program to train a group of South African professionals in gender reconciliation. For this reason, we describe the work in South Africa at some length here, including a detailed narrative of highlights of the Cape Town workshop. In keeping with the editorial policy throughout this book, the names of participants have been changed in the narrative, as well as some minor details, to protect the identity of the participants. Facilitators' names remain unchanged throughout.

### Need for Gender Reconciliation in South Africa

Gender violence and strife in South Africa have reached catastrophic proportions. Rape has soared since apartheid ended. According to U.N. statistics, South Africa has the highest incidence of reported rape in the world. Estimates vary, but conservative sources indicate that a woman is raped in South Africa every twenty-six seconds. This translates into more than 1.2 million rapes per year, a staggering number in a population of some 23 million females. Young girls have been increasingly targeted, partly fueled by the erroneous notion that one can be cured of AIDS by having sex with a virgin. A related factor is that younger girls are perceived as less likely to be contaminated with the HIV virus, and are therefore more desirable targets for rape. Certain hard to fathom patterns of rape have taken root, such as "mainstreaming," an insidious form of gang rape. If a young man gets in a fight or conflict with his girlfriend, he mainstreams her, which means his group of male friends gang rapes her as "punishment." Not only rape but domestic violence, sexual abuse, and sexual harassment in the workplace are also very widespread in South African society.

The AIDS crisis in South Africa is among the worst in the world. Approximately nine hundred people die each day in South Africa from AIDS. There are an estimated one thousand new HIV infections in South Africa daily. Many MPs, including Nozizwe, have lost family members to AIDS. Yet, unlike Nozizwe, very few MPs ever disclose that they have lost family members to AIDS. This creates an undercurrent of deep personal grief that many MPs share but never acknowledge or discuss with each other. This was another reason Nozizwe invited in Satyana's gender reconciliation work for MPs: she wanted to create a safe space for bringing forward the grief that AIDS has wrought in the personal lives of her colleagues. Nozizwe believes that doing so will also precipitate a more effective government response to AIDS, and to gender equity.

For background reference, it is useful to summarize briefly some basic information about South Africa. The African National Congress (ANC) is the ruling party that successfully ousted the terrorist apartheid government in 1994. The nation's population is about 47 million, and racial composition is approximately 75 percent black, 13 percent white, 9 percent mixed race ("colored"), and 3 percent Asian (primarily East Indian). The country is predominantly Christian, accounting for 80 percent of the population. Hindus comprise 1.2 percent of the population, Jews 0.3 percent, and about 15 percent do not identify themselves as members of any religion (Source: Wikipedia.com). Muslims account for significant percentages in some areas, such as the Western Cape.

## Current Political and Social Context for
## Gender Work in South Africa

Nozizwe Madlala Routledge became Deputy Minister of Health in 2004, and afterward she experienced increasing limitations on her ability to perform her role, including access to financial resources, for reasons discussed below. We only learned upon our arrival in Cape Town the full extent of the daunting challenges faced by Nozizwe over the past couple of years, in view of which her determination to go forward with the gender reconciliation pilot project in South Africa demonstrated a remarkable commitment on her part. In the end, we were all gratified that we persevered through multiple difficulties and delays, because the result was such an auspicious beginning.

The political climate in Cape Town at the time of our workshop included visible drama on several fronts directly relevant to our work. Three major issues were prevalent during our time there:

*Same-sex Civil Union Bill passed.* In the weeks just prior to the workshop, the parliament had been hotly debating a Civil Union Bill, introduced to formally recognize and legitimize same-sex marriage in South Africa. On November 14, the day that our gender workshop was concluded, this Civil Union Bill was passed by the National

Assembly. Response was strong on all sides, with gay and lesbian leaders applauding the bill and emphasizing the fact that it was the only legitimate response to the nation's constitution. The South African Constitution is widely regarded as one of the most advanced constitutions in the world regarding gender and human rights issues. The Bill of Rights (Section 9 of Chapter 2) specifically names "sexual orientation" as a fundamental human right and is one of several dimensions of human equality under the constitution. Nevertheless, Christian conservatives deplored the passage of the Civil Union bill. Christian Front leader Rudi du Plooy declared that, "By this act, the ANC has demonstrated that it will poke its fingers into the eyes of the Christians as an act of defiance to God's law. Sodomy is directly opposite to what God had intended and created."[1]

*Nozizwe and Deputy President reverse South African AIDS policy.* Nozizwe had been working under severely challenging conditions as Deputy Minister of Health because she had been gagged on speaking out about AIDS for the previous two years by her boss, the Minister of Health, Manto Tshabalala-Msimang. Together with South African President Thabo Mbeki, Tshabalala-Msimang had adopted a highly controversial position on AIDS—questioning the link between the HIV virus and AIDS and claiming that AIDS can be effectively treated nutritionally using a combination of garlic and beetroot. This position and resulting government policy had been severely criticized in the international AIDS community, and critics claimed that hundreds of thousands of lives had been lost in South Africa due to this irresponsible policy that flew in the face of all the available scientific and medical evidence. The crisis eroded President Mbeki's credibility and enraged international activists at the 2006 International AIDS conference in Toronto, embarrassing the South African government.

Nozizwe concurs with the mainstream view that responsible treatment of AIDS requires the dissemination of antiretroviral (ARV) drugs, which is the consensus of the scientific and medical communities. Because her superiors opposed this view, Nozizwe's hands had been tied politically, and she was denied access to political influence and government funds. So Nozizwe had been engaged in a challenging struggle to change government policy on AIDS—with very little success until the end of 2006, when things suddenly shifted due in part to international pressure following the Toronto conference. The Minister of Health fell ill in late 2006 and went into hospital, and Nozizwe moved steadily into the forefront of South African AIDS policy.

The situation came to a head on December 1, 2006 (World AIDS Day), when South Africa formally announced a major reversal in its AIDS policy. Under the leadership of Nozizwe and Deputy President Phumzile Miambo-Ngcuka, South Africa abandoned its earlier AIDS policy and rolled out a new policy that included multibillion-dollar plans to dispense ARV drugs widely in South Africa. ARV drugs were needed by some eight hundred thousand people but had been available to less than 25 percent of that number prior to this new policy. It was a major victory not only for Nozizwe but for hundreds of thousands of AIDS victims in South Africa. However, it put Nozizwe in hot political water for a time. She gave an interview to the *Daily Telegraph* in December 2006 in which she criticized the President and Health Minister for their earlier stance on AIDS. The government considered whether to take disciplinary action against her, including possibly firing her, but the South African press was hailing Nozizwe as a national hero, and the international community was rejoicing and crediting Nozizwe and Deputy President Miambo-Ngcuka with having rescued nearly a million South African AIDS victims. So the government backed down, and since then Nozizwe's standing within both the government and the nation has flowered beautifully.

*ANC Chief Whip Embroiled in Sex Scandal.* On top of these developments, a highly contentious sex scandal erupted in the South African Parliament just two days before our workshop began. The Chief Whip of the ANC, Mbuelo Goniwe, was accused of attempting to coerce a young parliamentary intern into a sexual liaison late one evening after a birthday party. The twenty-one-year-old woman reported the alleged incident, which led to a crisis among the women leaders of parliament as they grappled with whether to bring this incident forward into the public eye. Emergency meetings were held, bringing together prominent women leaders in parliament, several of whom had planned to attend our gender reconciliation workshop but cancelled at the last minute because they felt the need to tend to this unfolding crisis. The pressing drama of gender realpolitik in parliament overruled our program in gender reconciliation for these MPs—an irony that was not lost on the group.

On the morning of the third day of our workshop, the story broke in the headlines, "ANC Boss in Sex Scandal." The Chief Whip was temporarily suspended until the investigation could be completed. Nomawele Njongo, the intern at the center of the storm, was a personal friend of one of the parliamentary staff in our workshop, whom she contacted, seeking help. Nomawele had received numerous death threats via telephone calls and text messages on her cell phone, and she was very afraid. Several participants in our workshop expressed deep concern for her safety. The inside story that emerged in our group was that several leading male MPs in the parliament had strong-armed the young woman not to reveal what had happened to her, and they were enraged when she went public with her story. The attempt to silence her by prominent male MPs had in turn outraged leading women MPs, so the gender tension within parliament escalated quickly. Meanwhile Nomawele went into hiding, disposed of her cell phone, and contacted her friend in our workshop, seeking therapeutic help and legal protection.

On the day our workshop concluded, the ANC formally decided to conduct a full hearing into the matter. Afterwards, further allegations emerged that the Chief Whip had had sexual relations with other young women on parliamentary staff, and that he had fathered at least one or possibly two children with his employees on ANC staff. Meanwhile, the Deputy Chief Whip of the ANC, Andries Nel, attended our workshop for the first day and part of the second day before the crisis broke in the headlines. There was speculation that he might become the new Chief Whip, although such speculation was premature because the outcome of the hearing was still pending. The situation remained heated when we departed the country.

The hearing was completed on December 14, 2006, and the Chief Whip, Mbulelo Goniwe, was immediately expelled from the ANC party and removed as a member of South Africa's parliament. The ANC disciplinary committee had found him guilty of sexual harassment and of bringing the ANC party into disrepute. Goniwe is prohibited from holding public office for three years.

A similar development in another high profile case of sexual harassment occurred around the same time. On December 1, 2006, the High Court of Pretoria upheld the dismissal of Indonesian ambassador Norman Mashabane. Three years earlier, Mashabane had been found guilty of twenty-one counts of sexual harassment, including sexual harassment of his employee, Lara Swart. However, the Foreign Affairs Minister, Nkosazana Dlamini-Zuma, had overturned the guilty verdict, which led Swart to file an appeal. After a three-year legal battle, the Pretoria High Court vindicated Swart, upholding Mashabane's dismissal and quashing the reversal by the Foreign Affairs Minister.

In yet another high-level sexual harassment case involving a senior military general, Nozizwe officially challenged the Ministry of Defense in December 2006, wanting to know why the case had dragged on for three years and why the general had recently been promoted prior to the case being settled. She also highlighted a serious concern that there was not a single female present in the military courtroom's hearing of the case. At the time of this writing, the case is still pending.

## Participants in the Cape Town Workshop

Deputy Minister of Health Nozizwe Routledge invited approximately thirty-five Members of Parliament to the workshop, but many were unable to attend, so she opened it up to include leaders from other sectors, including the South African Council of Churches, women's organizations, and nongovernmental service organizations (NGO). In the end, there were twenty-five participants in the workshop, including fifteen women and ten men. All but one were either black or "colored," the nonpejorative term used in South Africa for persons of mixed race. There was one white person in the group, Nozizwe's husband, Jeremy Routledge.

**Facilitation Team**

Given the inherent intensity of gender reconciliation work, plus
the challenges of operating in the South African cultural context
rife with gender oppression, AIDS, and sexual violence—not
to mention the country's recent excruciating history during the
apartheid regime—it was important to have an abundance of highly
skilled staff for this event. We had been informed beforehand that
many of the participants belonged to the ANC and would likely
have suffered imprisonment and/or torture under the apartheid
regime. So we needed clinically trained staff on our team who
were comfortable working with participants who might regress
or become restimulated into past traumatic experiences. We also
needed sufficient staff on hand to confidently navigate through
a meltdown, should one occur. (As discussed in Chapter 7, a
"meltdown" is a powerful spontaneous deconstruction of "normal"
group process into an intensive cauldron of deep emotional release
and healing, usually involving several participants in cathartic
process or restimulated traumas simultaneously. See Chapter 7 for
more details and several examples.)

Quite beyond these clinical considerations, it was equally crucial
to incorporate black African facilitators in the mix, partly because
the Satyana Institute staff are white Americans, and also because
working in Africa we needed African consciousness and sensibilities
integrated into our facilitation team. With these considerations in
mind, we assembled a mixed-race facilitation team of exceptional
capacity and multiple skill sets. This gave us inner confidence going
in that our team could confidently handle whatever challenges
might arise in the group. The facilitation team consisted of authors
Will Keepin and Cynthia Brix, plus four co-facilitators, including
Julien Devereux and Janet Coster (both Satyana-certified facilitators
from the United States), Nomfundo Walaza from Cape Town, and
Karambu Ringera from Kenya. Janet Coster is a counseling psychologist from Santa Cruz, California, who specializes in gender issues and
spiritual counseling, and Julien Devereux is a clinical social worker
with a background in criminal justice, organizational development, and transpersonal psychology. Nomfundo Walaza is a clinical

psychologist, human rights activist, and director of the Desmond Tutu Center in Cape Town. Earlier she served for eleven years as executive director of the Trauma Centre for Survivors of Violence and Torture in South Africa. Karambu Ringera is a leading women's activist from Kenya who founded International Peace Initiatives, which sponsors grass roots peace work throughout Africa.

This facilitation team worked together well, and feedback from the group was enthusiastic. Keith Vermeulen, director of the parliamentary office of the South African Council of Churches, told us afterward, "Your mix of South African and African co-facilitation was inspired. Keep up the work, and keep working together!"

## Narrative Account of the Cape Town Workshop

As we recount the Cape Town workshop, we will also track in detail the experience of one particular participant, a woman whose name is Elana. By including Elana's experience at each stage of the process, this summary narrative will hopefully convey not only the essence of the workshop as a whole, but also something of the phenomenological experience of a particular individual who entered deeply into the gender reconciliation process.

### Days One and Two

The first evening (Day 1) and first full day (Day 2) of the workshop proceeded like most of our gender reconciliation events. Participants engaged in the ice-breaking exercises with a mixture of openness and trepidation, curious yet a bit uneasy about what was going to happen. Over time, a sense of safety grew and the atmosphere relaxed and deepened, becoming more personal and intimate.

### Love's Unfolding

To help instill basic skills for engaging in gender healing work and make them easy to remember—as well as to bring a light-hearted, playful element—we developed a simple acronym to encapsulate the essential skills and wisdom tools utilized in this work. The acronym is LOVE'S UNFOLDING, which represents the following:

LOVE'S = Listen . . . Open . . . Value diversity . . . Empathize . . . Speak your truth

UNFOLDING = Understanding . . . Nonjudgment . . . Forgive . . . Own your stuff . . . Laugh! . . . Discern . . . Inspire . . . Nurture . . . Gratitude

Each morning we introduced two or three letters of this acronym, drawing upon the group wisdom to guess the specific words involved. Then, for each word, we asked participants to embody that word in a physical movement or gesture. In this manner, over the course of the week the group choreographed a simple dance of "Love's Unfolding," which made for plenty of laughs while also supporting kinesthetic embodiment and learning.

Most days opened and closed with beautiful African songs led by Nomfundo. Music comes very naturally to South Africans, and their cultural heritage shines beautifully through their many songs, which they sang together effortlessly in gorgeous harmonies and elegant rhythms. Nomfundo led these songs with tremendous grace and enthusiasm.

On Day 2, we opened with further ice-breaking and community-building exercises, along with introductory presentations on principles of gender reconciliation. Especially important were the ethical guidelines and agreements that Satyana Institute has established for its gender reconciliation work, to which all the participants committed for the duration of the workshop.

The group began to grapple in earnest with gender injustice when we showed two ten-minute video clips summarizing respectively the pain suffered by women and the pain suffered by men. The video clips included excerpts from a documentary film on the "shadow" side of masculinity entitled *Tough Guise*, by Jackson Katz, and excerpts from testimony given at the Vienna Tribunal in 1993, when thousands of women from around the world testified at the United Nations Human Rights Conference in Vienna, Austria. We had selected and verified the relevance of these particular clips for a South African audience beforehand in planning meetings with Nomfundo.

In the afternoon, we did the silent witnessing exercise. It was especially powerful in this group, as participants witnessed the magnitude of gender injustice and suffering they had themselves directly experienced. It seemed that such an exercise was new to most participants, especially in a mixed group of women and men.

During the silent witnessing process, when the question was asked of the women, "Please stand if you have ever been hit or physically abused a man," one woman stood up, all by herself. This was Elana, a woman in her mid-fifties who explained later that by standing for this question she had finally found a way to acknowledge her own story without actually having to tell it. Later, we learned that Elana had never been able to tell her story to anyone before. Even in her women's circle over the years, whenever she had spoken about this story, Elana had always referred to it as a friend's story, and never revealed it as her own. So this act of standing for this question was, in itself, a mini-breakthrough for Elana.

## Day Three

On this day we did the Holotropic Breathwork process. The sense of safety and intimacy within the group continued to deepen over the course of this day, not only between breathing partners but also within the group as a whole. For the breathwork portion of the workshop, Nomfundo and Karambu temporarily relinquished their roles as facilitators and participated as breathing partners, because neither had ever experienced breathwork before.

Many participants had powerful experiences, awakenings, and insights during the breathwork, which served to deepen their participation in the workshop. As Karambu Ringera put it, "The breathing exercise was like an initiation into a whole new realm of self-awareness. It was a journey into who I am; what I need to see in my world that pointed to my work and role in this life." The breathwork served to convene the "group soul" and strengthen the invisible glue of the community, as it so often does. Some examples of experiences reported from the breathwork include the following:

Lloyd experienced a powerful energetic release during the breathwork. The energy blockage first appeared in his abdominal region, and he worked through the blockage using deep vocal sounds assisted by bodywork facilitation. This led to a deep, tearful release, followed by an expansive heart-opening experience.

Oni reported that she had a profound experience in the breathwork, despite her initial skepticism. During the introduction to the breathwork process, she said she had strongly doubted that anything of significance would happen for her. Yet, when she entered into the process, a powerful inner journey unfolded. She said that at one point she had a revelation that came to her as a clear vision and instruction. In her work, she has been experiencing an intensive conflict with a particular man, and this situation came up during her breathwork. A vision came to her that she needed to go visit this man's mother—not to talk to her, but rather to listen to her. This came as a clear instruction.

Malaika, a parliamentary researcher in her late thirties, has breast cancer that spread to her lungs. She had a powerful healing experience during the breathwork in which she received a clear inner instruction to "breathe out resentment, and breathe in forgiveness." She did this, and continued the practice for a long time during the session. Afterward, she reported that this gave her a deep peace, and, to her surprise, it also relieved (temporarily at least) her physical pain associated with the cancer. She inquired whether she should continue with the practice at home (breathing out resentment, breathing in forgiveness) and we encouraged her to do so, emphasizing that this practice had come to her as a spontaneous gift through her own inner wisdom. We told her that the practice is closely akin to the highly venerated Tibetan *tonglen* practice.

Elana had confided to the facilitators prior to the breathwork session that she was fearful that her abuse experience might come out during the breath session. She said that she had suffered thirty years of abuse from her husband, which were very painful memories for her, and she seemed afraid of losing her protective shield over this part of her past. During the breathwork Elana's abuse history did indeed resurface, and she followed the facilitators' guidance to keep breathing through it, regardless of what arose. Elana had a powerful experience with lots of tears over the two-hour session, and her energetic experience gradually shifted from tears of grief to tears of forgiveness and healing. Afterward, her eyes were shining, and Elana appeared to be in a place of release and peace. The next morning, when she arrived at the workshop, she said, "Today, I am a better person."

### Day Four

On the fourth day, we opened with small group work and then moved again into separate men's and women's circles. To deepen the work in the same-sex groups, we adapted the "truth mandala" process, which is a powerful tool developed by Joanna Macy. The truth mandala is a structured council process that creates a safe and supportive environment for participants to share the anger, grief, fears, and painful truths that are so often left unspoken and unexpressed and which then fester into unhealed pain. Rarely in contemporary society are we given an opportunity to bring such challenging truths into the open to be compassionately witnessed and released. The inevitable consequence is that these agonizing truths are suppressed and thereby create or reinforce what Eckhart Tolle calls the personal or collective "pain-body." The truth mandala process utilizes specific icons arranged in a large circle to symbolize different emotional expressions: rock for fear, dead leaves for grief, stick for anger, and empty bowl for whatever is missing or absent. The process supports people to bring forth taboo issues or whatever else needs to be aired and released.

Using the truth mandala, the women met to address two specific questions:

1. *What is your experience of pain as a woman?*
2. *What is most essential for men to hear, and understand, about your experience as women?*

The men met separately and addressed the analogous two questions about their own pain and experience as men. In both the women's and men's circles many stories began to surface. Most of what emerged in these circles was repeated the following day in the cross-gender truth forums, so we move on to describing the next day.

## Day Five

It has been said that "the shortest distance between a human being and the truth is a story" (Anthony de Mello). This was certainly borne out on this day, which was the crowning culmination of all the excellent work the group had done up to this point. Story after story came pouring out in the women's and men's truth forums. In many cases just the opportunity to recount a long-hidden, painful story to an open-hearted community of peers was itself a powerful healing experience. At one point we learned a popular saying in the Xhosa language, *Umntu Ngumntu Ngabantu*, which roughly translated means, "A person is a person through other people." This expresses the strong community spirit of the South African people, which became very evident, particularly in the final few days of the workshop as the group came together very powerfully.

The bulk of this day was spent in the process of cross-gender truth forums. As described previously, the format is deceptively simple: the women and men sit in two concentric circles, and the outer circle maintains silence and listens to the inner circle. Afterwards, the roles are reversed, so both the women and the men get a chance to be heard in silent witness by the other.

## Women's Truth Forum

The women went first into the inner circle as the men took their seats quietly around them. After a brief invocation the women began to come forward with their stories and other sharings.

Dana, a Member of Parliament, recounted that her teenage daughter had been raped about one year earlier by two boys. One of the boys was HIV positive. As a result, Dana's daughter was now HIV positive. Dana had suspected that her daughter had brought this rape upon herself, assuming that her daughter must have been "sleeping around." However, when her daughter was in the hospital after the rape, Dana learned that she had been gravely mistaken, and that her daughter was a virgin when she was raped. Dana was absolutely devastated—by the horror of the rape, by her daughter becoming HIV positive, and by her own mistrust of her daughter. "I am so angry with myself for suspecting my own daughter!" she kept repeating.

This story provided a poignant example of how the patriarchal system coerces and manipulates women into blaming themselves or each other for their victimization or traumatization—to such a degree that even a young girl's mother would blame her innocent daughter for "getting herself raped." Moreover, if a girl gets into trouble, it is seen as partly the mother's fault, which could also have been part of the reason for Dana's anger.

After Dana's story, several other women followed suit with their own stories—sometimes standing, sometimes crying, always with passion and sincerity. Some walked to the center of the circle to pick up the "talking earth" (a miniature replica of the earth), or one of the other icons from the previous day's truth mandala: the stone, dead leaves, or stick.

"Soldiers don't cry" is a strong admonition in South African society. Not only men but also most women in the ANC had adopted this same principle during the struggle against apartheid. They felt they could not allow themselves the luxury of tears, nor would they ever want their adversaries to see them "weak" or "defeated" in this manner. In the privacy of the women's circle the previous day some women had questioned whether they should allow themselves to cry in front of the men.

Yet, from the outset of the women's truth forum, this question was settled by necessity. During the opening story from Dana, several women had begun to cry and sniffle quietly, and this continued throughout their forum. The women handed one another tissues as needed. One woman from the parliament said she was able to cry for the first time in two years. When things became especially intense, the women would join hands and huddle a bit closer together, and Cynthia would remind them to center themselves in their breathing.

In many moments throughout the day the entire room was spellbound by what emerged. A few more examples from the women's truth forum follow:

"I never have permission anywhere to cry," Verena began slowly. She repeated this several times. "My husband doesn't want to know about it. And I cannot ever cry in the presence of my colleagues in the clergy."

Earlier, on the second night of the gender workshop, Verena had announced to the group, "I'm giving myself permission to cry," and she sat quietly crying in the plenary group as the evening drew to a close. Now Verena began to reveal more of her story. She said that her husband is light-skinned, as is her son. So Verena has the strange experience of being discriminated against disproportionately in comparison to her own family members, who are perceived as white (or nearly so). This creates a fundamental tension for her and her family members whenever they go out in public.

Verena is a pastor, and she was extremely eloquent and passionate at times, while at other times she seemed unsure of herself. She continued to share her personal experiences relating to racism and sexism.

"I hate white people!" Verena suddenly proclaimed emphatically, looking directly at Cynthia. Turning her gaze slightly toward Julien, who was sitting behind Cynthia in the men's witnessing circle, she added, "I especially hate white men!" Cynthia responded, "I hear you, Verena. Thank you for speaking your truth—so clearly and directly."

Verena sat in silence for a moment, then went on to give an articulate and impassioned account of the sexual shenanigans taking place among the clergy with whom she collaborates. She said that during retreats and conferences many of her male colleagues from various churches were having affairs or sleeping with their junior women colleagues. They would especially target younger, attractive female ministers for seduction and manipulate them into a box that they can't easily get out of. As a more seasoned, mid-career minister, Verena was privy to what the male ministers were up to, and the men knew it. So they would protect themselves and cover for each other, which included instructing their wives not to talk with or trust Verena. Consequently, many of the ministers' wives never engaged with Verena in a genuine way, while remaining utterly clueless about what was really going on. Verena lamented how the male ministers supported and covered one another's tracks, whereas she experienced neither the support of the ministers, nor their wives. "It's extremely painful to watch all this going on!" she exclaimed.

Then she recounted the story of a priest who had been pressuring her to sleep with him, and Verena would not submit to his advances. Finally, one day he came up to her, shortly before an upcoming retreat, and declared in a haughty voice, "I will have you at this retreat!" So Verena did not attend that retreat, nor did she feel she could tell anyone the real reason she stayed away. She also stressed that churches deny women the right to be who they are. As a pastor, her own church had required her to wear formal bland gowns, but she refused, and instead she wears more colorful, feminine attire.

"I hate men, and I hate my husband," Verena concluded. She recounted how she had divorced her husband but then went back and remarried him, under tremendous pressure from her father. But she explained that she only sleeps after her husband leaves early in the morning, and she drinks herbal teas to get to sleep so she doesn't have to be sexually involved with him.

The previous day in the women's circle, Elana had shared part of her story. But now, in the cross-gender truth forum, she came forward with her full story. Elana's husband beat her and the children regularly. "To protect the children, I used to beg him, 'Hit me instead!' But he wouldn't listen." Later, her husband raped her, which produced their fourth child, a girl. Elana acknowledged that she hated this child because of the rape, which greatly saddened her heart.

At one point, Elana's husband moved another woman into their home to be his lover. He and the new woman lived downstairs, while Elana and her children were relegated to the upstairs, where they had to sleep in the toilet room because it was the only sleeping space available. Elana was forced to work and give all her money to her husband, and to do all the cooking and cleaning. She was basically a slave. "He would never listen to me! Never!" she exclaimed. Her husband would drag her downstairs at times to make her do things for him. Sometimes, in fits of rage, he would throw her babies over the balcony, and Elana had to catch them in her bare hands to save their lives.

As time wore on, Elana became increasingly desperate and miserable. One day she refused to give her husband the money she had earned because she needed it to buy shoes for the children. He flew into a rage and came at her with a knife. Elana was cooking sausages over a hot stove at that moment, and to thwart the imminent attack she reeled around and threw the sausages and hot grease on him. She also hit his live-in lover with the frying pan. Her husband was not wearing a shirt at the time, so his chest was burned. Elana served a jail sentence for this action, and she felt unjustly imprisoned for having defended herself against being potentially murdered. "I didn't know what else to do," she explained. After some time, her husband bailed her out of jail because he wanted her home earning money and doing the chores. The cycle of abuse set in again. It mellowed somewhat over time but never came to an end until her husband died several years later.

More stories emerged, and then Nomfundo moved into the center, picked up the stone, and began to speak about a twelve-year-old girl she had treated at the trauma center. "This young girl was kidnapped, raped repeatedly, and then left to die in a grassy field near the Cape Town airport," she began slowly. "Early the next morning, an airport worker stumbled upon the girl lying in the tall grass." Nomfundo articulated her words with transparent anguish and precise diction. "She was naked, unconscious, covered with blood." Nomfundo held out the stone in front of her with both hands, as if asking it to absorb and bear the wrenching pain of the story. "The girl's body required surgical treatment to heal. Her sense of self and identity were completely obliterated by the experience. I've never treated anyone so utterly shattered."

As Nomfundo spoke, her eyes met the gaze of Kieran as he listened intently from his seat in the outer men's circle. Nomfundo moved toward the edge of the women's circle, reached out with both arms, and silently offered the stone to Kieran, as if to say, "Here, you take this. You are a man, and it was some of your male brothers who did this hideous violence to this girl. Please share in the horrific weight of this tragedy with us." Kieran received the stone and held it in his hands for some time while Nomfundo continued, then he silently handed the stone to the man next to him, who held it for a while and then passed it on. The stone slowly made its way around the silent men's circle.

Tears flowed copiously around the room, not only among the women. Several of the men had also been wiping their eyes, occasionally reaching for a tissue. When the stone was handed to Lloyd, he held it for a few moments, then dissolved into tears, and then he broke into loud sobbing. Given the strong taboo in South African culture against men crying in public, this was a remarkably poignant moment. The room was filled with a spellbound presence, infused with the sound of Lloyd's sobs. Two of the men moved over to join Lloyd at his side, offering hands of reassurance and support as he continued to weep. Nomfundo waited until Lloyd's crying subsided into sniffling before finishing her story.

One after another, the stories from the women's circle continued. At one point, one woman shouted, *Wathinta Abafazi, Wathnta Ibokodo!* and all the women laughed and nodded vigorously in enthusiastic agreement. It's a popular vernacular saying, "If you strike a woman, you strike a rock!," which expresses the solid strength of South African women.

A unique innovation in the forum process emerged spontaneously at one point when one of the women introduced into the circle a large bundle of slender stalks, each one made of light bamboo-like wood about two feet long. She distributed a pile of about twenty sticks to each woman in the circle and gave the following instructions. Whenever someone shared a story or experience, if it also applied to another woman in the group, the latter woman could acknowledge it by simply placing a stalk in the center of the circle. The women's sharing then continued, but this time, at the end of each sharing, other women would quietly add their stalks to the center, signifying in pregnant silence that a similar experience had happened to them as well. In this way, the power of the women's truth forum was magnified significantly, as everyone in the room could witness how prevalent these experiences were for the other women in the circle. The stalks were soon dubbed "me-too sticks," and this useful innovation continued for the remainder of the women's forum, and was adopted for the men's truth forum as well.

Toward the end, a woman named Boniswa took the "talking earth" and stood up. Speaking with passionate conviction, she implored the men to look beyond the appearances of women. "Most men usually only see us for our physical appearance—not for who we really are. Please! Look beyond the body, look beyond our outer appearances! We are women! To be truly known, we must be known from the inside outward, not from the outside in."

As the women's truth forum came to a close, the men were given a chance to reflect back what they had heard. Many women reported how healing it was to hear men acknowledging the specific details of women's pain. At one point Umoja stepped forward and placed his hands gently on each woman's back, in silent gratitude and acknowledgment.

After the women's truth form, something broke open in Elana. She grabbed one of the facilitators and started twirling her around in joy. "I'm doing so much better!" she beamed, "although I'm feeling partly bad, because I feel I betrayed my children. They went through all the abuse, too, and we all promised each other that we would never tell anyone what happened to us." Elana continued to chew on this last bit as the group broke for lunch.

## Men's Truth Forum

In the afternoon, it was the men's turn in the inner circle, with the women in silent witness around them. To speak openly about personal experiences relating to gender, women, and sexuality was a highly unusual experience for South African men—indeed, this was a first for nearly all of them. The process of preparing the men to address gender issues in this plenary format was greatly enhanced by the men's truth mandala the day before, in which many powerful stories had come forth. Nevertheless, some were still slow to come forward with deeper levels of their personal experience as men. The facilitators helped move the process along at points by sharing some of their own experiences as a way to support the men and give them permission to speak out in new ways. Two of the men, Howard and Craig, work professionally with battered women, and their presence also helped the other men in the group to embrace and open up about gender issues. An earlier guest faculty presentation from Dr. Kopano Retele, a specialist on men's issues in South Africa, had also helped to model a different way to be a South African man.

Once a few of the men took the bold plunge, the way was made easier for the others. This process is similar to men's work elsewhere in which a few courageous individuals initiate the process and others soon follow. A fruitful avenue of entry for some men in the circle was to speak about their daughters, for whom they held great love coupled with grave concern for their safety and well-being as they came of age in South African society.

The painful reality of everyday violence in South African society was brought home right at the outset. One of the men, Isaac, was getting a ride to the workshop with Melina each morning. That very morning, before Melina arrived at Isaac's home, a gunfight broke out on the street right in front of Isaac's house. His next-door neighbor is a woman who had been fighting with her ex-lover, with whom she had a child. That morning the ex-lover showed up at her house and began slapping the woman around. Then her current boyfriend came out with a gun, and the two men started a gun battle in the street. Had Melina arrived at Isaac's home a half-hour earlier, she would have driven right into the cross fire. Isaac didn't know whether anyone had been hurt.

Several of the men's individual sharings are summarized here briefly:

Umoja said that his wife had left him three times. Although he never explained in detail what had happened, he spoke about how painful it had been. He was reduced to feeling utterly worthless and rejected. He also spoke of deep concern for his two daughters. As a religious minister, he does not want to succumb to fear, he explained, but now that his daughters are coming of age, he prays that they will be protected from rape, sexual harassment, abuse, and AIDS—in a society rife with sexual violence. He conceded that there was only so much he could do, even though he feels concern and vulnerability on their behalf on a daily basis. Several men added their stalks to the center after his sharing, indicating their deep concern for their own daughters' welfare and safety.

Isaac is an earnest young man with an angina heart condition that he's had since birth. He began by relating a painful story from three years previously. He was with his three closest friends one day when suddenly a gunfight broke out in the neighborhood where they were walking. Caught in the cross fire, he and his companions scrambled to get out of harm's way as shots rang out all around them. Two of his friends fell to the ground as bullets tore through their flesh. Isaac and his third friend made it, but his other two friends both died that day. Isaac had been devastated by the loss. His soulful eyes welled up with tears as he recounted the story.

Isaac continues to carry a deep grief about the loss of these friends, which was further compounded by the more recent loss of yet another friend—to AIDS. Meanwhile, he is concerned about still another of his male friends, who is engaging in risky sexual behavior. Isaac has repeatedly warned him of the danger of contracting AIDS but the friend is not taking sufficient precautions.

Isaac spoke of his mother's response and advice to him about the tragic loss of his friends, which was to simply forget about them and move on. He shared other anecdotes about his mother: how she tried to raise him to be tough, "like a man," but it was against his intrinsic nature. He recounted a confrontation once with his brother in which he refused to fight. Overhearing this, his mother then instructed his brother to beat him up, which his brother proceeded to do. Isaac said the emotional pain of his mother's command to his brother was far greater than the physical pain of the beating itself.

Isaac works with abused women. Both he and another male participant, Craig, are employed by an NGO called Woman Awakened, which rehabilitates women who have been traumatized by domestic violence. Both were therefore much more sensitized to women's plight than most South African men, and their presence in the group helped greatly to raise awareness among the men in the group.

Lloyd was absent for most of the men's truth forum due to meetings in parliament. However, he had shared passionately in the truth mandala the day before. He spoke about how his team of colleagues had just prevailed in a major parliamentary battle that culminated in the passage of the Civil Union Bill for same-sex marriages. This had been a revealing process that demonstrated the degree to which various parliamentarians took seriously the Bill of Rights in the South African constitution, which guarantees equality for all citizens regardless of racial and personal differences, including specifically sexual orientation. Lloyd spoke of the need for taking the equality of women and men seriously, which it seemed not all MPs were equally committed to. Nevertheless, he maintained that the constitution of South Africa is the most advanced of any nation in the world regarding human rights and racial and gender justice. He added that for the urgent work of gender healing and reconciliation within the communities and religious congregations throughout South Africa, the constitution was a more powerful and effective tool than the Bible.

Lloyd also said that the Civil Union Bill may lead to the sanctioning of gay marriage in South Africa. He said he was hopeful, but it was uncertain whether this would come to pass.

Craig shared his thoughts about the spiraling tragedy of rampant sexual abuse and rape in South Africa. He expressed deep concern that young girls have increasingly become victims as rapists seek out younger victims in the hope of avoiding AIDS infection, or else because of the prevalent myth that having sex with a virgin is a cure for AIDS. Hence, many men infected with AIDS have been raping young girls, even infants.

Shortly before the workshop began, Kieran had shared his fear that as an American facilitation team we would come in with all the "answers" and do most of the talking. He referenced his frustration with trainers and facilitators from the United States in previous workshops he had done. He later told us he was pleased to find that we had come in not as experts but as learners.

Kieran opened his sharing by relating some childhood stories. Once, as a young boy, he had become frustrated with his sister while trying to put up a tent, and he started to hit her. He was supposed to stake down the tent, and he whacked her with the mallet, though not very hard, he said. For this he was beaten by his father—"hided until it drew blood," as he put it. "You *never* hit your sister, and you never hit a woman!" his father screamed at him. He was also beaten for childhood sex play.

Kieran expressed his passion for his work, which entails implementing the Alternatives to Violence Project (AVP) in South

Africa. He shared eloquently about how he had come from a position of white male privilege, at first taking all the associated benefits for granted. But witnessing events in Soweto during the apartheid regime changed him. He woke up and saw the incredible racism and injustice. As a result, many of his fellow countrymen were leaving South Africa in disgust and despair. But Kieran made the decision to stay and engage in the struggle against apartheid. He became involved in anti-apartheid activism, disseminating information and writing. Through this work he met Oni, who touched him deeply. Then he was arrested and spent a month in prison. Just after he was released, Oni was arrested, and she spent a year in solitary confinement. Not long after Oni was released, the two of them became a couple.

Kieran holds strong views about the value and importance of gender work, and he articulated them eloquently in his unassuming manner: "This work of gender reconciliation challenges the foundations of every major cultural institution in our society: the military, the church, the government, the corporations, the service professions, the educational system." Kieran paused, allowing the power of his words to sink in before continuing in his calm, confident voice. "In every case, these institutions are lopsided—conferring unfair advantages upon men, to be sure. But, at a deeper level, these institutions are structured in an imbalanced manner, favoring masculine over feminine values, which is harmful to everyone in society—women and men. To embark upon this work of gender reconciliation is to rattle the very foundations of our society, across the board. It is absolutely essential work."

Kieran went on to give a specific example, describing how innocent young men are profoundly betrayed by the military system, an arena he knows well. In every nation state, he explained, the military system soaks up tender young men—so young they have barely left their childhood behind—and conditions them to reject their own innate intelligence and sensitivity as human beings. They are trained to kill, taught not to think for themselves, trained to reject anything "feminine" as intrinsically weak and inferior, conditioned to regard women as objects of sexual pleasure, and drilled to obey superiors' commands without reflection or consideration, no matter how insane or irrational. Their budding sexuality in particular is coopted to serve military purposes, and their capacity for relational intimacy with women is severely impaired or destroyed. He said that the military system cannot function without this deep structural gender imbalance, which is imprinted ruthlessly and early in the young man's life—at a time when he is innocent, tender, impressionable, and not yet capable of standing on his own as an adult. In this way the young man's adult personality, mindset, and values are precisely molded to fit the needs of the military machine—and his humanity is betrayed.

Other powerful stories continued to emerge in the men's truth forum. One man spoke about his adolescent sexuality, which entailed masturbation with pornographic pictures of girls in magazines. These experiences were deeply imprinted and were later projected onto his relationships with actual women, whose bodies he compared to the idealized pictures in the magazines. After his sharing, every one of the men in the circle placed a stalk in the center, signifying that some version of this same experience was common to all of them.

Another man shared that many years back he had carried on a secret affair during his first marriage. His wife had trusted him completely, and when the affair came to light she was totally shattered by the betrayal of trust. Again, several stalks were quietly added to the central pile. He concluded his story by saying that they had divorced, and she remarried another man. Although she and he had remained friends afterward, he said the experience had caused her lasting damage.

The men's truth forum came to a close, and the women were given a chance to reflect back what they had heard and what was stirred in them. Verena summarized the feeling of many women when she said, "Just hearing men acknowledge these things helps so much. That's all I ever really wanted from my husband: if only he could have acknowledged what he did."

At this moment, a beautiful process of reconciliation suddenly began to unfold spontaneously within the group. It started when one of the women remembered how warm and nurturing it had felt when Umoja placed his hands gently on her back at the end of the women's truth forum. Recalling this, she moved forward and placed her hands on one man's back. The other women followed suit, placing their hands on all the men's backs. Then the women began to sing softly—a beautiful South African chant. As they continued singing, the men joined in, gently rocking back and forth. Then, after a short while, the men stood up, turned around, and faced the women. Everyone continued singing in two concentric circles, the women and men facing each other. Then the inner circle slowly began to rotate so that the women and men moved slowly past each other, with each woman making eye contact with each man, and vice versa. Radiant eyes and touching smiles filled everyone's heart as the chant continued, eventually culminating in a resounding conclusion. It was an exquisite ritual of reconciliation that lasted nearly half an hour—inspired naturally by the brave and beautiful work this group had accomplished together.

As the group shifted into break time, there were plenty of warm, loving hugs all around, coupled with many earnest and heartfelt exchanges and acknowledgments between various individuals in the group. The participants thanked one another deeply for taking part so authentically in such a courageous and intimate process together. It was beautiful to witness these wonderful women and men weave themselves back together into a warm and trusting community after such intensive and vulnerable communication among them.

On the final morning of the workshop, much of the time was spent in the honoring ceremonies which the women and men created for one another. After early morning planning circles were completed, amongst much joyful enthusiasm and playful banter, the two rituals were conducted.

## Men's Honoring Ceremony

The men went first and escorted the women into the room in pairs, carefully seating them in a semicircle. The women sat quietly, glancing at one another with quizzical looks as they surveyed the other end of the room, where the men had built a rather large, curious-looking structure. It was a kind of tower consisting of some twenty chairs, all carefully stacked and balanced, one upon the other. The structure took up more than a third of the room and reached nearly to the ceiling.

As the ritual opened for the women, the men announced that this tower of chairs represented the patriarchy. They proceeded to proclaim their commitment to dismantle and topple this oppressive structure—which holds both women and men in bondage to a system of oppression and injustice. The men then surrounded the tower of chairs. Reaching down in unison, each man pulled out one chair leg from the bottom simultaneously. The entire edifice of chairs came tumbling down with a resounding and dramatic CRASH! onto the floor. The skit was merely symbolic, but the power was impressive. The women were moved.

The men quickly straightened up the chairs, then lined up in a row and stood before the women. On behalf of all the men, Lloyd stepped forward and solemnly delivered the following declaration:

### Declaration to Our Sisters

Declaration presented by the men to the women in the men's ceremony for the women: *Acknowledgment of Women's Pain and Struggles, and Our Commitment to Bring Down the Structures of Patriarchy*

*We have met over the past five days in community as men, and in community with you as men and women. We have listened to each other's stories—some personal, others told on behalf of vulnerable, degraded, hurt, brutalized human beings—all for no other reason than that they are women, sisters, mothers, and girl children.*

*We have heard, too, that through the social structures of power and decision making, many of our brothers have abused our intended roles of caring and protection—for selfish power, and personal pleasure and gain.*

*The bonds of humanity have been broken.*

*We acknowledge that we have shared in the unfair and unjust advantage that has upset the Creator's intended balance of human relationships for love, companionship, and cooperation.*

*We have been complicit in breaking the intended dream of equality.*

*So now we come forward to say to you: we are sorry. We affirm that we want to start anew. Therefore, we now mark our foreheads with ash—the dust from which we have come, and to which we shall return—as an act to symbolize our sorrow, our apology, and our atonement.*

*And we come with a willingness to express, not our guilt—because guilt weighs us down and gives a burden we cannot bear—but rather, our responsibility. So we ask, will you accept our offer to take responsibility, as we commit ourselves to live out—and challenge and support all men everywhere to live and work for—gender equality, and thereby seek reconciliation?*

After this declaration was read, the men brought forward a small dish full of ash which they had obtained by burning the stick that had symbolized men's anger during the men's truth forum. Each man marked his forehead with ash. Then the men explained that they were going to wash and massage the women's hands. The men lined up with bowls of water, towels, massage cream, and chocolates—and began singing a soft chant as they started gently washing, drying, and massaging the women's hands, rubbing in moisturizing cream, and finishing with a chocolate. They continued in a row, tending carefully to each woman.

Afterward, the men lined up again before the women, and each man stepped forward and spoke to his personal complicity in the patriarchy and offered his own commitment of personal action to end the unjust oppression of women. For example, Howard said: "On behalf of all men who have hurt women, and for those women I myself have caused pain, I am very, very sorry. I commit to intervene in other men's unconscious complicity in perpetuating the patriarchy. In particular, I will never pass by a situation of violence without taking action, or overlook a nearby scream or similar sound of distress without checking up on it."

After each man had acknowledged his complicity and offered his commitment, the men brought closure to their ritual by bowing in silence before the women. They departed the room in silence.

## Women's Honoring Ceremony

Deeply moved, the women sat quietly for several minutes, taking in the power of the men's ritual offering. Then, inspired and charged up, they completed preparations for their own ritual.

A few minutes later, the women came out and escorted each man into the room, seating them carefully in a beautifully prepared circle. The light was dimmed, and stirring music was played as the women began a gorgeous dance of veils—each woman carrying one or more colorful, flowing veils of many different fabrics. The women began to weave in and out among the men, dancing ecstatically, whirling the veils around themselves and all around and between the men—draping them across the men's arms and legs and chests and sensuously sliding them across the men's faces and heads. The men sat enthralled with the colorful spectacle of dancing women, smiling eyes, and subtle sensuality as the women continued their dance for several minutes.

As Kieran remarked afterward, "The women became more and more beautiful as the workshop progressed!" and this was even more true now as the women danced with magnificent grace and open-hearted joy, their eyes shining with love. Actually, this phenomenon of mounting beauty had begun to gather increased momentum on the previous day after the women had opened their hearts and poured out their wrenching pain and anguish, which was then genuinely acknowledged and felt by the men. At that point, something deep within the women began to relax and let go, bringing them a deeper sense of inner peace and security. And with this inner release, the women's natural beauty and radiance began to stream forth naturally—unimpeded by fear, contraction, or judgment. This inner opening and expansion continued even more so now as the women danced for the men, offering their heart-to-heart blessings.

This process is something we have observed consistently over the years in facilitating gender reconciliation work. As the healing work progresses, and trust builds, the inner beauty of both women and men is released and begins to shine out—sometimes tentatively at first, like the petals of a flower opening to the sun. But as the gender reconciliation work unfolds, the fragrance and resplendent color of the soul's beauty and inner light is gradually and inevitably revealed—an exquisite emanation of our true nature. And when this takes place, people begin to glimpse what a huge price we are paying in our daily socially conditioned lives in which this extraordinary beauty and intangible fragrance is covered over by thick layers of social and cultural conditioning—so completely that most people have entirely forgotten that this inner beauty even exists.

After this sumptuous opening, the women stood in a circle alongside the men, and several of the women stepped forward, one at a time, each offering her personal blessing or testimony to the power of the work we had all been doing. Below are some of the testimonies offered by individual women to the men:

- "You have dedicated yourselves to walk this journey with us—giving all you have: your mind, spirit, soul, and body. Working together, we will close this gap between us."
- "I now realize that, as women, we are not alone. I appreciate the sacrifice you have made to take this journey with us, to commit yourselves to bring peace and the spirit of *Ubuntu* in our society."
- "You have come up unexpectedly with great courage, love, support, and words of wisdom to bring hope, light, and happiness. I would like to say that you have been wonderful throughout the workshop by being able to take this long journey with us."
- "Roar, young lions, roar! I have a great joy in my heart for the wonderful moments I spent with you!"

After several of these touching testimonies, the women broke out in a wonderfully glorious African song, bringing closure to their ritual. The men joined in, and the whole group was soon engulfed in joyous celebration of song and dance. The community dissolved into plenty of laughter, warm hugs, gentle tears, and deep gratitude, expressed in joyful reverie and intimacy.

## Integration and Closure

The final part of the workshop focused on integration, evaluation, and closure. Cynthia and Karambu outlined some of the major challenges that can arise when shifting back into familiar work and family environments, and summarized practical ways to carry the new skills and insights back into daily life. Then Karambu led a focused integration exercise, supporting participants to explore more deeply what some of the specific concerns and challenges were. Then, according to participants' stated needs and concerns, she facilitated the formation of several small groups to delve more deeply into the challenges of integration back into the workplace and home life. After lunch the plenary reconvened to hear reports back from the small groups, and each participant shared the next steps he or she planned to take. For example, Isaac came to clarity about the need for gender reconciliation work in his own village, and said that his first step would be to go back to the people in his village and truly listen to them. He realized it was important to begin by listening deeply in order to elicit from his fellow villagers what they most needed and wanted. Based on this, he would decide specific steps for introducing gender reconciliation work into his village.

In the closing circle, many expressions of appreciation and gratitude were made. In particular, several participants thanked Nozizwe profusely for her courage and foresight in convening this gathering, emphasizing that she had brought a much needed work between women and men to South Africa. We closed with a final performance of the Love's Unfolding dance, followed by a closing round of African song—with shining eyes and voices uplifted in joyous and resounding harmony. Everyone present knew that together as women and men we had blazed a unique and unprecedented trail of gender reconciliation in South Africa. In our hearts, we all hoped that this joyous conclusion was just the seed of an auspicious beginning for a new form of harmony and reconciliation between women and men in the great Rainbow Republic of South Africa.

## Elana's Follow-up

Elana had come to a place of deep forgiveness by the end of the workshop, and she said she didn't feel hate anymore. Her entire demeanor had changed, and she said she felt her story of abuse was finally out of her.

Two days after the workshop Elana invited Satyana's facilitators to attend a meeting of her women's group, to which she and four of the other workshop participants belonged. Two Satyana facilitators attended, along with five women who had been in the gender reconciliation workshop, each one wearing her name tag from our workshop. The women proceeded to speak enthusiastically about their experience of the gender work to the other women in the circle.

Then Elana recounted her follow-up story. The day after the workshop she went to visit her husband's grave, and there she forgave him for all the abuse. Afterward, she paid a visit to the home of his former lover (the woman who had moved into her home downstairs), with whom she had had no contact whatsoever for many years. When Elana knocked, the woman answered the door in a wheelchair. Elana explained that she had come because she wanted to forgive her. The woman was very grateful for this gesture from Elana, and invited her in. She told Elana that she had been thinking of her recently, and she explained that she believed the reason she was now in a wheelchair was because of what she had done to Elana. The two women had a remarkable healing conversation. Elana felt deeply released and free after this exchange.

Elana had returned to work the next day and was visibly radiant and peaceful. When her boss began discussing work matters early on her first day back, Elana interjected, "You didn't even ask about the workshop!" Her boss smiled and replied, "You don't have to tell us about the workshop. We can see it on your face!" Elana explained that all her coworkers commented on how different she looked. Then her boss inquired, "Do tell us about the workshop, please." Elana began speaking about the workshop, and the ensuing conversation with her colleagues was so engrossing that it lasted nearly six hours, until three o'clock in the afternoon.

## Introduction to Gender Reconciliation for Ela Gandhi's Community in Durban

Ela Gandhi, the granddaughter of Mahatma Gandhi, lives in Durban, South Africa. When she heard through our co-facilitator Karambu that our workshop was being conducted in Cape Town, Ms. Gandhi became enthusiastic and invited us to come to Durban to present an introductory program on gender reconciliation in her community. As it happened, she already had a two-day gathering planned for some twenty women in late November, with Karambu as facilitator, and she asked if we could change the program to present Satyana's gender reconciliation work instead. We responded that we were open to the idea in principle, but to be most effective the program required men to participate as well. We also advised her that in a two-day framework the work would be much less comprehensive than the Cape Town program. Ms. Gandhi encouraged us to come nevertheless, and she said she would get straight to work on finding men to join the workshop.

We designed a two-day format for a group that would likely include many more women than men. Will Keepin had a prior commitment to lead a retreat in India that could not be changed, so Cynthia Brix led the Durban program, with Karambu Ringera as co-facilitator. The program was a much abbreviated version of the gender reconciliation work we had presented in Cape Town. There were sixteen participants, including three men, from NGOs working for grassroots organizations, including a women's shelter for domestic violence, a community arts and garden project located in the Phoenix (Gandhi's settlement), the Mavela Creche, a children's center located in rural Durban, and employees of Satyagraha, an organization that promotes the Gandhian tradition of nonviolence. Racial composition of the group was six Indian, eight black, two mixed-race ("colored"), plus Cynthia and Karambu.

This workshop was a new experience for most, if not all, of the participants. For many, it seemed they were easing into experiential

ways of working in groups. For the most part the workshop proceeded according to familiar patterns. However, in the truth mandala only four people stood and spoke, including Karambu and
Cynthia, who modeled the process. A male participant opened the
mandala, and Ela was the final person to speak. The man who
did come forward spoke passionately about the betrayal he experienced from his parents and the ritual work he was doing to move
beyond this betrayal, though he did not give details. The fact that
others were not so forthcoming was understandable given that this
form of experiential work was new to most people and there had
not been time in this miniworkshop to cultivate the deeper work in
women's and men's circles that is so crucial to prepare participants
to share vulnerable truths in mixed company. Cynthia closed the
truth mandala with the reflection that "Perhaps our silence signi-
fies just how difficult it is to speak truth to our pain, our wounds,
our anger, our sorrow, our need. Yet this silence creates the space
for deeper wisdom to arise. Some would call this silence space for
God to speak."

This workshop was a very brief introduction to gender reconciliation, put together on short notice and again under suboptimal
conditions—especially with so few men present. Nevertheless, it
seemed to plant an important seed for bringing gender reconciliation to another part of South Africa. Ela Gandhi expressed strong
interest in holding a longer workshop in 2007, with invited guests
from the mayor's office and other governmental departments in
Durban. In the closing circle Ms. Gandhi said that she was very
gratified that the workshop integrated the spiritual dimension so
fully. She explained that her past experience in workshops was generally that either a particular educational training is given or that
the workshop is in essence a spiritual retreat. She said this was
the first time she had experienced a workshop that fully integrated
both transformative learning and spiritual components in a balanced manner.

## Conclusions and Future Potential for
## Gender Reconciliation Work in South Africa

"I have been looking for a long time to find a way to bring healing and reconciliation between women and men here in South Africa," Nozizwe told us after the event had ended. "And this work is the answer," she concluded. "We need much more of this work in South Africa."

Nozizwe's conclusion seemed to be widely shared by the other participants in the Cape Town workshop. Although this workshop was only a small beginning, conducted under conditions that were far from ideal, this pilot program in gender reconciliation clearly touched the hearts of these South African men and women deeply. We heard unanimity of voices calling for the infusion of gender reconciliation work into South African society. Some participants said that our gender reconciliation program should be implemented in every province, others stressed that it should take place again every year, others said that every citizen of South Africa should experience it, while still others focused on the urgent need for it within specific sectors such as the parliament, the churches, or the academy.

The Deputy Chief Whip of the ANC, Andries Nel, strongly recommended to us that we schedule our next program on gender reconciliation for Members of Parliament at an optimal time of parliamentary recess in South Africa, when more MPs could attend more readily. Keith Vermeulen, director of the parliamentary office of the South African Council of Churches (SACC), expressed interest in convening a special gathering on gender reconciliation for leading pastors and clergy in South Africa. His colleague, Themba Mntambo, a Methodist minister who also serves on the SACC, also expressed enthusiasm about this prospect.

Jeremy Routledge (Nozizwe's husband) works with Phaphama, an NGO that works on alternatives to violence (AVP). He told us this was the best workshop that he and Nozizwe had ever been to, and he expressed interest in implementing gender reconciliation work within several networks, including (a) the Quaker Peace Network-Africa, a network of Quaker peace activists in Africa (Rwanda, Burundi, Kenya, Uganda, DRC, South Africa), (b) the

Alternatives to Violence Project (AVP) network in Africa, which includes Nigeria, Namibia, Zimbabwe, and Sudan, in addition to the countries already mentioned, and (c) possibly at the men's and women's prisons at Pollsmoor.

The unanimous enthusiasm for this work expressed by participants in this pilot project naturally led us to ask: why is there such a strongly perceived need for gender reconciliation in South Africa? Indeed, while most countries across the globe could benefit tremendously from gender reconciliation, it seems that the current social and psychological climate in South Africa is, on the whole, more ripe for gender reconciliation work than other places we have worked. Several possible reasons come to mind as likely contributing factors:

First, South Africa has just come through a profound and unprecedented healing process through the work of the Truth and Reconciliation Commission (TRC). For an entire nation to rise to this level of mature responsibility to heal and reconcile its own racism through a systematic program of spiritual forgiveness is unprecedented in modern history. And yet, just as racism is a form of structural inequality that arbitrarily privileges one group of human beings over another, so too is gender injustice. Having embarked in earnest upon reconciling the one issue (racism), the other (gender and sexism) naturally cries out for healing and reconciliation, which to date has yet to begin.

Second, the Rainbow Republic is a new, young nation—with a fresh new beginning supported by a new constitution that many analysts agree is the most advanced human rights constitution in the world. In particular, the constitution guarantees every citizen of South Africa gender justice, including choice of sexual orientation. A Gender Equity Commission has been established to implement this noble vision in society, although by all accounts it has yet to achieve significant progress. So there is a clarion call for tackling the ancient problem of gender oppression. Moreover, at this moment the Rainbow Republic is just twelve years old, entering its adolescence as it were, so it's time to address issues of gender and sexuality. Notwithstanding this cute metaphor, we asked Nozizwe if there might be anything to this, and she confirmed that indeed the nation is entering an adolescent phase, which can be seen in many aspects of the society. In particular, gender reconciliation needs to be implemented sooner rather than later—before age-old patterns and "patriarchal" imbalances are allowed to take root and become entrenched as the social norm.

Finally, beyond these overarching factors there are the immediate and highly disturbing symptoms of a nation plagued by rampant sexual violence, rape, sexual harassment, and AIDS—all of which have reached epidemic proportions in South Africa. An ironic byproduct of the fall of apartheid is the dramatic rise of rape and sexual violence in South Africa. The AIDS crisis is extreme, and is exacerbated by sexual aggression and violence. Recent high profile sexual harassment cases resulting in the dismissal of the ANC Chief Whip Mbuelo Goniwe and the Indonesian ambassador Norman Mashabane highlight the pervasive extent of sexual harassment in South Africa, and will likely pave the way for other victims to step forward and demand their day in court. All these factors taken together in this burgeoning nation call for a literal revolution of consciousness and awareness in regard to sexuality and gender equality. Indeed, perhaps the nation of South Africa—fueled by dire necessity, an explicit constitutional mandate, and the recent success of the TRC in healing the racism of apartheid—will lead the way in gender reconciliation for other nations to follow.

# CHAPTER 11

# *Lessons from a Decade of Gender Healing*

By love has appeared everything that exists.
By love, that which does not exist, appears as existing.

—Shabestari

People from many walks of life have experienced Satyana's gender reconciliation work since its inception fifteen years ago. In all, about seven hundred people have participated in one or more five-day programs. Professionals attending the workshops have included physicians and health professionals, psychotherapists, social workers, environmental activists, government officials, clergy and religious leaders, academics and teachers, graduate students (and undergraduate and high school students), artists and musicians, Zen monks and nuns, social activists, politicians, blue-collar workers, Catholic nuns and priests. As emphasized in earlier chapters, gender injustice and oppression are universal afflictions—on both personal and political levels—that virtually defy race, ethnicity, class, age, and sexual orientation. Introducing the work in other countries such as India, Croatia, and South Africa has supported the healing of gender relations in cross-cultural, multiracial, multiethnic, and interreligious contexts.

To assess the value of Satyana's gender healing work and its effects on participants' lives, probably the best approach is to turn to those who have direct experience with the work. This chapter summarizes feedback, insights, reflections, and learnings from past participants in Satyana's gender reconciliation work. Special emphasis is given here to survey results from professionals with extensive experience in Satyana's work. These longtime participants have returned to the work multiple times, reflecting their commitment to awakening deeper places of healing and reconciliation in themselves, in their communities, and in society as a whole. Many of them consciously intend—by courageously delving into the depths of their own gender healing and reconciliation—to serve as a healing force or conduit for their brothers and sisters across the globe, and it is largely through this selfless intention on behalf of others that they discover the deeper spiritual dimensions of the work.

## Written Evaluations from Participants

At the conclusion of each gender reconciliation event we have gathered written evaluations from participants. This feedback has been utilized over the years to assess the impact and value of the work from participants' perspectives and to make improvements in the process, fine-tune the exercises, and provide specific feedback for the facilitation team. Taken as a whole, these evaluations have provided a great deal of useful information and encouraging feedback reflecting a high degree of enthusiasm and validation for the gender reconciliation work.

As examples of this feedback, the following are a few direct quotes that convey the tenor of much of the feedback we receive in written evaluations. The first three participants quoted below attended two or more workshops, the others attended just once.

*I was deeply moved and changed, and am profoundly grateful for the whole experience. I see more about how I re-enact dysfunctional gender scenarios, despite my conscious commitment to change. Satyana Institute's vision [of gender reconciliation] is unique, and uniquely valuable to the world.*
—Peter Rutter, M.D., author of *Sex in the Forbidden Zone: When Men in Power Betray Women's Trust*

*An extraordinary and gentle journey into the painful feelings of separation between men and women. Witnessing ourselves and each other with truth and compassion, we begin to see the unity and perfection of our lives.*
—Seisen Saunders, Sensei, Zen teacher, Maezumi Roshi and
    Bernie Glassman lineages

*The most valuable aspect of the gender work was simply having the opportunity to discuss, openly, unafraid, with an extremely well-intended mixed group, issues that mean so much, and that we "framed" the whole exchange in spiritual terms.*
—Carol Lee Flinders, Ph.D., author of *At the Root of This
    Longing: Reconciling a Spiritual Hunger with a Feminist
    Thirst*

*The workshop opened more doors in my heart. It also brought light within me to ensure that I understand problems our society is facing. This program should rotate in all South African Provinces.*
—Sello Mukhara, African National Congress (ANC),
    Parliamentary Caucus of South Africa

*This workshop makes me a new woman and a new mother. I forgave my husband, and I forgive men. We must have these workshops each year.*
—Delores Ismail, The Women's Centre, Cape Town

*My conviction grows daily that what you're doing with gender reconciliation is an absolutely untapped educational experience. It was a change-making workshop on a profound level and is making a really large difference in my ministry.*
—Rev. Robert Thayer, Unitarian Universalist minister

*The love that unfolded was incredible!! Thank you for being part of the healing process of and for Africa!!*
—Karambu Ringera, Director, International Peace Initiatives,
    Nairobi, Kenya

Notwithstanding the upbeat enthusiasm of these reflections, they were all given in written evaluations at the end of events, and such evaluations tend to be of rather limited value for assessing the true impact of the work. There are several reasons for this. First, evaluations at the end of workshops are typically biased in a favorable direction, coming at the end of a process that usually concludes on a very positive note—a time when participants are feeling especially good and generous. Second, the majority of these evaluations do not generally delve deeply into the underlying reasons behind their specific feedback, whether enthusiastic or otherwise. This is natural because participants are focused on completion and closure with one another and the group, and many are eager to get back home. Third, and more important, such evaluations by their nature do not provide insights into how the work is integrated into participants' lives in the days and weeks after the workshop ends, which is the true test of the work. So there is no information about the lasting effects of the work in people's daily lives—"where the rubber meets the road," so to speak. Finally, such evaluations generally only focus on one particular workshop, and thus they don't shed light on the deeper or long-term impacts of the work, particularly in the case of people who engage in the work extensively over time.

## Qualitative Survey of Certified Facilitators

For the reasons cited above, we chose to perform a qualitative survey with a smaller number of people who had extensive experience in the gender reconciliation work rather than a quantitative survey of a larger number of participants with less experience in the work. However, in taking this approach, we do not deny the value of these more summary evaluations such as those quoted above. Indeed, in view of their favorable nature, a more systematic survey and analysis may be called for at some point down the road to probe both the benefits and limitations of the gender reconciliation work in this broad context.

To obtain a more indepth assessment of Satyana's gender reconciliation work, including its longitudinal effects over time, we conducted an informal qualitative survey of a small number of professionals who are deeply familiar with Satyana's gender reconciliation process.

The women and men surveyed were chosen because they completed Satyana's professional gender reconciliation training program, and each of them has between six and ten years of experience with this work. These people can therefore portray—for better or for worse—the deeper effects and long-term impacts of Satyana's gender reconciliation work. Of course, from a statistical perspective, because these are self-selected professionals who chose to engage deeply in Satyana's work there is the possibility of a systematic bias in their responses. Nevertheless, these are the people who have the most experience with the work and know it best, and we believe their survey responses give the most comprehensive and accurate account of the strengths and weaknesses of Satyana's gender reconciliation work to date. Taken together, these survey responses constitute an informal, preliminary longitudinal study that could motivate a more formal evaluation at some point in the future. The detailed survey responses are presented in Appendix B. The remainder of this chapter summarizes the major findings from the survey.

## Common Themes in the Survey

Certain themes emerged repeatedly from the survey respondents quoted in Appendix B in relation to their experience of the effects of Satyana's gender reconciliation work. These themes included (1) the importance of the spiritual dimensions of the work, (2) increased compassion and understanding, (3) deepened relationships in marriage and with children, (4) integration of gender reconciliation in the workplace, and (5) the importance of intra-gender dynamics in the work. Among these, the most frequently voiced themes were the importance of the spiritual aspects of gender reconciliation work and the increase of compassion experienced through the work.

Several respondents spoke about the deepening of their intimate partnerships or marriages, including decreased psychological projections in relation to their respective spouses or partners. In some cases the gender reconciliation work fostered a deep healing that had not otherwise been forthcoming in intimate partnerships or marriages. Relationships with family members also had positively improved and expanded, especially with sons and daughters.

Integration of the gender work within the workplace was another prominent theme. The majority of the respondents—men and women alike—stated that they use what they experienced and learned in Satyana's gender work in their work environments on a regular basis. Several respondents asserted that they are now unable and unwilling to remain silent about gender injustice and oppression in the workplace. Two of the women said they were more aware of gender injustice and were no longer afraid to directly confront people or the issues, despite the fact that speaking about gender issues in the workplace is not always welcome.

Intragender aspects of the work also emerged as a key theme within these reflections. Participants often come to gender reconciliation work expecting primarily to confront issues with the opposite sex. Not infrequently, however, critical issues arise within the women's group or the men's group and this intragender aspect becomes one of the most crucial elements in the work. We have seen several examples of this earlier, such as in Chapter 3. During Satyana's yearlong training program, the women's group had to work through some deep-seated intragender conflicts among themselves before they were even ready to begin broaching issues with the men. All the male respondents highlighted the intragender aspects of the work and expressed a deeper connection with other men that inspired each of them independently to take up a new leadership role working with men.

The survey asked for ways to improve Satyana's gender reconciliation program, and several suggestions emerged, most of which pertain to the practical challenges of expanding the institutional capacity to deliver the gender reconciliation work, as demand for it grows. Specific suggestions are reproduced in Appendix B, and are being accounted for in Satyana Institute's planning for the future.

The benefits of Satyana's gender reconciliation work, as gleaned from the survey responses, are summarized in the following eleven points:

1. *Increased awareness and experiences of the spiritual dimensions of gender healing and reconciliation*

2.  Increased compassion for others and sensitivity to their life's challenges

3.  Heightened awareness of pervasive gender dynamics—on gross and subtle levels—that play out in individuals, interpersonal relationships, and social and cultural contexts

4.  Noticeable healing of long-standing gender wounds, often bringing new freedom and energy into family, work, and social contexts

5.  Increased awareness and sensitivity to intragender dynamics, and deeper same-sex relationships

6.  Improved communication in intimate relationships with spouse and family members of both sexes

7.  Deepened capacity for intimacy and increased confidence and ability to share honestly in group settings

8.  Direct experience of the tremendous healing power of community, as well as the power of cultural conditioning

9.  Renewed optimism regarding intimate relationships and harmonious collaboration between women and men

10. Increased ability and willingness to address challenging gender patterns operative in daily life at home, work, and in social settings

11. Increased awareness and experiences of the "transcendent" or archetypal nature of masculine and feminine principles manifesting in all creation

In closing, all the survey respondents strongly endorsed the wider dissemination and implementation of Satyana's gender reconciliation work. The support and enthusiasm from this group of professionals illustrates their deep commitment to carrying this work forward. All the survey respondents expressed a conviction that gender healing and reconciliation is absolutely needed, and they consistently affirmed that Satyana's model offers a practical pathway for bringing greater peace and harmony between women and men into the world.

# CHAPTER 12

# Divinity of Duality: Restoring the Sacred Balance of Masculine and Feminine

*The most vital issue of the age is whether the future progress of humanity is to be governed by the modern economic and materialistic mind of the West, or by a nobler pragmatism guided, uplifted, and enlightened by spiritual culture and knowledge . . .*

—Sri Aurobindo, *The Life Divine*

Tension was visceral in the room as the Catholics huddled together on one side and the Protestants on the other. The impasse in this Northern Ireland community had become so thick it could be cut with the proverbial knife.

Activist Danaan Parry had taken on the daunting challenge of facilitating a series of workshops to reconcile the bitter differences that were fueling open warfare in this troubled land during the early 1990s. Over the previous weeks Parry had already facilitated several sessions with this group, during which grievances and accusations had been aired at length on both sides. Strained relations had been mounting steadily, and when he walked into the room on this day, Parry knew instinctively that his only hope for making any headway through the quagmire was to take an entirely new tactic.

"Today we're going to do something completely different!" Parry announced cheerfully, catching the group off guard. "For a good while now, we've been hearing the challenging issues on both sides of this conflict. I've heard them many times—and you've all heard them a lot more than I have. So today we're not going to focus on all that," he continued forcefully. "What I want to know from you today is this: What is it like to be a woman in Northern Ireland?" Parry paused, then continued with a slight twinkle in his eye, "What is it like to be a man in Northern Ireland?"

The people glanced at each other with quizzical expressions and looked up at Parry with bewilderment, wondering what this could possibly have to do with their dilemma. After all, their troubles were all about religion, the war, and the pain of lost family members. But Parry persisted, "I really want to know, what exactly is it like to be a woman in Northern Ireland? And what's it like to be a man in Northern Ireland?"

Walking around the room, Parry began to motion with his arms. "Let's have all the women move over to this side of the room," he instructed, pointing with one hand, "and all the men on the other side," indicating with his other hand where he wanted the men to gather.

When the group was reconfigured with women and men on opposite sides of the room, Parry guided them into a simple storytelling process. He asked the people in both groups to take turns telling their individual stories about their lives in Northern Ireland. He instructed each group to listen very carefully to the different stories to discover if there was anything the women shared in common, or anything the men shared in common.

So the women began telling their stories, bringing forward wrenching tales of husbands and sons killed in the violence, fears for the safety of their children, the constant threat of new violence breaking out. As the Catholic and Protestant women looked at one another and listened to each other's stories, they soon discovered that they were all living through the exact same nightmare. A natural empathy emerged as they identified with one another's sorrows, horror stories, and fears—and before long they were in tears, holding each other, commiserating in mutual grief and compassion. The men had a parallel heart opening and healing experience as they listened to one another and discovered their shared pain across the religious divide, as men living in a war-torn society.

By the end of the afternoon, there were many long, healing hugs within the women's and men's groups. Through the doorway of gender a profound healing bridge had been created across the devastating religious chasm in this community. Both sides came to realize that they had thereby taken their first major step toward mutual healing, understanding, and peace.

This anecdote from the inspiring work of the late Danaan Parry illustrates what is perhaps the most fundamental principle of gender healing work:

• A key turning point in gender reconciliation comes when individuals perceive the truth of the "other" gender as their own experience. Through this doorway of empathic identification, a deeper underlying unity is discovered; namely, that *there is no other*. Gender reconciliation provides a practical and universal doorway for awakening to the oneness of all of humanity.

The heart melts in empathic identification, and, through this inner doorway, people are awakened to a deeper underlying unity. Gender healing can facilitate this awakening, regardless of participants' religious faith, cultural background, philosophical belief, or spiritual orientation. The human heart is universal, and when it opens, union happens. When the clouds clear, the sun cannot help but come out, and it becomes self-evident that the source of light is one, was there all along, and illuminates everything equally. An analogous realization takes place for human beings when the shared heart opens in community: the essential oneness of humanity becomes self-evident; it was there all along, and unites all hearts equally. In these moments, it doesn't make any difference what religion or beliefs people hold, what their gender identities are, what their professions are, what their education level is. None of that matters when the oneness of humanity is revealed.

The foregoing anecdote also illustrates how gender reconciliation work can be applied in arenas of human conflict quite beyond gender injustice. This Northern Ireland community was deeply divided along religious lines, and Parry ingeniously bisected the group according to gender, which was effectively "orthogonal" to the religious division, and the result was a powerful healing bridge in this deeply conflicted community.

Clearly, this same process has wide potential application in other war-torn regions of the world. Powerful healing work between Palestinian and Israeli women—as facilitated, for example, through the Global Peace Initiative of Women founded by Dena Merriam— draws on this same principle.

Other key insights from more than fifteen years of gender reconciliation work are summarized briefly below. We have already addressed these points at considerable length at various points throughout the book, so we simply summarize them briefly here:

- Gender injustice is universal; the basic dynamics are largely the same across different cultures, although the specific manifestations differ in form and intensity.
- Given proper facilitation and structured support, groups of sincere women and men can explore together challenging gender issues that are ordinarily taboo, and experience healing and reconciliation of deep-rooted gender-based conflicts that are often regarded as altogether intractable.
- Effective gender healing and reconciliation requires methods and facilitation skills that go quite beyond mere dialogical and psychological approaches in order to tap the deeper wellsprings of the human spirit.
- The model for gender reconciliation documented in this book (developed by Satyana Institute) has proven effective in widely diverse groups and settings, and is transferable to dissimilar cultures.
- The key to success in gender reconciliation work is not how much expertise participants have in gender issues, but rather their sincerity of intention and willingness to engage in the process, allowing it to unfold in its own integrity.

- By addressing challenging gender issues in a group or community
  a "collective alchemy" occurs that greatly enhances the
  transformative power of the work. This remarkable synergy goes
  well beyond what can happen in a one-on-one interpersonal
  context, be it between husband and wife, client and therapist,
  parishioner and priest, or student and teacher. The synergy of
  community amplifies the potential for healing, and certain social
  and cultural gender dynamics can only be healed in groups or
  community settings.

## Spiritual Wisdom: Unity beyond Duality

The gender crisis is ultimately a collective spiritual crisis. As Martin
Luther King, Jr., emphasized in regard to racial inequity, the issue was
never blacks versus whites, but rather justice versus injustice. So too
in the case of gender inequity, the issue is not men versus women, but
justice versus injustice. Yet both the women's and men's movements
have tended to frame the issue in polarized terms and confine their
analyses to conventional psychological and sociological paradigms.
The larger spiritual dimension has largely been omitted altogether.
Contemplative monk and author Bede Griffiths observed about the
men's movement that "it's all on the psychological dimension—there
is nothing beyond the psyche. That is where most Western people
stand today—imprisoned in the psyche. We have lost the awareness
of the spirit." Spiritual feminist writer Carol Lee Flinders makes
a similar observation about the women's movement: "Feminism
catches fire when it draws upon its inherent spirituality—when it
does not, it is just one more form of politics, and politics has never
fed our deepest hungers."

In her extensive cross-cultural research, historian Gerda Lerner
was astonished to discover a striking pattern in the origins of gender
oppression that was replicated in every ancient culture she examined:
"The most important thing I learned was the significance to women
of their relationship to the Divine, and the profound impact that the
severing of that relationship had on the history of women."[1] Lerner
concludes that the rise of women's oppression was directly coupled
to the decline of women's connection with the Divine. The logical

implication is that the end of women's oppression is intricately tied to women reclaiming their connection to the Divine. This implies that there is a fundamental link between "feminism" and spirituality—a connection that has yet to be widely recognized or embraced. Yet this connection is fundamental, and the authors would extend Lerner's conclusion to apply to men as well. As men reconnect more deeply to their divine origins, they naturally tend to become more loving, more committed to serving others, and more prepared to take responsibility for their role in healing and transforming the culture.

By invoking a "higher" or "spiritual" dimension of consciousness, the gender crisis can eventually be resolved—or, rather, dissolved. Only on this level can the duality of opposites be transcended in a higher unity. Then the genders become complementary aspects of a larger, magnificent unity. Without this possibility of transcendence, the debates and struggles between women and men will be endless, and hopes for a genuine resolution are futile. Einstein's oft-quoted observation is applicable here: a problem can never be solved on the level of consciousness that created it. So too the "battle of the sexes" will never be won by either "side"; another level of consciousness must be brought in that is beyond that which gave rise to the battle in the first place. Such consciousness is cultivated in the wisdom traditions of all human societies. Yet, this spiritual dimension of human consciousness has been denied or largely deemphasized in Western culture for at least several hundred years. This is why the Indian sage Sri Aurobindo has observed that the key question of our time is whether humanity will continue down the materialistic path mapped out by the West, or follow a nobler paradigm that invokes the spiritual wisdom of humanity, uplifting and reuniting the human family.

## Denial of Divinity and the Cure of Grace

To deny the sacred has long been the signature strategy of the "patriarchy," and it has been devastatingly effective over many centuries. Through systematic denial of the divine or sacred dimension of life, the direct connection to the divine Source that is innate in every human being is blocked or thwarted, and the forces of temporal power and worldly influence can then take over all aspects of human society. With the divine thus usurped, the society is beholden to, and easily manipulated by, the major institutions of social and cultural power: politics, religion, corporations, government, military, education, economics, the media.

Denial of divinity is essentially what Gerda Lerner was so surprised to discover in her cross-cultural research on the origins of patriarchy. Yet this strategy was applied not only to women, it is actually the oldest patriarchal trick in the book: deny the sacred, and take control. This fundamental strategy has been applied systematically, in one form or another, to every dimension of human society. It was used by religious institutions to ruthlessly eradicate mystical wisdom and the feminine mysteries, replacing them with the ecclesiastical authority of priests and clergy. It has been adopted in market economics to reduce the earth to a mere physical object, thereby enabling relentless exploitation of natural resources and unbridled pollution of the natural environment to fuel an insatiable appetite for material wealth. It is consistently applied by governments, corporations, and other social institutions to render strong and sound human beings into unthinking, compliant pawns—mere cogs in a soulless machine. It is used to control sexuality—desacralizing the inherent divinity of *eros*—by rendering it immoral in the case of religion, or reducing it to lustful indulgence in the case of secular institutions such as the military or the corporate media. Throughout the past few thousand years, systematic denial of divinity has served to trick otherwise ethical, upstanding citizens into betraying their own souls and condoning unspeakable evils at times, and into forgetting the sacred at *all* times. This collective forgetting of the sacred origins and divine essence of humanity has become so deep and all-embracing that we have forgotten that we have forgotten. Entire societies or nations have sometimes been swept up in the grip of a collective delusion or demonic trance, unleashing tremendous forces of destruction. The power of these systematic manipulations and dark forces in human society must never be underestimated, and they have been the lament of many prominent social analysts, such as scholar Reinhold Niebuhr in his potent book *Moral Man, Immoral Society*.

Yet this bleak, disturbing picture is *not* the whole story! Nor is it the most important or the deepest truth of human existence—far from it. For as Martin Luther King, Mahatma Gandhi, Desmond Tutu and many other voices have contended emphatically, pessimists like Niebuhr and others, however brilliant, have missed one absolutely fundamental factor: love. By neglecting the power of love and its immense capacity for transformation in society, social pessimists overlook what King has called "the cure of grace." Indeed, love is the greatest power in the universe. Love can transform every darkness and bring in a profound grace that reawakens the magic and sacred in life. And for this, it is *not* necessary that the masses of humanity all suddenly awaken to love. All that is required is for a critical mass to awaken to love, and this relative minority of people will, over time, expand and effect a transformation that can eventually touch the hearts of billions.

"The mystic is the pupil in the eye of humanity," as Sufi mystic Ibn Arabi observed, and just as physical light enters the body through the tiny pupil of the eye, divine light enters humanity through its relatively small (but growing!) number of sages, mystics, and sincere devotees of divine love in every tradition across the globe. Working through individuals of pure heart in every land, a web of light and love is now being woven all across the planet that will become the foundation for a new civilization of love. This "inner net of the heart" is laying the invisible groundwork for a major transformation of consciousness—through a subtle network of light and love that vibrates at a higher frequency than collective darkness. Love functions at higher orders and more refined levels of energy that quietly undermine and dissolve the lower orders of energy that comprise darkness.

### Gender and Spiritual Identity

Gender healing and reconciliation work leads naturally and inevitably to fundamental questions about who we are as human beings, and what is the true nature of our identity. The question of gender identity can be viewed as a form of asking the question "Who am I?" and seeking the answer somehow in relation to gender. This question—"Who am I?"—is the right question to ask, as reflected for example in the profound self-inquiry practice of the great Indian sage, Ramana Maharshi. But to restrict this question to the domain of "gender identity" arbitrarily limits a profound inquiry to a relative dimension. The question "Who am I?" is the beginning of a deep spiritual journey, which, when pursued far enough, will eventually leave behind all questions of gender and move into the realm of pure being or spirit.

In pursuing the question "Who am I?" we come first to the realization that we are not our bodies or personalities. As we realize this ever more deeply, we identify less and less with our bodies, our masculine or feminine qualities, our sexual identities, and ever more strongly with something larger that is universal and transcends gender altogether. Our true identity has nothing to do with gender, or our bodies, or our sexuality. It has to do with our spiritual essence, or soul, or Atman, or Great Spirit, or Buddhist nonself—there are many names for it.

Thus, the question of gender identity, carried far enough, will inevitably lead beyond gender altogether. Gender is not an end in itself, and gender identity is but a small piece of a far more profound puzzle. As the self-enquiry process unfolds, we begin to see gender differences and conflicts in a whole new light, and new resolutions begin to emerge in ways we could not have imagined. Thus, gender becomes a vehicle for awakening to deeper levels of self-realization, and not an end in itself.

### Gender Healing and Integrative Medicine

The growing field of integrative medicine strives to synthesize a diverse range of approaches to health and healing—balancing traditional Western modalities with other methods including Eastern approaches and traditional indigenous systems of healing. Satyana's gender reconciliation work was presented at the World Congress of Integrative Medicine in 2007, held in Santa Fe, New Mexico. Through this conference it became evident that gender reconciliation work is a form of collective healing that is resonant with certain emerging advances in integrative medicine.

One of the most prominent models of integrative medicine was developed over a period of twenty years by Dietrich Klinghardt, MD. Klinghardt posits five fundamental levels of healing, based on the ancient yoga sutras of Patanjalii that specify five bodies in the human being; the physical body and four "subtle" bodies. Klinghardt has applied this five-level model of healing to accurately diagnose and treat a broad range of clinical disorders ranging from physical diseases to emotional, mental, and soul-level disturbances. The five levels of healing in Klinghardt's model are: the physical body, energy body, mental body, intuitive body, and the soul level. A principal feature of Klinghardt's clinical model is that these five levels are hierarchically organized, meaning that healing at a particular level has beneficial healing effects on the levels below it, but not on levels above it. Thus, for example, an effective treatment modality at the mental level will have healing effects on the lower levels of the energy body and the physical body, but not on the higher levels of the intuitive body and soul level. At the low end of the spectrum, healing on the physical level—the primary focus of Western medicine—affects only the physical body. At the high end of the spectrum, healing on the soul level has cascading healing effects on each of the lower levels (physical, energy, mental, and intuitive bodies).

Viewed from the perspective of Klinghardt's model, gender healing and reconciliation could be seen as operating primarily on the soul and intuitive levels, with attendant beneficial effects on the three lower levels. Many of the healing experiences reported in earlier chapters of this book seem to support this interpretation, and Klinghardt's work provides a kind of independent clinical validation of the crucial importance of healing at the soul and spiritual levels, without which a true and complete healing of the individual and the human community is not possible.

Another key innovation in integrative medicine is a powerful new form of psychotherapy that has emerged in recent years known as "family constellations," developed by the German psychotherapist and former priest, Bert Hellinger. The basic premise of this approach is that when a particular family member is excluded or violated or marginalized in a significant way, the entire family system is afflicted, often for several generations afterward. The resulting family system remains "constellated" in a particular way that often produces all manner of psychological difficulties and challenging symptoms for later family members that cannot be healed or transformed until the excluded person or experience is somehow recognized and reintegrated back into the conscious awareness of the family system.

Although Hellinger's work is primarily focused on family systems (and to a lesser extent on organizational systems called "systemic constellations"), it seems that Hellinger's basic framework could be profitably expanded to encompass entire human cultures and civilizations. For example, the denial and exclusion of sacred aspects of gender and sexuality in Western society could be seen as having created a "cultural constellation" of gender injustice and disharmony—one that cannot be healed or transformed until the sacred dimension of gender is reintegrated back into the society. Whether or not such a generalization of Hellinger's ideas is legitimate, the basic principle here is sound: when something essential is denied, the result is a dysfunctional system that cannot recover until that essential element is reclaimed or restored. This is basically what has happened in virtually every human society in relation to gender. The remedy is to reclaim the sacred dimension of gender and eros—the spiritual union of masculine and feminine—at every level from the individual, to the intimate couple, the family, the community, the society, and the globe.

## Spiritual Love, Androgyny, and Beyond
What is spiritual love? What is the nature of the deepest love? How does love reconcile male and female? What is divine love? In broaching such questions about love, we begin by invoking Rumi's caveat:

> No matter what I could say to explain and elucidate Love,
> inadequacy overcomes me when I come to Love itself. . . .
> Love cannot be contained within our speaking or listening,
> Love is an ocean whose depths cannot be plumbed . . .
> Whatever you have said or heard is but the shell:
> the kernel of love is a mystery that cannot be divulged.

Silence! Silence!
For the allusions of Love are reversed;
the meanings become hidden from much speaking.[2]

Yet, we must speak of love, however inadequately, because love
is the entire foundation, the means, and the goal of gender reconciliation work. So let us be brief in words, and trust a deeper wisdom to
emerge from the ensuing silence.

The mysterious relation between love and healing is beautifully
characterized in a passage by the great mystic St. John of the Cross in
which he speaks about how the wound of love is cauterized by love,
in a manner that cures yet also further wounds:

The cautery of love effects a wound of love in the one it
touches. Yet there is a difference between this loving cautery
and the cautery produced by material fire. The wound left by
material fire is only curable by other medicines, whereas the
wound effected by the cautery of love is incurable through
medicine; for the very cautery that causes it, cures it, and by
curing it, causes it. As often as the cautery of love touches
the wound of love, it causes a deeper wound of love, and thus
the more it wounds, the more it cures and heals. The more
wounded the lover, the healthier the lover is . . . to such an
extent that the entire soul is dissolved into a wound of love.
And now, all cauterized and made one wound of love, it is
completely healthy in love, for it is transformed in love.[3]

Thus, the wound cures, and the cure wounds. The process of
gender reconciliation is similar. To go directly into the gender wound
is certainly painful—it tears at the heart, which is why people sometimes feel they can't "take it," or don't want to go there. Yet in that
tearing open the heart cries tears of blood, and in this very flow the
healing begins. The cure is effected by the tears of the heart. A broken heart is an open heart, and through it, a larger invisible healing
power can enter. As it is said, "God enters through a wound," and
when people's hearts break open together, the tears of their love

flow together and become the healing balm for the wound. Thus the wound cures.

Yet, that very cure prepares the ground for yet another level of wounding, as the next layer of healing is broached. The process then continues in a cycle of wound and cure, wound and cure, ever deepening as it goes. Gradually, as participants' hearts break open ever further, they begin to merge into one another simultaneously, advancing steadily toward becoming one large shared heart in which perception of individual selves—and separation of male and female—is ground down and dissolved, until all become one.

In the end, we are no longer man and woman, no longer "gendered" beings, because gender is partial, and we have become whole. We no longer identify with only a part, or just one side, when all parts and all sides dwell within us. Male and female become united within us in a sacred androgyny. The soul unites male and female, and goes beyond both, as we become one being with all. The coupling of sexual intercourse is a physical symbol of this larger union. Sexual union provides a temporary, finite glimpse of this eternal, infinite union.

In this unitive realization, we recognize that it was always so; we were never separate, and male and female were never really two. Such an integral androgyny is often found naturally in highly realized spiritual masters of either sex. For example, as J. G. Bennett observed about the great Christian mystic St. Teresa of Avila, "Men encountered in St. Teresa a woman who was more fully a man than they were, while she was also fully a woman."[4]

This experience of unitive androgyny is closely related to mystical love, in which there is a loss of the separate self—the identity of I, me, and my personality—followed by a radical union with the Divine. The price for this profound gift of divine grace is small, although it seems exceedingly high to the ego. Rumi describes it eloquently:

This Love sacrifices all souls, however wise, however awakened—
Cuts off their heads without a sword,
hangs them without a scaffold.

We are the guests of the One who devours his guests;
the friends of the One who slaughters his friends.

Although by his gaze, He brings death to so many lovers,
Let yourself be killed by Him. Is He not the water of life?

Never, ever grow bitter. He is the Friend who grows gently.
Keep your heart noble, for this most noble Love
Kills only kings near God, and those free from passion.

We are like the night, Earth's shadow. He is the sun.
He splits open the night with a sword soaked in dawn.[5]

All inner darkness, illusion, and obscurities are shattered by the sword of divine light. Love kills the lover; cuts away everything that opposes it, dissolves all partial and separate identities, until nothing is left but the lover's burning heart, which is then merged into the object of his or her love. As the Sufi mystic Alansari put it, "Know that when you lose your self, you will reach the Beloved. There is no other secret to be learned, and more than this is not known to me."

Thus the lover sacrifices his or her life to the Beloved, and they become one. All duality is dissolved in a higher unity. With this realization comes the startling discovery that the lover always was the Other, there never were two in the first place. The separate self never actually existed; it was an illusion all along.

Different traditions speak of this mystical process in different terms. Christ said, "No one hath greater love than this: to lay down one's life for one's friends." In spiritual love, the "friend" is the Beloved, God Her/Himself. We lay down our lives for God, and into God. This means giving up our very identity, everything we hold most dear, for our Beloved. As Muhammad put it, "Those who die before they die . . . do not die when they die."

The pinnacle of gender reconciliation work bears a resemblance to this mystical union, though perhaps not quite so extreme or exalted. Yet, not infrequently in gender reconciliation work women and men discover and behold the living unity of male and female within themselves. The experience entails a kind of uplifting revelation in which the sacred feminine and divine masculine are experienced as dwelling in glorious dynamic union together, deep within the heart. Men look upon and behold the radiantly beautiful women, who mirror back to them their own inner feminine divinity. Women behold the strong and powerful men, who mirror back to them their own inner divine masculinity. Both women and men are mutually uplifted, embraced, and transported in profound mutual blessing transmitted from and through one another. The veils of separation are lifted, and the ecstatic dance of masculine and feminine divinity is suddenly unmasked and revealed. As one participant who is a long-standing Sufi practitioner described it, "I saw God, in a whole new way."

The Flemish mystic, Jan Ruysbroeck, succinctly describes the multilevel experience of seeing the Divine: "You behold what you are . . . and you are what you behold." This seeing or beholding takes place in the heart, in the core of one's being—it is not a mental concept or idea. The duality of lover and Beloved, of male and female, dissolves into one loving: no separation, no subject and object, only love. In a related, beautiful passage, Meister Eckhart describes the experience of union with God: "The union is so entirely one, that this 'I' and that He become one *is*, and act in the world as one is-ness."

Gender reconciliation work inevitably leads us to, or toward, this unitive experience. It's one thing to read about the experience or hear about it, but when it actually happens to you, it's quite a different thing. Suddenly you glimpse the real miracle of the masculine and feminine. You behold this glorious, cosmic, interpenetrating, interreceptive tapestry—alive and shimmering before you, and within you—and you are part of this scintillating tapestry. And, on another level, you *are* the tapestry!

"Divine duality" is thus a misnomer, because there is no duality in divinity—it is One. Yet it manifests itself in lover and beloved, male and female, human and divine, matter and spirit—always a unity, but with two aspects. Gender reconciliation is a work of love that leads to the eventual dissolution of gender identity. Notwithstanding the value of today's expanding spectrum of gender identities that break free from the narrow and rigid conditioning of the past, gender healing work ultimately leads to liberation from "gender identity" altogether, or it is not yet completed. The separation between masculine and feminine disappears in the gender-reconciled heart, then reappears again, in an eternal dance. All human beings are both masculine and feminine—and neither. All dualities merge, and we are rendered one whole being, and one humanity.

## Disidentifying with the Gender War

In his relevant work, Eckhart Tolle underscores the primacy of today's crisis of relations between women and men: "As the egoic mode of consciousness and all the social, political, and economic structures that it created enter the final stage of collapse, the relationships between men and women reflect the deep state of crisis in which humanity now finds itself."[6] Tolle's diagnosis of this crisis is that women and men are unwittingly identified with the pain-body, the collective aggregate of unhealed pain endured by women and men down through the ages that has become frozen and lodged in the deeper layers of individual and collective consciousness. As he puts it, "Many volumes have been written, and many more could be written, about the ways in which unconsciousness is brought out in male-female relationships. But . . . once you understand the root of the dysfunction, you do not need to explore its countless manifestations."[7] For Tolle, this root is unconscious identification with the pain-body, which typifies normal dysfunctional relationships between women and men.

Tolle elaborates further in his more recent book *A New Earth*, and hints at the solution:

> The greatest achievment of humanity is not its works of art, science, or technology, but the recognition of its own dysfunction, its own madness . . . To recognize one's own insanity is, of course, the arising of sanity, the beginning of healing and transcendence . . . [In particular] when identification with [the pain-body] ceases, the transmutation begins.[8]

Tolle speaks about how interpersonal conflicts can be trans-formed by the presence of disinterested, compassionate witnesses. The spacious presence of witnesses tends to awaken a similar wit-nessing consciousness within each of the warring parties—and they begin to disidentify from their battle stations that were created by their pain bodies.

Tolle is affirming in another way what we have experienced first-hand over several years of practicing gender reconciliation work. Bringing the painful insanity of gender conflicts skillfully into the open-out of the hidden "safety" of home, bedroom, sangha, church, or workplace into the light of group or community awareness—serves to deconstruct and transform those very conflicts. This was articulated in Chapter 2 as the third principle of gender reconcili-ation; namely, that gender healing work is most effectively done in groups or communities. Disinterested, compassionate witnesses are part of what the group or community provides—people not directly engaged in a particular gender conflict or process who can therefore more easily withdraw projections, disidentify with their pain-bodies, and maintain a compassionate field of presence for their peers.

This is the central principle operative in the silent witnessing exercise and the cross-gender truth forums. Of course, at any point during the gender healing process, specific issues and group dynam-ics may shift such that the dispassionate witnesses and protagonists/antagonists switch places. In whatever manner the process unfolds, a group or community of conscious, compassionate participants creates an optimal container or temenos for transmuting gender conflicts courageously brought forward into the light. Naturally, the process works best when carried out by people who are well-intentioned and sincere about moving beyond past wounds and hurts and building a culture of respect, dignity, and flowering love.

Tolle emphasizes that for the healing process to succeed fully, com-batants on all sides must relinquish their victim identities, not only on a personal level, but on the collective level as well. For example, he says that women are correct in their perception that the collective female pain-body is due in large part to male violence inflicted on women and repression of the female principle throughout the planet over millennia. But if a woman derives a sense of self from this fact, "what men did to women," it could keep her imprisoned in a collective victim identity. This "may give her a comforting sense of identity, of solidarity with other women, but it is keeping her in bondage to the past and blocking full access to her essence and true power."[9] The same could also be said for men who identify with the collective male pain-body. The parallel insight here would be that the men's movement is quite right in documenting and articulating a morass of injustice that has been perpetrated exclusively against men, but if men establish their identity from this pain, they may lock themselves into an irreconcilable conflict, and lose access to their true power.

This is not to deny the legitimacy of the pain and injustice that has been perpetrated against either men or women. Both sides' claims are legitimate. It is rather to step back and affirm that true gender justice and equality will never emerge from identification with collective pain, no matter how justified, and that the true transformation and healing begins with the process of disidentifying with the pain and actively moving toward love and forgiveness, however tentatively at first.

### Toward a New Civilization of Love

Gender oppression is universal, and all societies would benefit tremendously from authentic gender healing and reconciliation. The whole of humanity is in profound need of a kind of "Truth and Reconciliation Commission" in regard to gender injustice and sexism. Humanity as a whole must one day face unflinchingly the full agonizing truth of gender oppression and sexism in our consciousness, our societies, our families, our relationships—our very legacy as a species. We must cultivate a vast forgiveness for the ruinous violations of women and girls, the profound betrayal of men and boys, and the persecution of all those who haven't conformed to narrow, rigid heterosexual stereotypes. Humanity will never be able to move fully forward into its next phase of evolution, toward a new civilization of love and harmony, without first reconciling gender imbalance at a far more profound level than has yet been achieved in any contemporary society.

The Vietnamese Buddhist master Thich Nhat Hanh has said that the next Buddha will emerge not in the form of an individual, but rather in the form of a community of people living in loving kindness and mindful awareness. Gender reconciliation work is one of many seeds sown in this field that are beginning to germinate at this time. Just as an individual evolves spiritually over time, so too society evolves in its collective consciousness and spirituality. A new level of conscious evolution is now on the brink of awakening in humanity—a new era in our understanding and expression of gender, intimacy, and sexuality—for which all gender healing work to date has been but preparation. There is a particular level of work that can only take place in groups and communities of women and men, and not in intimate partnerships or nuclear families.

A new dawn of a higher form of love between men and women is coming—one that is already beginning to show itself. This new form will unravel the illusion of romantic love and eventually replace it with a nobler and more universal form of love between men and women. It will not deny the expression of physical intimacy and love, but it will elevate the erotic impulse from largely physical bonding to a form of spiritual communion. It will entail not simply spiritualized sexuality, as has been focused on extensively in the West in recent years. The intimate interplay between archetypal manifestations of Divine Feminine and Divine Masculine will become more accessible to suitably prepared souls, and this in turn will bring a magic and delight back into humanity and to the earth that has been lost for millennia. As the abuses of the feminine are faced squarely and transmuted over time, a certain innocence and purity will once again return to the hearts of human beings. The magical dance of the masculine and feminine, which is our birthright as human beings, will come back to reenchant our lives once again.

As this reenchantment comes to pass, if there remain women's or men's movements at all, their purpose will be to serve beyond themselves, rather than to champion their own causes. Women, men, and people of all sexual orientations will work for the well-being and spiritual liberation of one another. As service to others continues to develop in society at large, an altogether new magic will begin to appear which has not been seen for thousands of years, and the relationship between humanity and the earth will then begin to shift rapidly.

Perhaps this seems like pure fantasy, but in fact we have directly and consistently witnessed the seeds of this process taking place, in microcosm, in more than forty events involving seven hundred people in Satyana's intensive retreats and programs. The women's and men's circles begin by addressing their own wounds, their own needs—which is important and necessary, because we have to go through this. But by the end of these gatherings, the men are totally focused on honoring and uplifting the women, and vice versa. The women's and men's circles become entirely focused on supporting and celebrating each "other," and as they do this the greatest gifts come forward, and the real magic—and fun!—begins. Each of these groups serves as a kind of "alchemical incubator" in which women and men are jointly pioneering new forms of unprecedented healing and mutual harmony—reclaiming the awe and living magic of the dance between masculine and feminine in human life. In so doing, these workshops are forging new ways and models for women and men that will one day spread to become the norm on a much larger societal scale. Thus these nascent groups, alongside other similar spiritual groups and communities, are planting seeds of grace that will infuse society and eventually transform it. This process could be viewed as the alchemical principle operating in reverse: "As below, so above." What is now taking place and emerging on a small scale within the microcosm of certain spiritual groups and communities will one day become a lived reality in the larger human family.

The gender healing work described in this book is just a beginning, but it lays the groundwork for a new harmony and balance between the masculine and feminine in our hearts, in our relationships, and in our communities. Because everyone is affected by gender conditioning, the process of gender reconciliation is one of the most direct routes to awakening the collective heart of a community or group. The work naturally awakens a community's capacity for compassion and forgiveness; it provides a direct and natural avenue to heartfelt communication and awareness. It also serves to restore a sense of the sacred interconnectedness of all life, including humanity's interdependence with the nonhuman world.

The prevailing view of the "gender war"—as a battle between women and men—is misplaced. Gender disharmony is, at root, a collective spiritual crisis: a war waged by humankind against itself—driven by a denial of the sacred essence of masculine and feminine and a tyrannical separation and imbalance of masculine and feminine principles. This imbalance is manifest at all levels of society, from the individual human psyche, to the family, to community, nation, and finally to the entire human family, and our relationship to our planetary home.

The human heart has the capacity to transcend and heal these rifts. A startling power emerges when human beings gather to explore and reconcile their differences in community. The potential contribution that gender reconciliation offers to the future of humanity is enormous, and has only just begun.

Let us close with a prayer, which is adapted from the same mystical poem we opened with in Chapter 1 (p. 32) written by the Indian poet Jnaneswar:

Without the God,
There is no Goddess,
Without the Goddess,
There is no God.
How sweet is their love!

Embracing each other,
They merge into One,
As darkness merges with the light
At the breaking of dawn.

When we discover their Unity
All words and all thoughts
[and all books!]
Dissolve into silence . . .

# ACKNOWLEDGEMENTS

So many people and organizations have contributed to this project in substantial ways that it's difficult to know where to begin in acknowledging them. There is a saying in South Africa that "a person is a person through other people," and this is certainly the case in this work.

The author(s) are deeply indebted to the following philanthropic foundations for providing financial support to Satyana Institute's Gender Reconciliation project: the Shaler Adams Foundation, Hidden Leaf Foundation, the Kalliopeia Foundation, the Cunningham Family Grant Fund, the Roy A. Hunt Foundation, the San Francisco Foundation, the Tides Foundation (Caritas Fund), the Giant Steps Foundation, and the Rockwood Fund. We are also grateful to the Nathan Cummings Foundation for providing start-up funding for Satyana Institute over three years in the late 1990s, and to other supporters of Satyana's work including the Fetzer Institute, Gaia Trust of Denmark, Selby-Fong Spirit-in-Community Fund, Tides Foundation (Hormel Fund), and The Philanthropic Collaborative.

We owe a special debt of gratitude to Margaret Schink for her unwavering support of our work on multiple levels, not only generous financial support, but also sustained spiritual and moral support through thick and thin over the years. Her persistence and faith have been a continual source of personal and professional blessing over the years. We are also grateful to Linda Cunningham who has given generously of her skills and resources to support this work on several levels to help birth this work into the world. A special thanks goes to Bill Melton and Patricia Smith for providing the first grants to support the development of what evolved into Satyana's gender reconciliation work. We are also deeply grateful to many individual donors—too numerous to mention here—who have graciously donated to this work over the years.

Among funders and close friends of Satyana Institute, we acknowledge certain key individuals who have been special longtime supporters of the gender work, and who have held the sustained vision with us over many years—despite the inevitable ups and downs. These individuals include Dave Brown, Lowell Brook, Tara Brown, Terry Hunt, and Hildur and Ross Jackson. Many others have also supported this work and held the vision with us, and we thank each of them for their inspiring commitment and service to this project.

The author(s) are deeply grateful to the Board of Directors of Satyana Institute who have provided years of selfless service with nary a wavering complaint. We especially wish to acknowledge major contributions from our faithful lawyer Seth Henry, from Jed Swift who co-founded the Institute, from Kelly Green (deceased), and from Linda Cunningham—all of whom gave tirelessly of their time and energy to building the organization and structure of Satyana Institute. We also gratefully acknowledge the emerging services of Bernie Zahlea, and the crucial contributions from Andre Carothers early on, without whose support and guidance the institute may never have taken form.

Turning to our fellow facilitators, the author(s) owe a tremendous debt of gratitude to Diane Haug, whose contribution to Satyana's gender work has been paramount over many years. Diane co-facilitated our yearlong professional training and numerous other gender workshops, bringing her tremendous spiritual depth and impeccable clinical expertise to the intensity of gender healing work. We are also grateful to and inspired by other collaborating facilitators, including Nomfundo Walaza of the Desmond Tutu Center in South Africa, Karambu Ringera of International Peace Initiatives, and Peter Rutter who combines a unique Jungian approach with leading expertise in the arena of sexual harassment.

The author acknowledges his deep gratitude for the tremendous contribution of contributing author Molly Dwyer, who devoted more than three intensive years of her life to Satyana Institute's work. Molly made important contributions to many aspects of the gender reconciliation project, and to other Satyana projects.

The author(s) are honored to express gratitude to the team of Satyana certified facilitators, many of whom have contributed valuable time and energy to co-facilitate this work for little or no monetary compensation. We gratefully acknowledge the thirty-three courageous professionals who completed our yearlong professional training program—enduring the sometimes grueling alchemy of the gender-healing cauldron!—and we have been inspired by their commitment and selfless service to the cause of gender healing in the world. Among these, fifteen have thus far persevered to become Satyana certified facilitators: Cynthia Brix, Janet Coster, Linda Cunningham, Julien Devereux, Shawn Galloway, Shell Goldman, Jay Hartstein, Corky Hewitt, Shirsten Lundblad, Gwenn Marie, Stephanie Shelburne, Alan Strachan, Carlotta Tyler, and Marcia Wolff. We would be remiss if we did not particularly honor and give special thanks to: Julien Devereux who has given so generously of his time and remarkable skills in facilitation and organizational development over many years; to Janet Coster and Alan Strachan who enthusiastically gave of their time more than once as co-facilitators; to Linda Cunningham, Shawn Galloway, and Lynda Griebenow who donated their time as co-facilitators, and to Carlotta Tyler whose combined skills in facilitation and organizational development provide a valuable addition to our strategic planning committee. A special thanks goes to Darcy Cunningham for her skillful leadership and co-facilitation of the certification training program, and for her excellent job preparing the professional training manual.

Beyond these colleagues, we acknowledge our gratitude to many key past collaborators whose names are listed in the Introduction to this book. Among these, a special warm thanks goes to Johanna Johnson. We also particularly thank Heart Phoenix, John Seed, Anne Yeomans, Jeffrey Weissberg, Allen Kanner, Amy Fox, and Rachel Bagby. A special gratitude is due to Sharyn Faro and Bonnie Morrison, clinical psychologists who provided invaluable clinical training over six years of collaborative facilitation of Holotropic Breathwork for their clientele.

I owe the greatest debt of gratitude to my spiritual teacher, who wishes to remain anonymous, and to the superiors in the lineage. I am also deeply indebted to my mentor Father Thomas Keating whose wise counsel and spiritual support have been invaluable. I am deeply grateful to Llewellyn Vaughan Lee for many powerful learnings, and for his profound teachings and mastery in alchemy, mysticism, and the emerging global oneness.

I am very grateful to certain friends and close colleagues who have provided sustained professional and personal support over the years, especially Richard Tarnas, Robert McDermott, Hildur and Ross Jackson, Charles Terry, Betsy McGregor, Duane Elgin, and Michael Abdo. A special expression of gratitude goes to mentor and friend Stanislav Grof, whose contributions to transpersonal psychology—particularly the development with his wife Christina Grof of Holotropic Breathwork—have played a major role in my life and work. For some twenty years I have applied breathwork in many different venues (not just the gender work), and it has consistently served as a profound practice to awaken and expand the consciousness of many participants and students over the years. My gratitude goes out also to earlier important teachers and mentors, including Ravi Ravindra, Barbara Findeisen, and Joanna Macy.

The author(s) gratefully acknowledge the powerful and inspiring contributions from several distinguished Guest Faculty in Satyana's professional training programs, including: Andrew Harvey, Carol Flinders, Mahnaz Afkhami, Christopher Kilmartin, Lucia Ticzon, Angeles Arrien, Larry Robinson, Rina Swenson, Robert Gass, and Stuart Sovatsky.

We heartily thank our editor Regina Sara Ryan at Hohm Press for handling the editing and publication process with such skill and grace, and our publicist Megan McFeely for serving the larger dissemination of Satyana's gender work. Warm thanks go also to Joan O'Donnell of Harvard's Peabody Museum for providing the first round of editing, and for her sensitive reflections on subtle issues in the manuscript. A heartfelt thanks goes also to Doug Childers for his sharp editorial work and wise counsel regarding the publishing world. Many thanks go to other key friends and supporters who have been visible advocates for this work, including Jane Calbreath, June Katzen, and Selma Naloor.

The author(s) are very grateful to Sister Lucy Kurien of the Maher project in India for her profound inspiration and collaboration on gender healing work in India, and for providing retreat space for completing this book. Deep thanks are due also to the Medical Mission Sisters and their Holistic Health Center in Pune, India for providing a beautiful retreat space where portions of this book were written.

We are pleased to acknowledge our inspiration and gratitude to South African Deputy Minister of Health Nozizwe Madlala Routledge, for her courage and leadership in orchestrating the introduction of Satyana Institute's gender reconciliation work to Members of Parliament and prominent leaders in the South African Council of Churches and NGO sector. We also wish to express special thanks to Bernedette Muthien for organizing Satyana's first trip to South Africa in 2003, and for introducing us to Deputy Minister Nozizwe Madlala Routledge.

Finally, I would like to acknowledge my family, especially my parents Bob and Madge Keepin to whom this book is in part dedicated. My parents have provided consistent love and support throughout my life, while not always quite understanding what I was up to, yet trusting (or praying!) that it was all worthwhile. My sisters, brother, and multiple nieces and nephews have been a gracious support, and I particularly acknowledge my nieces Mikaela Keepin and Alexandra Gramps, both of whom have generously volunteered their services to the women and children of Maher in India. It is a great joy and privilege to acknowledge my closest colleague, Cynthia Brix, who joined Satyana Institute's gender reconciliation work in 2001. After five years of fruitful collaboration, the nature of our partnership shifted dramatically two years ago, and in 2007 Cynthia and I were married. To Cynthia and to all of the wonderful people and supporters mentioned herein, my heart goes out in gratitude and love.

# APPENDIX A

# *Outline of Satyana's*
# *Gender Reconciliation Model*

The stages of Satyana's gender reconciliation process are outlined below. These stages are laid out here in orderly sequential fashion, but in practice these distinct stages often interweave and overlap, depending on the particular event and cultural context. The outlined steps generally take place over a five-day period, although they are discernible in every gender reconciliation event, regardless of its length. The timeline given here is for the usual five-day format.

**Days 1–2: Preparation/Invocation**
- Following welcome and introductions, the workshop begins with a participatory invocation that unifies the group in its collective intention for cooperation, mutual healing, and reconciliation.
- Ethical guidelines and agreements are established for the group or community, which helps to build a collective temenos or "group container" of trust, integrity, and safety for all. Principal guidelines include: strict confidentiality; taking responsibility for one's process; honoring and not judging the experience of others; mindful communication; being attentive and sensitive to the group process (practices are included for "maintaining presence"); and refraining from sexual interactions or romantic encounters with others in the group. These guidelines protect the safety, integrity, and intimacy of the gender reconciliation process. Abstaining from "normal" social patterns of sexual or romantic contact also awakens insight into the nature and depth of participants' sexual

conditioning and how it impacts their lives. A unique form of intimacy is invoked by honoring these guidelines.

- The group engages in periods of contemplative practice, further opening individual participants and the group as a whole to the spiritual dimension. This aspect can be adjusted, either highlighted or conducted more subtly, depending on the particular social context of the workshop.

- Exercises for awakening sensitivity and nonverbal communication are included to heighten awareness of the multilevel communication that characterizes gender healing work. These preliminary steps are essential, and help to build a container in which deep and fruitful work can be done in the often unpredictable and sometimes volatile process of gender healing and reconciliation.

### Days 2–4: Immersion and Transformation

- The group begins to examine gender-related disharmony and injustice, considering the nature and forms of gender conflict that occur in the larger social and cultural arenas. This is done through multimedia presentations focusing on the afflictions of gender imbalance suffered independently by women and by men—followed by processing in small breakout groups.

- A "silent witnessing" exercise is conducted that awakens in each individual, and in the group as a whole, an awareness of the shadow side of gender conditioning and its pervasive and profoundly destructive impact on individuals across all boundaries of gender, sex, culture, race, and class. A series of gender-related questions is asked of the women and men (separately, usually), enabling each group to witness ways in which the other group (as well as their own) has experienced unfairness, violation, shame, injustice, and so forth, due to gender conditioning. The questions culminate with such queries as: Have you ever been physically abused? Have you ever feared for your personal safety because of your sexual orientation? Have you ever been raped or forced sexually against your will? Have you ever suffered from domestic or intimate violence, or feared for your personal safety in your own home? After each question, participants who have experienced these things are invited to stand up (if they choose), while the rest of the group sits in silent witness. In this process, potent gender issues become suddenly poignant and personal, without the detailed stories having to be revealed.

- The focus shifts from the collective/impersonal to the individual/personal as participants share stories of their own gender-related challenges and experiences. These stories—poignant, humorous, harrowing, or tragic—stir emotions, awaken memories, inspire insights, and deepen the group bond. Here, in the personal domain, we begin to see consistent themes of sexuality, power, and identity woven into gender issues.

- Certain "hot-button" gender issues often emerge in the group that carry a charge that is potentially polarizing. By this point in the workshop some of these volatile issues and concerns have usually arisen, releasing into the group an accompanying energetic charge or tension.

- The group begins to explore experientially what has emerged up to this point. Because words can only take us so far, the tools used here include contemplative practices and experiential breathwork.

- The breathwork process adds another dimension to the work. Participants enter into an inner journey using the breath as a vehicle for self-enquiry. Breathwork opens inner energy centers in the body, psyche, and spirit, and it activates the mysterious "inner" healing power that is widely associated with breathing practices in many different spiritual traditions. Breathwork serves to invoke the "group soul" and cultivates a unique form of intimacy within the group. It also begins to build group skills and capacity within the community for navigating through powerful emotional and archetypal energies and collective healing states, which are essential for the deeper levels of gender healing and reconciliation work. Breathwork is sometimes of necessity omitted from shorter events, but its absence considerably reduces the depth to which the gender work can go, and also limits the capacity of the group for "alchemical" healing.

- Key gender issues have now been evoked within the group process and explored collectively and internally. The group then breaks into separate women's and men's circles to explore these issues more deeply in parallel same-sex groups. Different techniques are utilized in these circles—depending on the circumstances and context—including council process, truth mandala, psychodrama and related techniques, conflict facilitation, interactive games and physical movement practices, healing circles, and so on.

- The women's and men's circles rejoin in plenary for a mutual exploration of those issues that have released the most energy or charge in their respective groups. Various methods are used to facilitate this interactive dialogue and inquiry, depending on the nature of what has emerged. Often the cross-gender truth forum is utilized at this point, in which women and men convene in separate concentric circles, with the outer circle in silent witness of the inner circle, then reversing these roles so that each group is witnessed by the other. Other techniques include interactive dialogue processes, psychodrama, conflict facilitation, and interactive family therapy modalities.

## Days 4–5: Consecration, Integration, and Closure

- The larger group separates again into men's and women's circles in order to create rituals for honoring and celebrating the "other" group. The men design, choreograph, and conduct a ritual to honor and bless the women, and to exalt the feminine. The women do the same to honor the men, and the masculine. Facilitators do not guide or program these rituals, but leave them entirely up to the participants so they are spontaneous and serve to draw forth the creativity and unique energy of the participants. Depending on the depth of the healing work that has preceded them, these rituals are often surprisingly profound and moving ceremonies in which a palpable sense of Divine Feminine and Divine Masculine qualities are often experienced or glimpsed. These rituals are not just "icing on the cake," but are an essential and integral element of the gender reconciliation process—

bringing consecration and closure to one level of the work, and thereby also establishing the ground and trust for a subsequent deeper level of the gender work to unfold.

- After the two rituals are performed, the community focus shifts toward integration and closure. Integration includes consolidation of key insights and learnings from the experience; precautions and skillful practices for taking the lessons and insights back into the participants' home lives and workplaces; and closing council process, plus other completion practices.

Each of the above stages is a critical component of the process of gender reconciliation work.

**Application to Lesbian, Gay, Bisexual, and Transgender Issues**
As discussed in Chapter 1, Satyana Institute has always welcomed LGBT individuals to our programs, and we uphold the importance and legitimacy of LGBT issues. One-third of our thirty-three professional trainees in our gender reconciliation training program identified as LGBT, and we have worked with numerous LGBT co-facilitators over the years.

In most of Satyana Institute's gatherings that have combined heterosexual and LGBT participants, a profound level of gender healing work has resulted that would not have occurred in the same way had the group not been so diverse. Gender identities are expanding today beyond traditional male and female roles, not only in the gay, lesbian, bisexual, and transgendered communities, but also among many heterosexuals, particularly in younger generations. Youth are increasingly resisting rigid classification as either male or female—demanding more fluid and inclusive gender identities and roles. Expanding gender identities create new challenges and opportunities for gender reconciliation, and this has created great richness as well as challenges within Satyana's gender healing programs. It has also created challenges at times. Older participants are often comfortable in their identities as either women or men (whether straight, gay, or bisexual), whereas younger generation participants may feel alienated or oppressed by this polarized classification. Heterosexuals may appreciate an exercise or process that is viewed as oppressive or biased by gender-diverse participants, and vice versa. These differences have the potential to become a source of dynamic tension in a group, and, if properly handled, this can serve to move all participants more deeply into their hearts, thereby awakening a deeper unity within the group.

In our workshops that have combined heterosexual with gay, lesbian, and bisexual participants, we found the gender reconciliation process generally works quite well without any need for major adjustments in the format or design of the process. Indeed, such gatherings have generally been powerful learnings and heart-opening experiences for everyone in attendance.

That said, we have experienced a few cases in which the diversity of gender identity among the participants was so broad as to create some frustration for everyone involved. For example, in some (but not all) events that combined heterosexual and transgender participants, both subgroups have at times been frustrated by not being able to focus sufficiently on their own issues and concerns. One challenge that can arise is that transgender participants attending the program may not be comfortable joining either a women's or a men's breakout circle. This reluctance is entirely understandable because transgender individuals identify neither as women nor men, and so to be forced to choose between the two categories feels to them like a repressive violation, one that is based on a predominant heterosexist bias in the culture from which they feel gender healing work should provide relief and liberation.

In these cases, we have responded in different ways, depending on the circumstances. In instances where there were a substantial number of transgender participants we have modified the entire workshop design by creating three breakout groups: men, women, and a third group labeled either "transgender" or another appropriate label chosen by the transgender participants themselves. This has generally proven successful given sufficient workshop time, and has resulted in a rich experience for all participants. The workshop format is reconfigured to make room for three breakout groups and three cross-gender truth forums, ensuring that each of the breakout groups (men, women, and transgender) has a chance to be heard in silent witness by the other two. A total of three rituals is also required in this case, in which each subgroup designs a ritual to honor and bless the other two groups. One disadvantage of this format is that there is less time for each of the truth forums and the rituals, and the process is necessarily considerably more structured and less flexible to ensure that each of the three breakout groups receives its due share of time and attention within the limited time frame of the workshop.

In cases where there have been only a few transgendered participants (three or fewer), this approach is not practical because it would devote such a large portion of workshop time to just a few participants, leaving the remaining participants feeling that their concerns are disproportionately addressed. In these situations, we readily concede that our gender reconciliation model is not an ideal framework, and we ask the transgender participants to make the difficult choice between joining either the women's or men's breakout groups. If they have difficulty deciding, we ask each one how they were raised as children (i.e., either as a girl or a boy) and suggest they join that group, since gender reconciliation work has so much to do with undoing gender conditioning. Beyond this, either the entire Satyana model would need to be redesigned, which we have not undertaken, or perhaps the transgender participants are better served by seeking a different modality of gender healing work that more directly serves their needs.

In summary, different groups of people have different issues and needs, and we have learned that it's not always possible or necessarily desirable to try to create a gender healing program that suits the needs of every person and all constituencies. It is sometimes best for gender programs to be designed and focused on the specific needs of particular constituencies. For example, there are billions of heterosexual women and men across the globe who have no issues whatsoever about their sexual orientation or gender identities but who are struggling mightily with toxic cultural conditioning in relation to social strictures governing their lives as women and men. For most of these people, heterosexual gender reconciliation work is their deep need. To forcefully or ideologically expand the focus to include LGBT issues would not only be irrelevant, it would derail the process and prevent them from doing the deep gender healing work they urgently need to do. Meanwhile for others, LGBT issues are paramount, and for them to engage in gender healing work between heterosexual women and men would be irrelevant or counterproductive.

Thus LGBT issues are not everyone's concern, just as Muslim "honor killings" or Hindu "bride burnings" are not everyone's concern. However, what links all these diverse interest groups is the gender oppression they all share and the violation of fundamental human rights constellated around gender. The human rights abuses of the LGBT community *are* everyone's concern, just as the human rights abuses of Muslim women *are* everyone's concern, as are the abuses of oppressed human beings everywhere. Thus the unifying theme for all forms of gender oppression is the larger question of universal human rights.

# APPENDIX B

# *Qualitiative Assessment of Satyana's Gender Reconciliation Program: Survey Responses*

To assess the efficacy and long-term impacts of Satyana's gender reconciliation work, the authors conducted a qualitative survey of professionals with six to ten years experience with this work. An overview of this survey and its principal findings are presented in Chapter 11. This Appendix summarizes some of the survey details, and presents the detailed responses we received from each survey respondent.

We sent out a total of twenty-nine surveys and received ten back. The bulk of this Appendix reproduces the highlights of the ten detailed survey questionnaires we received back. The responses came from three men and seven women, all of whom are professionals in various fields who completed Satyana Institute's yearlong gender reconciliation training for facilitators, which was conducted outside Boulder, Colorado, from November 2001 – November 2002. This professional training program consisted of four weeklong training modules and was attended by a total of thirty-three trainees. It was to this training group that we sent out the survey (apart from two people who have since passed away, and two others for whom we no longer have contact information). A fifth weeklong certification training module was conducted in May 2005, for which fifteen of the original thirty-three participants—six men and nine women— returned for final certification training as facilitators of Satyana's gender reconciliation work. Nine of the ten survey respondents completed this certification program.

One of the most auspicious aspects of Satyana's gender reconciliation project is that our certified facilitators are committed to carrying Satyana's gender reconciliation program to wider audiences. As will become evident, many of the following comments reflect strong support of Satyana's mission, and further underscore the importance of bringing conscious gender awareness, healing, and reconciliation into other realms of society.

Eleven specific headings are utilized to organize the survey responses below. These headings, selected based on the survey, are as follows: (1) Relationship with self, (2) Intimate relationship(s), (3) Relationships with family, (4) Work environment, (5) Men/women relationships, (6) Lesbian, gay, bisexual, transgender (LGBT) and heterosexual relationships, (7) Memorable moments of gender work, (8) Changed societal perspective, (9) Most valuable aspects of the work, (10) Suggestions for improvement of the work, and (11) Implementation of the work—globally. Not all respondents addressed every question in the survey; in these cases, the corresponding headings are omitted from their responses below.

Presented below are the ten survey responses, each of which begins with a brief biography of the respondent. The reader will note that the responses are repetitive in various ways, and this forms the basis for formulating common themes and impacts of the gender work. The benefits of Satyana's gender healing work, as gleaned from these surveys, are summarized in eleven points which are presented in Chapter 11.

## Julien Devereux L.C.S.W., L.C.D.C.

Julien is a consultant and coach in clinical social work and organizational development and management. He has a background in criminal justice, addictions counseling, and human services administration. He serves on the senior staff at Eupsychia Institute in Austin, Texas, where he leads training programs in Integrative Breathwork.

*Relationship with self.* Satyana's work challenged me on many of my assumptions about gender. Some changed, some didn't, but all were examined. What did occur is reconciliation or integration between the two aspects [masculine and feminine] of myself. It was no longer necessary to wall off parts of myself out of a homophobic fear of being too feminine or fear that I would hurt someone if I expressed my masculine sense of power. Within myself, I now feel the inner marriage of the feminine and masculine. There is not a battle going on between my head and my heart. I can actually balance and integrate these two aspects of myself and feel whole.

*Intimate relationships.* My relationship with the most important woman in my life, my wife, has deepened into an unshakeable friendship that still has deep passion after thirty-four years together. I no longer project onto her intentions that came from my early development with an alcoholic, abusive, sick mother, but experience her as who she is without past baggage from my assumptions about "all women."

*Relationships with family.* My relationships with my daughters initially drove me to this work because they were afraid of me, and I reached a point of awareness that I did not want to teach them to fear male authority figures. I also began to see the impact of social conditioning on them in middle school, which limited their opportunities and eroded their confidence and self-esteem. Following the gender work, my relationships with my daughters went through several years of transformation in which they had to get used to the changes in me and risk a deeper connection. At times I worked too hard to achieve this, but in the long run we have a great relationship in which they can tell me anything, and I have the ability to simply listen and love them, rather than trying to give them advice and fix them.

*Work environment.* As a social worker, organizational consultant, and life coach, I use what I learned in this work in almost every session. I openly talk about gender issues as they manifest in the lives and social structures of my clients. This is not always welcomed or attended to, but I believe that I can no longer be silent on this issue, because it is so fundamental to all human dynamics. The first way that we are taught to be separate is through gender. Is it a boy or is it a girl? It has to be one or the other. After this is determined, all the social constructions and constrictions begin to be taught, beginning with whether the blanket is pink or blue. What the training has done for me is allowed me to see these dynamics everywhere and not be blind to them.

*Men/women relationships.* As a result of Satyana's program I started doing men's work through the Mankind Project and I still meet weekly with men to work through the deconstruction of attitudes and feelings that prevent me from a full integration with my true self that has both masculine and feminine dimensions. Through the gender reconciliation work, I have been able to be available in a compassionate way for other men and to allow myself to be supported, nurtured, and loved by men without confusing it with being homosexual or weak.

In my professional work, women often tell me that I feel safe to be around. At one time I would have taken this to mean that I am not much of a man or that I am a wimp. Now, it is the deepest compliment to me, and I feel a deep sense of healing whenever I hear it. In my work facilitating breathwork for Eupsychia, many women come to heal from sexual trauma and I am able to help them process through it without triggering their trauma. I believe this is a direct result of my work in gender reconciliation.

*LGBT and heterosexual.* My first really good friend, Tom, who was gay, joined me in the yearlong training and died during that year. I learned so much from him and yet I don't think we would have ever been friends if I hadn't attended earlier Satyana workshops. I learned so much about the broad range of human sexuality in this work that totally took me by surprise. The most surprising was the fact that there are more than two genders and that those who don't fall neatly into the two socially approved genders have already done a lot of integration work with their masculine and feminine sides because they had to in order to survive.

*Memorable workshop moments.* There are so many that it is hard to pick out a few. In one of the early workshops, I was challenged by a woman to not sit on the sidelines in this struggle culturally, but rather to be one of the men that were actively challenging patriarchy. I have been doing so ever since. Another moment was being challenged by one of the women in the training because I had come on to her sexually. After being challenged and deeply reflecting on it, my realization was that I had no skill at nonsexual intimacy with a woman. At a certain point of feeling close, the only option I knew was to sexualize it. This understanding shook me to my toes, and I began to work at acquiring a new level of skill at being close emotionally, physically, and intellectually without projecting my sexual fantasies on a woman.

*Changed societal perspective.* I have noticed how difficult the struggle has been for women to be heard and understood and how difficult it is for them to be leaders in society while being attacked and discounted because they are women. I have also noticed that they need encouragement, support, and role models to step forward and lead. I have a deep desire to help them take over the world as soon as possible to assure its survival and to help counterbalance the centuries of masculine dominance that has now become so dangerous and self-destructive. I believe that it's important that men join women in that struggle or it will never succeed. I am one of those men.

I've noticed that in the men's work that I'm involved in, so many men are isolated, alone, afraid, and depressed. They have a hard time showing up to do work because they know that it will pull the old rug out from under them. So they often drift away and don't come to group or relapse to drinking or sexually acting out. They all know that what they were taught about being men is NOT TRUE but they don't know what to do about it.

*Most valuable aspects.* Again, there are so many dimensions it is hard to say, but I think what distinguishes Satyana's work from other work is the recognition that gender work is essentially spiritual, and if it is not addressed from that perspective it is incomplete. In other words it is fundamentally transformative and nothing will be the same after experiencing it. This also makes it difficult to explain and even more difficult to engage people in it. The other dimensions that are important are the awareness exercises and the ability for this work to connect the personal with the spiritual or collective through the path of the heart. The experiential nature of the processes assures that participants don't simply reduce this to theory for discussion but actually are able to have it transform their perspective.

*Suggestions for improvement of the work.* My primary concern is there is not enough money or capacity to respond to the need that exists for this work.

*Implementation of work—globally.* This process is reliable, repeat-able, and universal enough that it should be replicated and further developed in any situation that will allow it. It is a fundamental building block in transforming society into a peaceful, sustainable way for humans to be in the world together.

## Gwenn Marie, M.A.

In a long communications career, Gwenn Marie produced and host-ed several TV series, pioneered the use of corporate satellite televi-sion networks, and led creative marketing teams for global brands. She owns and manages a serene and peaceful California desert inn with her husband, Rich Caldwell.

*Relationship with self.* The gender work has become part of the fabric of my life, every day. It informs all of my relationships, all the time. I see and interact with both women and men with the lens of our learning and insights. It's much easier to be happy! Very profound and positive impact. By deepening my compassion for masculine and feminine energies, I have opened a lot more "space" and respect for yin-yang forces within myself. Satyana's work helped me realize how much time I spend in "masculine mode," and how difficult it has been to tap into and express my feminine. It's opened my eyes to how many opportunities I miss to act from my feminine when I'm in "alpha male" superdrive mode; there is no room for the feminine.

The work also opened me to feeling and expressing the universal feminine grief that shrouds human experience today—war and vio-lence are huge wounds to the feminine. No wonder so many women can't sleep and suffer from "lack of desire" in the sexual domain! The feminine is in excruciating pain. How can women feel truly and vibrantly alive and contribute from the feminine when war and vio-lence completely degrade and destroy the human life that comes from our wombs? I can feel how deeply in touch with feminine grief I am, and it has opened huge new channels of compassion for myself and other women. I strongly believe that if warring men truly understood how human destruction insults and wounds the feminine psyche, they would stop and come back to the embrace they most need from their women.

*Intimate relationships.* Most importantly, I find my "field of compassion" has expanded as a result of this work, for which I will be forever grateful. I have much more "room" for my dear spouse; I'm far less triggered by certain behaviors. I'm far more willing to work to "remember" and respect what drives the masculine viewpoint and actions. The conversation has opened huge new terrain for us that we traverse daily, and it has sharpened our communications skill sets. I'm learning how to communicate in ways my husband can "hear," which means we're both happier most of the time!

*Relationships with family.* I'm a fascinated observer of interpersonal dynamics within the family. The work has enabled me to offer thoughtful counsel about relationships with "the other" to my adult children, which seems to resonate for them. Our family "drama quotient" is extremely low, which makes for more satisfying relationships.

*Work environment.* I use the Satyana work in every facet of my life, including a very busy professional and business context. I believe it helps me be a more effective leader and collaborator, open to new ideas and not reacting from "victim," even when interacting with challenging people. The depth of the work touches my public life in every way. And people do notice the difference!

*Men/women relationships.* I've found a deeply authentic connection with men, as a partner. The work has helped me experience far less anger and resentment toward men, which has opened many new possibilities for collaboration, friendship, and satisfaction. The work has helped me understand and appreciate the masculine experience in ways I'm sure I never would have. For this I am most grateful. Thank you!

I listen to women's complaints about men from a different perspective—I simply won't play there. Women must take responsibility for our own emotional ecology and stop blaming men for everything. My viewpoints about women's responsibility to assume leadership for shifting dynamics are not always popular. Too many women comfortably reside in blame and refuse to do the work. A new voice is being called for, not the shrill, demanding voice of "victim," but the calm, reassuring voice of "partner." Women have no idea of our true power!

*LGBT and heterosexual.* The gender work has enriched these relationships, though I've always had plenty of room for people with sexual preference and drives different than my own. The opportunity to interact closely with gay, lesbian, bisexual and transgendered friends in such a deeply intimate and caring way was very enrichening.

*Memorable workshop moments.* During the yearlong training I had exceptional experiences in our breath work. In one session, I was introduced to and invited to say "yes" to The Void. I experienced pure nothingness for the longest time. It was a tremendous opening. During the certification training (May 2005), I also experienced a breakthrough to my grief in the women's circle during the truth mandala exercise where we individually entered a place divided into quadrants, with sticks, stones, and other artifacts, and we moved among them, expressing insights and emotions. I tapped into a grief so huge and overwhelming it nearly consumed me. Accepting the gift of that grief was memorable.

*Changed societal perspective.* I'm aware of the absence of an authentic feminine voice in the world political landscape, those who speak from the wisdom of the feminine. We have Nancy Pelosi and Hillary Clinton, and Angela Merkel, but they speak, act, and lead from the masculine dynamic. Women have learned so well to be "like men," which isn't helping anything.

*Most valuable aspects of work.* Being in the crucible of discovery together. Seeing how we are all wounded. Gaining a new understanding of our divine design—we are meant to complement, to partner in wholeness. Broadening and deepening perspectives. Getting out of the blame game. Accepting responsibility for my own role, the parts I've played in the past, and new possibilities for the future. Meeting and coming to know an extraordinary group of people.

*Suggestions for improvement of the work.* First of all, THANK YOU for seeing it, studying it, and formulating a starting place to "deal and heal" with each other. What a huge endeavor! My only suggestion for improving the work is in designing and executing more useful follow-up mechanisms, activities, and forums that would keep us connected and inspired.

*Implementation of work—globally.* Yes, of course! It's tempting to think that the world is actually divided into states, countries, political parties, religious sects, and other factions—a false and dangerous assumption. The real organizing principle of everything is masculine/feminine. Until we heal and balance that dynamic (calm the masculine, embrace the feminine), we will continue to repeat useless cycles of war, violence, abuse, and genocide. The masculine/feminine dynamic is the DNA of all life and our experience in it.

### Shirsten Lundblad, M.Div., L.M.T.

Shirsten is a professional musician, certified yoga teacher, and massage therapist. She completed her divinity degree at Harvard Divinity School, performs and records with Inanna, Sisters in Rhythm, and Referendum, and teaches classes in sacred chant and percussion.

*Relationship with self.* I have a greater appreciation for the impact of gender injustice and its personal and political impact for men and women.

*LGBT and heterosexual.* I have done a lot of community process in my life, and I found the gender reconciliation work to be some of the most profound work I have ever experienced. And yet, at the same time, I have had a difficult time translating that experience into a language or system in daily life that seems to have any impact, other than how deep transformative experiences can't help but find their indirect expression in one's daily life.

I have long felt that there is another piece of the work that involves lesbian, gay, and transgendered people exploring this and teaching it together, as some of our experiences in the world in relation to gender are both subtly and profoundly different from those of heterosexual people. This first became apparent to me in the same-sex groups that we had in our yearlong training. That is not meant to imply that lesbians all trust each other without reservation (especially when one adds dynamics of race and class). And yet there are some trust issues regarding competition for male attention and male-affiliated power that are not experienced in the same way with lesbians. Some of our wounding is also different, and some is the same. I do not wish to capitalize on the differences, and yet it has felt to me that there is a puzzle piece that needs to be fit in here more intentionally to complete the picture and ultimately the healing work ahead of us.

Transgendered people have helped me to begin to explore some of the differences between sexuality and gender, which is also very important to sort out in this inquiry and group process.

*Changed societal perspective.* As we ponder the concept of "sacred marriage" I wonder how the "marriage myth" functions in the psyches of those of us who are not given public sanctity, privilege, and associated rights of such a basically common and celebrated ceremony. It is not something that I was as aware of until recently, with all the attention that this question has been given, and now having the opportunity to drive down any public highway in America and see bumper stickers saying: "One man + one woman = marriage."

*Most valuable aspects of work.* I definitely appreciate the spiritual context for this work, in that I have long felt that feminism and spirituality are intimately connected. All my feminist studies in seminary emphasized how the personal IS indeed political. And that our spiritual lives express themselves in our sociopolitical interactions and involvements.

*Implementation of work—globally.* I think this work is some of THE MOST PROFOUND AND IMPORTANT WORK THAT WE CAN BE DOING TO HEAL OURSELVES, and to prevent the annihilation of the species and the planet.

## Alan Strachan, Ph.D., M.F.T.

Alan has a private psychotherapy practice in Santa Cruz, California, focusing on issues such as gender healing, clarifying life purpose, and relationship as a spiritual path. He was formerly the staff psychotherapist at the Stanford Research Institute. Alan is currently writing a book about the unconscious forces operating in the presidency of George W. Bush and in the collective psyche of the American people.

*Relationship with self.* This work has absolutely helped the masculine/feminine integration. I have a much greater self-awareness and self-acceptance of how my personal identity encompasses both "masculine" and "feminine" traits, and greater sensitivity to how gender issues affect others. I'd had a series of powerful dreams about this issue—psychospiritual androgyny—for years before attending the training, and having the opportunity to process "male/female" issues in a therapeutic community was very, very beneficial. I've come to a much greater acceptance of my inherently androgynous nature.

*Intimate relationships.* Satyana's work has had a profound and positive impact on my marriage. In addition, the training inspired me to form a peer-facilitated men's group. It's been going for three years and has been wonderful—a place for caring men to be able to share openly, belying the oft-repeated stereotypes about men not being willing or able to communicate their feelings.

*Work environment.* I bring my increased awareness and sensitivity to my psychotherapy work with clients. I understand and appreciate with more clarity and empathy the particular issues that men and women each face in our gendered society. I am able to empathize with women and talk to them about the debilitating effect our patriarchal society has on women—which carries a particular healing impact, coming from a man. I have also been moved to respond to political circumstances in which I felt gender prejudice was in evidence and needed to be ameliorated.

*Men/women relationships.* I've become more open to exploring friendships with a wider group of men, and not just dismissing almost all of them as emotionally stunted and therefore poor candidates for authentic friendship.

I have increasing sensitivity, in particular, to the debilitating, denigrating, psychologically and physically violent impact of the patriarchal emphasis of U.S. society on women.

*Memorable workshop moments.* There are too many to count—literally. Many, many incredibly deep experiences, including deeply healing moments with my wife, the profound pleasure of bonding with the men in the men's groups, transformative breathwork sessions, some of the didactic presentations (particularly when they connected with the spiritual foundations of the work), spending many sleepless nights processing deep fears and learning essential lessons, getting to know people and getting to be known—falling in love over and over again—and an extraordinary experience of one-ness that has continued to resonate to this day.

*Changed societal perspective.* Yes. I'm even more sensitive to the unconscious assertions by both men and women that our stereotypic gender roles are hardwired rather than largely being the product of social conditioning. It's the "men are from Mars and women are from Venus" bias writ large, which, in my truly balanced and dispassionate way, really pisses me off (!). It's a profound disservice to the deeper truth of who we are.

*Most valuable aspects of work.* Doing deep work on our personal identity (taking ever greater responsibility for our thoughts, feelings and actions), and doing so in relationship with others who are also doing that deep work. My wife and I had done very deep gender work in and between ourselves prior to the Satyana training, but it was vitally important for us to then do this work in community. It took us to a level of healing that would have otherwise been impossi-ble. The spiritual base of the work, and the way that was manifested in concrete, embodied ways, was absolutely essential.

*Implementation of work—globally.* Absolutely needed. It is badly needed in this country [U.S.] and throughout the world. Gender issues/biases/prejudice/violence is pandemic, and a tragedy that increased awareness and sensitivity could avert. It would be a revelation—and revolution—for the human race to engage in this work.

## Royda Crose, Ph.D.

Royda is a psychologist, hypnotherapist, gerontologist, wellness specialist, and author of the book, *Why Women Live Longer Than Men, and What Men Can Learn from Them* (Jossey Bass, 1997). She hosts a radio show, "Women's Issues, Women's Voices" in Columbia, Missouri. Royda co-founded the first legal abortion clinic in Dallas in the 1970s, and she has an extensive background in women's health, lifespan wellness, and gender differences in aging.

*Relationship with self.* The first Satyana gender reconciliation workshop I attended in 1996 was very healing for me. It was actually life-changing, so much so that I then sent my adult children to subsequent workshops so that they might also have the benefits.

*Intimate relationships.* It opened me to more fully identify with and express my bisexuality, which has resulted in experiencing intimate relationships with women for the first time in my sixties.

*Relationships with family.* It has opened up communication in our family with increased understanding of masculine and feminine perspectives or ways that we view situations and experiences.

*Men/women relationships.* The gender work helped me to have more compassion for men. I became aware of the wounds that men suffer living in a patriarchal society in ways that I had never considered or even known about before. I don't feel that the program influenced my relationships with women much at all.

*LGBT and heterosexual.* Satyana's unit on this in the training was very helpful. I especially liked and am using the multidimensional grid that was presented. It has helped me to understand my own bisexuality. I had previously done quite a bit of work in human sexuality so I was already involved with this aspect of the program, as far as comfort level, knowledge, and social relationships.

*Memorable workshop moments.* Most memorable was the work I did at the end of the first workshop (1996) when I was in a lot of pain and confusion. Two of the facilitators (both men) and many of the participants stayed after the closing to work with me in order to gain some closure. In the training, the thing that stands out was my experience when two other participants—a woman and a man—were in conflict and I became enraged with what I felt later was the rage of my great-grandmother and my grandmother, rather than my own. It seemed that a deep cellular genetic rage of past generations of women in my family was triggered and I was the vessel to express it for the first time, long after both these abused women had died. I am still mystified by what happened. I had never felt such rage before, and I felt safe enough to express it.

*Changed societal perspective.* As a psychologist, I believe that this gender work has made me a better therapist for both male and female clients. My depth of understanding has grown, my compassion has expanded, and my ability to listen without being triggered myself has improved.

*Most valuable aspects of work.* Bringing men and women together in honest, open dialogue, in a safe supportive environment. If I had to sum up my experience with the gender reconciliation work it would be (1) these workshops gave me a safe place to engage my deep-seated rage, which was much greater than I had ever imagined, and (2) this work gave me insight about the wounding that the patriarchy has caused for men, which subsequently opened me to much greater compassion for the male species, whom I had hitherto regarded only as my oppressors. I could now see firsthand from the men in this work that we are all oppressed and wounded, and both genders need healing. This realization gave me greater appreciation for the impact that the women's movement has made toward healing for women—something that men may have yet to fully accomplish for themselves.

*Implementation of work—globally.* I think this gender work is one avenue to healing wounds and resolving violence that exists on many planes and in many environments. It is one path to building peace on the planet.

## Shawn Galloway

Shawn is a professional musician, artist, author, and workshop facilitator with a strong background in men's work. He has released several CDs, including the multimedia experience entitled *I Choose Love*, which was inspired by Satyana Institute's gender reconciliation work and has been enthusiastically received across the country. Shawn released a CD last year entitled *Love Will Overcome*, and he has written theme songs for several organizations, including The Peace Alliance, The New Energy Movement, and Go Gratitude.

*Relationship with self.* The gender reconciliation work has given me a deeper sense of inner peace related to my own internal relationship between the feminine and masculine aspects of myself. I feel more in communion with Divine Love.

*Intimate relationships.* Increased understanding, compassion, and insight for both sexes. We are both equally wounded, and when we realize this, we can then support each other in the healing process; first by upholding each individual's relationship with Divine Love, and then by coming together to express our spirits in ways that support both ourselves and our community.

*Relationships with family.* It helped me heal the wounding I received from a mother who was very active in the women's movement during the '70s and '80s, and the fallout for me as a male teenager growing up. I was able to set some strong boundaries within myself and with my mother, which enabled me to release the shame I held as a man from the constant male bashing I was surrounded by and not pass this on to my daughter.

*Men/women relationships.* Being a man, I have come into deep acceptance of who I am and how I am programmed in human form. Satyana's gender trainings empowered this strength in me and allowed me to build healthy relationships with other men, and to honor our uniqueness as men together.

I see women as a Divine reflection of the woman within me. I love and honor women and all that they face on their path, knowing that the way I relate with them is the way I relate with myself. The gender work enabled me to dive deeply into this understanding of my inner struggles with women and offered a healing that I fully embrace today.

*LGBT and heterosexual.* I realized that gender identities are not about sexual preference, but about the internal relating people hold within themselves between the feminine and masculine energies. I also realized the great value that the LGBT population brings to a community; they dance between worlds, and can become great bridge builders for healing gender relations.

*Memorable workshop moments.* Most memorable was when I realized how my internal masculine and feminine were at war with each other and how, in creating dialogue between them, they came into harmony and balance. Another crucial moment for me was when an older woman stood up and said that she had come to the realization that women have to protect men as much as men have to protect women. I felt years of holding women's pain melt away from me when I heard this.

*Suggestions for improvement of the work.* The single most important issue in gender work for me is healing the internal conflict between the feminine and masculine energies. I would strongly suggest that this be the most important intention of the work, and that all harmony and balance comes out of this principle.

*Implementation of work—globally.* Absolutely needed. When we as men and women are affirmed and honored by our own gender, then we have the power and strength to meet the complimentary gender eye to eye, and together we can begin building communities that honor both equally.

## Janet Coster, M.A., P.M.F.T.

Janet is a psychotherapist and spiritual director in private practice in Santa Cruz, California. She has a professional background in dance and the performing arts. As a pastoral, marriage, and family therapist, Janet serves a broad clientele of diverse sexual orientations, including heterosexual, gay, lesbian, bisexual, and transgender.

*Relationship with self.* Through gender reconciliation work I experienced intrapersonal healing at a very profound level of my being. This experience built a larger container for holding global pain that is beyond one individual's capacity to hold. It thereby supported my own courageous immersion into the deep individual gender wounds I have personally sustained.

*Intimate relationships.* My marriage partner and I were given a much deeper understanding of how gender healing MUST occur within the community context, since gender conditioning/wounding begins at that level. This level of support led to our being able to risk speaking openly about how profoundly gender wounding has affected us as individuals, and thus in relationship. Although we had been very actively working on this healing between ourselves, the group support became a bridge toward a much deeper, much needed experience of interpersonal healing within the context of our relationship.

*Relationships with family.* I have worked on even greater levels of understanding, tolerance and forgiveness for the unhealthy gender role modeling I was given so early in life, and for the very specific ways by which particular men in my life demonstrated misogynistic, inappropriate, and hurtful behavior toward me.

*Work environment.* I have been able to cultivate a more defined and concrete sense of how to begin approaching and healing the effects of cultural gender conditioning in all our lives. In particular, this has emboldened me—both in my counseling practice and in community and international work—to openly name and work with the societal levels of gender conditioning and wounding. Working at this larger contextual level is very healing and vitally important, as opposed to working only on an individual story level. Doing so immediately brings a sense of support, relief, and understanding to clients and others—and gives them a way to begin examining how collective levels of conditioning have affected them. I am witnessing major healing changes in my clients (and others), as I now hold this same larger space and understanding for others that was previously held for me (in the gender reconciliation trainings).

*Relationships with men.* I now carry a much greater sensitivity to—and compassion for—the profound level of wounding that men also bear from the cultural conditioning they receive. I have a deeper understanding about how ALL of us are "losers" in the current cultural setup. A critical distinction I now make is this: although generally speaking it is true that on a *cultural* level, (1) men receive many more "perks" and (2) there is much greater inequity and violence toward women on multiple cultural/global levels, nevertheless, on a *human personality* level, both men and women suffer, suffer, suffer. It is an endless circle of suffering, whereby everyone—women and men—are terribly affected. Conversely, wherever there is healing and reconciliation on any of these levels, both women and men will benefit. This deeper *interpersonal* understanding and compassion that I now experience with regard to men represents for me yet another proof of my healing/forgiving *intrapersonal* experience.

*Relationships with women.* I was able to do an important healing piece with the women in our gender reconciliation circle. So much wounding occurs between women, and I have been the recipient of plenty of this in my life—oftentimes just for being an attractive and intelligent woman. There is a cultural setup whereby women threaten (and are threatened by) one another, and therefore we project onto and mistreat one another, thereby reifying and reinforcing the domination model inherent in the larger culture. I was able to openly share and cry and cleanse some very old wounding on this level. I was heard and held and received by others around this. This has enabled a deeper forgiveness (reconciliation) process, starting from the inside out, which has had unending ramifications.

*LGBT and heterosexual.* I have always been open to other expressions of self and self-identification. The yearlong program helped to further educate me and to further expand my awareness and deepen my sensitivity to LGBT concerns. My counseling practice, which was already inclusive of gay/lesbian/bisexual people, has quite naturally expanded to include working closely and comfortably with transgender people. I have learned a lot and have been able to give a lot in order to support the particular challenges experienced by transgender folks. They demonstrate for us all—with daily embodiment—the struggle to balance both masculine and feminine energies within.

*Memorable workshop moments.* There are many: the faces of those who became my beloveds. The willingness to unveil ourselves to one another, and the courage and risk-taking concretely demonstrated through the levels of intimacy we reached together. Often, at first, our stories of deep anger and pain were the only gifts we had to give to one another. What a testimony that we were able to both give and receive such gifts! The personal risk that my marriage partner and I took to open our shared relationship to the circle. The final celebration of our yearlong training—i.e., a time when women and men came together at a much deeper level of truth and intimacy than where we had begun. In a year's time, we were able to move demonstrably past the profound wounding each of us brought in—with its resultant bitterness, mistrust, and anger—to an expression of much greater love and trust. We were able to swap gender dress and gender roles, tell gender jokes on ourselves, and share together our tears and deep belly laughter.

*Changed societal perspective.* For decades I have been painfully aware of dominating societal setups regarding gender dynamics. I have been aware of how the religious realm has too often glibly served as an oppressive hierarchy, adding its sanction to the societal setup, rather than challenging it in the name of true kenosis and transformation. Although the serious ramifications of all of this have been openly named by some, they continue to be ignored by our "tribal consciousness" world. Gender wounding and gender discrimination therefore continue to be—for women AND men—a silent holocaust whereby countless souls and lives are destroyed internally and/or externally.

What has changed, and continues to change, in relation to these societal and religious dynamics is my self. A direct healing result of practicing gender reconciliation in our supportive group trainings (while also doing the work intensively in my marriage partnership) is that, increasingly, I am less and less "hooked" by my personal story of gender wounding. I am experiencing more and more inner cleansing and freedom from the toxic effects of gender wounding. I therefore find myself in a paradoxical position of being more compassionate and forgiving of the world for having contributed to my personal wounding, while, at the same time, I am increasingly less willing to allow it to go on. This leads me to take an even stronger activist stance in the world.

*Most valuable aspects of work.* Most foundational of all, I believe, is the spiritual base of the work. It is absolutely ESSENTIAL. Without it, I could not have participated, nor do I think the work can be sustained.

*Suggestions for improvements of the work.* I just want to express complete gratitude for the grace avenue that is opened through the gender reconciliation work, and for the willingness of all (Satyana and participants everywhere) to be channels for that grace!

*Implementation of work—globally.* Most definitely needed! We have all seen what the world is like when we are not owning and healing these places inside and out. Gender reconciliation work is healing on both a personal AND global level, and both levels are essential. I have experienced this firsthand, personally and with the groups I have both participated in and helped to facilitate. The alchemical process of grace, transformation, and reconciliation truly does begin to take place. People's self-containers are enlarged by the group container, which in turn honors both the micro and the macro perspectives.

## Carlotta Tyler, M.S.O.D.

Carlotta is an organizational development consultant and executive coach who works primarily with women leaders. She is a specialist on gender issues and dynamics in the workplace. Carlotta conducted twenty-seven years of longitudinal research on four continents with over fifteen hundred women, focusing on ways that women organize to do work and women's interpersonal dynamics in groups of women.

*Relationship with self.* I had done extensive integrative intrapsychic work prior to taking the gender reconciliation program. Part of my goal in taking Satyana's training was to further integrate the masculine with the well-accessed feminine, but not using a Jungian model of those words. Anima, to me, is a male definition of the feminine, which does not concur with my experience of these dimensions, having lived this lifetime as a female. The concepts are inherently biased.

*Intimate relationships.* Greater balance, understanding, calm.

*Relationships with family.* I have had increased empathy for my son during a recent divorce. Loving kindness, open heart, maintain appropriate boundaries, reflect.

*Men/women relationships.* I have more empathy for my son and his father, and increased empathy and insight on male behavior and ways to engage in dialogue around interpersonal gender dynamics.

*LGBT and heterosexual.* I have greater appreciation of the spectrum of sexual identity and behaviors, and my impression expanded that these are not fixed conditions, but have the potential to fluctuate along a continuum from "male"-defined to "female"-defined over a lifetime. I gained insights into role reversal in heterosexual couples and the capacity for a "straight" marriage to combine with homosexual behaviors without a breach. I learned the value of the contracted marriage.

*Changed societal perspective.* I have developed a more acute lens on interfemale dynamics, especially around indirect aggression, power issues, confusion and dynamics, indirect woman-on-woman projections from mother, sister, daughter life experiences. I have a greater understanding of the sacrifices exacted from white males by the patriarchal culture for white male entitlement, privilege.

*Most valuable aspects of work.* Satyana's program is valuable as an active laboratory for working on the process of gender appreciation based on direct experience. Given a safe container with highly skilled group technicians, as well as gender reconciliation specialists, this work cultivates the ability to cut through and resolve masses of limiting beliefs, woundings, confusion.

*Implementation of work—globally.* Absolutely. I think it is important to call it something other than "gender reconciliation," as this name calls up implied expectations that in the timeframe offered the work will resolve, or reconcile, these differences. I did not have the experience of the work actually doing that. I would rather call it exploration across gender, as I do in my work: "Gender Appreciation." But whatever it's called, this work is a fine beginning down a lifetime path.

## Corky Bridgeforth, M.Ed.
Corky is a retired elementary school teacher who specializes in body/mind/spirit connection. She is trained in yoga, homeopathy, Brain Gym, vision therapy, and other areas, and recently married again.

*Relationship with self.* I first came to gender reconciliation work because I was convinced that it is possible for both masculine and feminine energies to be expressed in a truly balanced way, intrapersonally and interpersonally. This balance can lead to a beautiful dance between the masculine and feminine that creates something greater than either can be without the other. I simply wanted to learn how to dance through my life experiences with that sort of balance.

This work gave me many glimpses of that perfection. It also showed much more than I even wanted to know about how sadly lacking that perfect gender balance is in so many places in our imperfect world! As a result of much personal growth, I have been given an opportunity to create that sort of balance in my relationship with my new husband, Jack.

*Intimate relationships.* I have gained a much deeper understanding and acceptance of who and where men are, which allows me to be more present, less needy, and more assertive in my dealings with them. This was perhaps the most significant growth for me. This inner work helped me to stand tall as a single woman in the world, to take good care of myself, and to seek and create a new, much more balanced intimate relationship. I am blessed. My relationship with Jack allows me to be a good wife, but also to experience the role reversal, allowing my husband to be a good wife for me when I was the one leaving home to be the breadwinner. Sometimes women need wives, too, and men need good husbands.

*Relationships with family.* I'm a better listener. I have less need to win or be in control because I have more sense of personal power.

*Work environment.* Gender work taught me the power of maintaining clear, strong, assertive feminine energy in the face of shadow masculine and shadow feminine behavior. I am much more attuned to gender issues in general, and find myself quite willing to confront these issues when they appear.

*LGBT and heterosexual.* I have gained a much greater understanding and acceptance of the issues LGBT people face in their journey toward wholeness.

*Memorable workshop moments.* The closing rituals stand out in my mind as transformative. High points: breathwork, spontaneous music, small group interactions, guest speakers, ever-deepening dialogue, single gender work, silent witnessing. How important it was to be able to wrestle with our differences, challenges, confrontations, and disagreements, and still be able to look at each other through the eyes of the Beloved!

*Changed societal perspective.* I developed much greater sensitivity to gender dynamics in society as apparent throughout our media, news, computers, movies, and so on. In my teaching world, I had many opportunities to observe gender dynamics within families—i.e., fathers and daughters versus mothers and daughters, subtle conditioning, role modeling, parental expectations, mass media advertising, toys, and so forth.

*Implementation of work—globally.* There is real benefit in implementing gender reconciliation work widely throughout the world community. The more we can learn to really understand and dialogue with one another—individually and globally—across our different ways of being, the healthier will be our society at all levels.

## Linda Cunningham, M.A.

Linda is a retired co-founder of HellerCunningham, an international organization development consulting firm. She came to Satyana's gender work after a deep immersion in women's experience of the sacred through the Women's Well in Concord, Massachusetts. Currently, Linda works with women who are reclaiming their lives following abusive relationships. She also works with men in prison, training them in alternatives to violence (AVP).

*Relationship with self.* Furthering gender healing work in the world is a major focus of my life. When I can't be actively doing gender work with Satyana, then I concentrate on working with women to help them change their lives. I have been doing this since the '60s as an active feminist—and now I have wedded feminism with spirituality.

*Work environment.* I have been a feminist most of my life. My studies of the patriarchy and its role in the oppression of women and girls led me to an indepth study of the Divine Feminine. This in turn led me to Satyana's gender reconciliation work that seeks to liberate and support both the Divine Feminine and the Divine Masculine.

*Men/women relationships.* I strive to see the Divine Masculine in the men I meet—even if they don't consciously identify with this in themselves. This has been especially helpful working with men in the prisons, where the system depends on dehumanization—to keep both prisoners and guards towing the line.

Gender reconciliation work has also expanded my work of helping women to increase their self-esteem and reclaim their divinity, which has been denied them by all the major religions.

*LGBT and heterosexual.* I have always worked closely with gay people, so I entered this arena with a great deal of sensitivity. My knowledge of LGBT issues expanded in the yearlong program and in subsequent challenging gender workshops I helped to facilitate in South Africa and Massachusetts.

*Memorable workshop moments.* My first Satyana workshop was at Ghost Ranch in New Mexico. The setting was deeply spiritual, and it permeated the work. I remember one woman standing up for herself in challenging unwanted attention from a man in the group. I felt like a guardian mother: all the power of the Divine Mother was present.

During the yearlong training, one memorable moment was the first women's gathering. It was so long, contentious, and difficult—

AND we all hung in there. I was so struck by the pain in that room—and by the courage to name it and to begin to explore and respect our differences. That truth forum was dynamite!

Other memorable moments: feeling genuinely loved by the men, with no edges or motives, just flowing love. That was a first for me, and it moved me deeply. I love the way we wrestled with the difficult times—and did not run from them. What character and dignity there was in this group!

During Satyana's certification training in May 2005—there were seventeen of us in Colorado—my heart so overflowed with love I thought it would burst. The love within and without was so powerful—beyond anything I had ever experienced before. I feel these bonds are forever—that we will be there for each other no matter what. And things weren't all "nice." We confronted one another and opened to new awareness in each moment—ALL in a community of love and respect.

The honoring rituals from both the men and the women at the end of the certification training were the most extraordinary and moving of all the many I have experienced. It was the deepest, the richest expression of pure love between men and women, and the Divine in both.

*Changed societal perspective.* I have been deeply sensitized to gender dynamics since I was in my twenties. As a woman who worked in corporations and universities it was impossible not to experience incredible discrimination based on gender. Unfortunately, this still exists, though sometimes in more subtle ways since we have passed laws to try to give women some rights that men have always had. We have a long, long way to go.

*Implementation of work—globally.* To my knowledge, this is the only gender work that comes from a spiritual base and not just a foundation of righting centuries of wrong. I believe the world needs this approach now more than ever, and that political movements for justice will be more powerful if they come from a spiritual base or perspective. Satyana's work on consciousness is so very powerful, profound—and has both challenged and shaped my images of the Divine. I wish it could be taught everywhere.

## Improvement of Satyana Gender Reconciliation Model

An important aspect of assessing any program is considering ways to improve the work. In this survey only a few participants responded to this question. Nevertheless, it is useful to take a closer look at the responses we did receive, and to add more detail that emerged in later follow-up with some of the respondents.

Julien wrote, "My primary concern is that there is not sufficient capacity to respond to the need that exists" for this work. His legitimate concern is that Satyana-trained facilitation staff and resources are insufficient to meet the demand that may be forthcoming, particularly as this book is published. This concern is corroborated by the enthusiastic response we received in South Africa alone. Satyana Institute is forming a strategic planning group to address these and other issues as the gender work continues to grow.

Carlotta wrote, "Overall, the work is inspired. Ensure that group facilitation skills are to the level of NTL Institute or Gestalt Institute graduates, with some field experience in other than gender reconciliation work. The container MUST be safe for all. The operating norms must be more inclusive of group-dynamics related issues." Carlotta's suggestions are particularly important as we move toward implementing new training programs.

Gwenn wrote, "My only suggestion for improving the work is in designing and executing more useful follow-up mechanisms, activities, and forums that would keep us connected and inspired." This points to a crucial dimension of the work that will become ever more important as it continues to grow. There is room for new creative work here to support participants who have gone through the work with ongoing follow-up and to develop self-generative processes for advancing gender reconciliation work more widely.

Shawn wrote, "The single most important issue in gender work for me is healing the internal conflict between the feminine and masculine energies. I would strongly suggest that this be the most important intention of the work."

Shirsten suggested that the work could be augmented in ways that address more specifically the needs of the LGBT community, which is certainly true, as touched upon in Appendix A.

Finally, Linda has made a number of suggestions for streamlining the organizational structure of Satyana Institute and for offering a shorter introductory format, which has been implemented.

Most of these suggestions are now being incorporated or accounted for in strategic planning for the next phase of Satyana's gender reconciliation work.

In closing, every survey respondent strongly endorsed the wider dissemination and implementation of Satyana's model of gender reconciliation. The support and enthusiasm from this group of professionals demonstrates their deep commitment to carrying this work forward. All of them affirmed that gender healing and reconciliation work is absolutely needed, and that Satyana's model offers a practical pathway for bringing greater peace and harmony between women and men into the world.

# ENDNOTES

## Chapter 1

[1] See Robert Gilman, "Essential Peacemaking," *In Context*, no. 34 (1993): 52-54.

[2] Samuel Shem and Janet Surrey, *We Have to Talk* (New York: Basic Books, 1999).

[3] Robert Bly and Marion Woodman, *The Maiden King: The Reunion of Masculine and Feminine* (New York: Henry Holt and Co, 1998).

[4] Aaron Kipnis and Elizabeth Herron, *What Women and Men Really Want* (Novato, Calif.: Nataraj Publishing, 1995).

[5] Riane Eisler and David Loye, *The Partnership Way* (Brandon, Vermont: Holistic Education Press, 1998).

[6] Llewellyn Vaughan-Lee, *Awakening the World: A Global Dimension to Spiritual Practice* (Inverness, Calif.: Golden Sufi Center, 2006, 66-83).

[7] Quoted in Andrew Harvey, *The Essential Mystics* (Castle Books, Edison, N.J., 1996, 50-52).

## Chapter 2

[1] Alice Bailey, *A Compilation on Sex* (Lucis Trust, London, 1990, 13-15).

## Chapter 3

[1] Bill Moyers, *A Gathering of Men*, 1990 television program produced by Betsy McCarthy, directed by Wayne Ewing, Mystic Fire Video, Burlington, Vermont.

## Chapter 5

[1] Andrew Harvey, *Light Upon Light: Inspirations from Rumi* (Berkeley, Calif.: North Atlantic Books, 1996, 104).

## Chapter 6

[1] J. Hanus, "The Culture of Pornography Is Shaping Our Lives," *Utne Reader* (Sept/Oct 2006): 58-60.

[2] Carly Milne, *Naked Ambition: Women Who Are Changing Pornography* (New York: Carrol and Graf, 2005); Candida Royalle, *How to Tell a Naked Man What to Do* (New York: Fireside Simon and Shuster, 2004).

3   Pamela Paul, *Pornified: How Pornography Is Transforming Our Lives, Our Relationships, and Our Families* (New York: Times Books, Henry Holt, 2005).

4   J. Stoltenberg, *Refusing to Be a Man* and *What Makes Pornography Sexy* (Minneapolis, Minn., Milkweeed Editions, 1994).

5   Daniel Odier, *Desire* (Inner Traditions, Rochester, Vermont, 2001, 8-9).

6   Sahajayoginicinta, quoted in Miranda Shaw, *Passionate Enlightenment* (Princeton, N.J.: Princeton University Press, 1994, 188).

7   Miranda Shaw, "Everything You Always Wanted to Know About Tantra . . . but Were Afraid to Ask," *What is Enlightenment?*, Lenox, MA, Issue No. 13, Spring-Summer, 1998.

8   Ibid.

9   Amarananda Bhairavan, *Kali's Odiyya—A Shaman's True Story of Initiation* (York Beach, Maine: Nicolas Hays, 2000).

## Chapter 8

1   Stanislav Grof, *The Adventure of Self Discovery* (Albany, N.Y.: SUNY Press, 1988, 171).

2   For a complete description and detailed clinical data, see Stanislav Grof, *The Adventure of Self Discovery* (Albany, N.Y.: SUNY Press, 1988).

3   Stanislav Grof, *Psychology of the Future* (Albany, N.Y.: SUNY Press, 2000, 215-217).

4   See, for example, the Contemplative Mind Project, based in Northampton, Massachusetts (www.contemplativemind.org).

5   Bernie Glassman, *Bearing Witness* (New York: Harmony/Bell Tower [Crown]), 1999.

## Chapter 9

1   "India Dealing With Infanticide," BBC News Online, www.collegenet.com/elect/app/app?service=external/Forum&sp=2194

2   Shiva/Shakti, Krishna/Radha, and Rama/Sita are three of the numerous divine consort couples among the gods of Hindu mythology. Shiva is the god of dissolution, and Shakti is his consort, the goddess of manifestation. Krishna is a human incarnation of Vishnu, the god of preservation, and it is Krishna who speaks as God in the Bhagavad-Gita. Radha is Krishna's beloved consort. Rama is the god in the Hindu epic *The Ramayana* who saves humanity by slaying the evil Ravana, and Sita is Rama's beloved divine wife, whom Indian women idealize and seek to emulate.

## Chapter 10

1   Quoted in *Cape Times*, November 15, 2006, Cape Town, South Africa. Full text of du Plooy's quote available online at www.christianfront.org.za/news/civilunionbill.htm.

## Chapter 12

1   Gerda Lerner, *The Creation of Feminist Consciousness: From the Middle Ages to 1870* (New York: Oxford University Press, 1993): quoted in Carol Flinders, *At the Root of this Longing, Reconciling a Spiritual Hunger and a Feminist Thirst* (San Francisco: HarperSanFrancisco, 1999, 126). *See also* Gerda Lerner, *The Creation of Patriarchy* (New York: Oxford University Press, 1986).

2   William C. Chittick, *The Sufi Path of Love: The Spiritual Teachings of Rumi* (Albany, N.Y.: SUNY Press, 1983, 194-195).

3   St. John of the Cross, "The Living Flame of Love," in *The Collected Works of Saint John of the Cross*, Kieran Kavanaugh, and Otilio Rogriguez, translators (Washington, DC: ICS Publications, 1991, 600).

4   J.G. Bennett, *Sex: The Relationship between Sex and Spiritual Development* (York Beach, Maine: Samuel Wieser, 1981, 50).

5   Andrew Harvey, *Light Upon Light: Inspirations from Rumi* (Berkeley, Calif.: North Atlantic Books, 1996, 79).

6   Eckhart Tolle, *The Power of Now, A Guide to Spiritual Enlightenment* (Novato, Calif.: New World Library, 1999, 130).

7   Ibid., 135.

8   Eckhart Tolle, *A New Earth: Awakening to Your Life's Purpose* (New York: Dutton, 2005, 14 and 183).

9   Eckhart Tolle, *The Power of Now, A Guide to Spiritual Enlightenment* (Novato, Calif.: New World Library, 1999, 141).

# INDEX

# OTHER TITLES OF INTEREST FROM HOHM PRESS

## YOGA MORALITY
*Ancient Teachings in a Time of Global Crisis*
by Georg Feuerstein

The spiritual and moral teachings of Yoga can serve as a life raft for those who want to live with integrity and without fear as humanity heads into turbulent waters. The book is a hard-hitting critique of the media hype surrounding Yoga, and an exploration of Yogic philosophy and practice to discover what it means to be a mature, moral person. It addresses the question: How are we to live consciously, responsibly, authentically, and without fear in the midst of mounting turmoil?

"Georg Feuerstein is not only vastly knowledgeable about the history and literature of spirituality, he is also a genuinely wise human being."
— Richard Heinberg, core faculty, New College of California, and author *The Party's Over: Oil, War and the Fate of Industrial Societies*

Paper, 320 pages, $19.95                    ISBN: 1-890772-66-6

• • •

## THE SHADOW ON THE PATH
*Clearing the Psychological Blocks to Spiritual Development*
by VJ Fedorschak
Foreword by Claudio Naranjo, M.D.

Tracing the development of the human psychological shadow from Freud to the present, this readable analysis presents five contemporary approaches to spiritual psychotherapy for those who find themselves needing help on the spiritual path. Offers insight into the phenomenon of denial and projection.

Topics include: the shadow in the Work; notable therapists; the principles of inner spiritual development in the major world religions; examples of the disowned shadow in contemporary religious movements; and case studies of clients in spiritual groups who have worked with their shadow issues.

Paper, 300 pages, $17.95                    ISBN: 0-934252-81-5

**To Order: 800-381-2700, or visit our website, www.hohmpress.com**

# OTHER TITLES OF INTEREST FROM HOHM PRESS

### AS IT IS
*A Year on the Road with a Tantric Teacher*
by M. Young

A first-hand account of a one-year journey around the world in the company of a *tantric* teacher. This book catalogues the trials and wonders of day-to-day interactions between a teacher and his students, and presents a broad range of his teachings given in seminars from San Francisco, California to Rishikesh, India. *As It Is* considers the core principles of *tantra*, including non-duality, compassion (the Bodhisattva ideal), service to others, and transformation within daily life. Written as a narrative, this captivating book will appeal to practitioners of *any* spiritual path. Readers interested in a life of clarity, genuine creativity, wisdom and harmony will find this an invaluable resource.

Paper, 840 pages, 24 b&w photos, $29.95          ISBN: 0-934252-99-8

• • •

### THE ALCHEMY OF LOVE AND SEX
by Lee Lozowick
Foreword by Georg Feuerstein, Ph.D.

Reveals 70 "secrets" about love, sex and relationships. Lozowick recognizes the immense conflict and confusion surrounding love, sex, and tantric spiritual practice. Advocating neither asceticism nor hedonism, he presents a middle path—one grounded in the appreciation of simple human relatedness. Topics include: • what men want from women in sex, and what women want from men • the development of a passionate love affair with life • how to balance the essential masculine and essential feminine • the dangers and possibilities of sexual Tantra • the reality of a genuine, sacred marriage. . .and much more.

" ... attacks Western sexuality with a vengeance." — *Library Journal.*

Paper, 300 pages, $16.95          ISBN: 0-934252-58-0

**To Order: 800-381-2700, or visit our website, www.hohmpress.com**

# OTHER TITLES OF INTEREST FROM HOHM PRESS

*KISHIDO*
*The Way of the Western Warrior*
by Peter Hobart

The code of the samurai and the path of the knight-warrior—traditions from opposite sides of the globe—find a common ground in *Kishido: the Way of the Western Warrior*. In fifty short essays, Peter Hobart presents the wisdom, philosophy and teachings of the mysterious Master who first united the noble houses of East and West. Kishido prioritizes the ideals of duty, ethics, courtesy and chivalry, from whatever source they derive. This cross-cultural approach represents a return to time-honored principles from many traditions, and allows the modern reader from virtually any background to find the master within.

Paper, 130 pages, $12.95          ISBN: 1-890772-31-3

• • •

*YOU HAVE THE RIGHT TO REMAIN SILENT*
*Bringing Meditation to Life*
by Rick Lewis

With sparkling clarity and humor, Rick Lewis explains exactly what meditation can offer to those who are ready to establish an island of sanity in the midst of an active life. This book is a comprehensive look at everything a beginner would need to start a meditation practice, including how to befriend an overactive mind and how to bring the fruits of meditation into all aspects of daily life. Experienced meditators will also find refreshing perspectives to both nourish and refine their practice.

Paper, 201 pages, $14.95          ISBN: 1-890772-23-2

To Order: 800-381-2700, or visit our website, www.hohmpress.com

# OTHER TITLES OF INTEREST FROM HOHM PRESS

## THE ANTI-WISDOM MANUAL
### A Practical Guide to Spiritual Bankruptcy
by Gilles Farcet, Ph.D.

What if the spiritual path turned out to be a road to hell paved with good intentions?

Most spiritual books tell us what we *should* do, or how we *should* view things. *The Anti-Wisdom Manual* takes a different approach. It simply describes what people *actually do* to sabotage their own progress on the spiritual path, whatever their chosen way—Christian, Buddhist, Native American, Muslim, Jewish, or any other. Think of it as a handbook in reverse. Using humor and irony, while based in clarity and compassion, the author alerts readers to the common traps into which so many sincere seekers easily fall.

Paper, 176 pages, $14.95                    ISBN: 1-890772-42-9

• • •

## THE WAY OF FAILURE
### Winning Through Losing
by Mariana Caplan

This straight-talking and strongly inspirational book looks failure directly in the face, unmasking it for what it really is. Mariana Caplan tells us how to meet failure on its own field, how to learn its twists and turns, its illusions and its realities. Only then, she advises, is one equipped to engage failure as a means of ultimate "winning," and in a way that far exceeds our culturally defined visions of success.

Paper, 144 pages, $14.95                    ISBN: 1-890772-10-6

To Order: 800-381-2700, or visit our website, www.hohmpress.com

# OTHER TITLES OF INTEREST FROM HOHM PRESS

## TO TOUCH IS TO LIVE
*The Need for Genuine Affection in an Impersonal World*
by Mariana Caplan
Foreword by Ashley Montagu

The vastly impersonal nature of contemporary culture, supported by massive child abuse and neglect, and reinforced by growing techno-fascination are robbing us of our humanity. The author takes issue with the trends of the day that are mostly overlooked as being "progressive" or harmless, showing how these trends are actually undermining genuine affection and love. This uncompromising and inspiring work offers positive solutions for countering the effects of the growing depersonalization of our times.

"An important book that brings to the forefront the fundamentals of a healthy world. We must all touch more." — Patch Adams, M.D.

Paper, 272 pages, $19.95                                    ISBN: 1-890772-24-0

• • •

## HALFWAY UP THE MOUNTAIN
*The Error of Premature Claims to Enlightenment*
by Mariana Caplan
Foreword by Fleet Maull

Dozens of first-hand interviews with students, respected spiritual teachers and masters, together with broad research are synthesized here to assist readers in avoiding the pitfalls of the spiritual path. Topics include: mistaking mystical experience for enlightenment; ego inflation, power and corruption among spiritual leaders; the question of the need for a teacher; disillusionment on the path . . . and much more.

"Caplan's illuminating book . . . urges seekers to pay the price of traveling the hard road to true enlightenment." — *Publishers Weekly*

Paper, 600 pages, $21.95                                    ISBN: 0-934252-91-2

**To Order: 800-381-2700, or visit our website, www.hohmpress.com**

# OTHER TITLES OF INTEREST FROM HOHM PRESS

## STAINLESS HEART
*The Wisdom of Remorse*
by Clelia Vahni

Anyone who has ever felt guilt will find both comfort and direction in this clearly written and compassionate book. The "stainless heart" is Clelia Vahni's description of the pure, essential nature of the human being. This heart, however, is rarely touched. One reason for this impasse, the author states, is that we have built walls around the heart out of shame, or have held ourselves apart so we don't get hurt or hurt others any more because we are afraid of the pain that guilt carries. Guilt is different from genuine remorse, the author argues. Guilt destroys us, while true remorse is the entry into truth, to a clear vision of life "as it is," and thus to a transformed relationship to ourselves and others. "The voice of remorse," she writes, "is a call from our stainless heart, challenging us to make the effort necessary to live by its wisdom."

Paper, 160 pages, $12.95                              ISBN: 1-890772-40-2

• • •

## YOGI RAMSURATKUMAR
*Under The Punnai Tree*
by M. Young

This is a richly detailed and thoroughly researched biography of the beggar saint of Tamil Nadu—Yogi Ramsuratkumar. From the lyrical to the factual, this book is filled with stories of Ramsuratkumar. Personal accounts of those who knew the beggar well reveal the life story of a saint unique even in the long history of India. *Yogi Ramusuratkumar: Under the Punnai Tree* occasionally takes a broader view and explores how Ramusuratkumar's life fits into overall themes of the spiritual path. A literary and pictorial feast for those who love India's rich heritage and a must read for spiritual seekers of all traditions.

Paper, 726 pages, 72 photos (color and b&w), $39.95   ISBN: 0-890772-34-8

To Order: 800-381-2700, or visit our website, www.hohmpress.com

# ABOUT SATYANA INSTITUTE

The Satyana Institute is a non-profit service and training organization. The mission of Satyana Institute is to support individuals, organizations, and communities to combine "inner" work of the heart with "outer" service in the world. The Institute has two program areas: Power of Reconciliation and Leading with Spirit. For more information, please visit *www.satyana.org*.

Power of Reconciliation is a project of the Satyana Institute that organizes workshops and training programs for healing and reconciliation between women and men in several countries. Program offerings range from introductory weekend workshops to six-day intensive programs, and are conducted in a broad range of contexts including service organizations, parliamentary and governmental departments, religious organizations and congregations, psychotherapeutic settings, spiritual and intentional communities, and academic institutions. The project also conducts programs periodically to train qualified professionals to become certified facilitators of the Power of Reconciliation model.

For more information, please visit *www.powerofreconciliation.org*. To schedule an event for your organization or community, please contact *reconciliation@satyana.org*.

# ABOUT THE AUTHORS

**William Keepin, Ph.D.,** has facilitated more than forty intensive gatherings in five countries for healing and reconciliation between women and men. He is President of the Satyana Institute and founder of the Power of Reconciliation project. Trained in mathematical physics and in transpersonal psychology and eastern meditation disciplines, his scientific work on global warming and renewable energy influenced environmental policy in many countries. He is co-editor of *Song of the Earth: The Emerging Synthesis of Scientific and Spiritual Worldviews* (Permanent Publications, 2007). Will leads spiritual retreats and supports women's projects in India.

**Cynthia Brix, M.Div, M.A.,** is Program Director of the Satyana Institute and Co-Director of its Power of Reconciliation project. She is the former Unitarian Universalist campus minister at the University of Colorado-Boulder. Her background is in wellness management and gerontology, and she co-chaired the Race Relations Committee for the City of Muncie, Indiana. A student of Eknath Easwaran's Passage Meditation, Cynthia has led meditation workshops at Unitarian Universalist conferences, and she co-leads spiritual retreats and supports women's projects in India.

**Molly Dwyer, Ph.D.,** completed her doctorate under the guidance of cosmologist Brian Swimme, and served as Co-Director of Satyana Institute's Gender Reconciliation Project from 1999 to 2002. Molly received the 1999 Vickers Award from the International Society for the Systems Sciences for her paper "The Emergent Feminine." Her first novel, *Requiem for the Author of Frankenstein*, will be released in 2008.

### Contact Information
*www.satyana.org*
*www.powerofreconciliation.org*
*www.divineduality.org*

See **About Satyana Institute** on previous page.